Film, Negation and Freedom

Film, Negation and Freedom

Capitalism and Romantic Critique

Will Kitchen

BLOOMSBURY ACADEMIC
NEW YORK • LONDON • OXFORD • NEW DELHI • SYDNEY

BLOOMSBURY ACADEMIC
Bloomsbury Publishing Inc, 1385 Broadway, New York, NY 10018, USA
Bloomsbury Publishing Plc, 50 Bedford Square, London, WC1B 3DP, UK
Bloomsbury Publishing Ireland, 29 Earlsfort Terrace, Dublin 2, D02 AY28, Ireland

BLOOMSBURY, BLOOMSBURY ACADEMIC and the Diana logo are trademarks
of Bloomsbury Publishing Plc

First published in the United States of America 2024
Paperback edition published 2025

Copyright © Will Kitchen, 2024, 2025

For legal purposes the Acknowledgements on p. viii constitute an extension
of this copyright page.

Cover design: Eleanor Rose
Cover photograph: Malcolm McDowell in *O Lucky Man!*, 1973, dir. Lindsay Anderson
© Moviestore Collection Ltd / Alamy

All rights reserved. No part of this publication may be: i) reproduced or transmitted
in any form, electronic or mechanical, including photocopying, recording or by means
of any information storage or retrieval system without prior permission in writing from
the publishers; or ii) used or reproduced in any way for the training, development or
operation of artificial intelligence (AI) technologies, including generative AI technologies.
The rights holders expressly reserve this publication from the text and data mining
exception as per Article 4(3) of the Digital Single Market Directive (EU) 2019/790.

Bloomsbury Publishing Inc does not have any control over, or responsibility for, any
third-party websites referred to or in this book. All internet addresses given in this
book were correct at the time of going to press. The author and publisher regret any
inconvenience caused if addresses have changed or sites have ceased to exist,
but can accept no responsibility for any such changes.

A catalog record for this book is available from the Library of Congress.

Library of Congress Cataloging-in-Publication Data

Names: Kitchen, Will, author.
Title: Film, negation and freedom : capitalism and romantic critique / Will Kitchen.
Description: New York : Bloomsbury Academic, 2023. | Includes
bibliographical references and index.
Identifiers: LCCN 2023013064 (print) | LCCN 2023013065 (ebook) |
ISBN 9798765105535 (hardback) | ISBN 9798765105542 (paperback) |
ISBN 9798765105573 (epub) | ISBN 9798765105566 (pdf) |
ISBN 9798765105559 (ebook other)
Subjects: LCSH: Penn, Arthur, 1922–2010–Criticism and interpretation. |
Anderson, Lindsay, 1923–1994–Criticism and interpretation. | Motion
pictures–Philosophy. | Capitalism. | Romanticism. | LCGFT: Film criticism.
Classification: LCC PN1998.3.P4525 K58 2023 (print) | LCC PN1998.3.P4525
(ebook) | DDC 791.4302/33092–dc23/eng/20230609
LC record available at https://lccn.loc.gov/2023013064
LC ebook record available at https://lccn.loc.gov/2023013065

ISBN: HB: 979-8-7651-0553-5
PB: 979-8-7651-0554-2
ePDF: 979-8-7651-0556-6
eBook: 979-8-7651-0557-3

Typeset by Deanta Global Publishing Services, Chennai, India

For product safety related questions contact productsafety@bloomsbury.com.

To find out more about our authors and books visit www.bloomsbury.com and
sign up for our newsletters.

Contents

List of figures vi
Acknowledgements viii

Introduction 1

Part One
1 No way out: Romanticism in the films of Arthur Penn and Lindsay Anderson 19
2 Romanticism after Auschwitz: The tradition of critical philosophy 47
3 Empty infinities: Freedom and the doctrine of action 77

Part Two
4 The artist's calling: *Mickey One* (1965) 107
5 Enemies of promise: *O Lucky Man!* (1973) 141
6 Dialectic of enlightenment: *The Missouri Breaks* (1976) 177
7 The tyranny of spectacle: *Britannia Hospital* (1982) 207

Appendix 243
Bibliography 244
Index 252

Figures

1	*Mondaufgang am Meer* (*Moonrise Over the Sea*, 1822)	3
2	*O Lucky Man!* (1973)	13
3	*Ladri di biciclette* (*Bicycle Thieves*, 1948)	20
4	*If....* (1968)	27
5	*Alice's Restaurant* (1969)	31
6	*If....* (1968)	37
7	*Bonnie and Clyde* (1967)	39
8	*Mickey One* (1965)	41
9	*Is That All There Is?* (1992)	44
10	*Four Friends* (1981)	98
11	*Mickey One* (1965)	108
12	*Mickey One* (1965)	114
13	*Mickey One* (1965)	118
14	*Mickey One* (1965)	120
15	*Mickey One* (1965)	123
16	*Mickey One* (1965)	129
17	*Mickey One* (1965)	131
18	*Mickey One* (1965)	133
19	*Mickey One* (1965)	137
20	*O Lucky Man!* (1973)	142
21	*O Lucky Man!* (1973)	152
22	*O Lucky Man!* (1973)	157
23	*O Lucky Man!* (1973)	160
24	*O Lucky Man!* (1973)	163
25	*O Lucky Man!* (1973)	166
26	*O Lucky Man!* (1973)	168
27	*O Lucky Man!* (1973)	175
28	*The Missouri Breaks* (1976)	179
29	*The Missouri Breaks* (1976)	184
30	*The Missouri Breaks* (1976)	194
31	*The Missouri Breaks* (1976)	197
32	*The Missouri Breaks* (1976)	200

33	*Britannia Hospital* (1982)	208
34	*Zéro de conduite* (1933)	210
35	*Britannia Hospital* (1982)	215
36	*Britannia Hospital* (1982)	217
37	*Britannia Hospital* (1982)	221
38	*Britannia Hospital* (1982)	225
39	*Britannia Hospital* (1982)	228
40	*Britannia Hospital* (1982)	229
41	*Britannia Hospital* (1982)	232
42	*Britannia Hospital* (1982)	235
43	*Britannia Hospital* (1982)	237
44	*Britannia Hospital* (1982)	240

Acknowledgements

Many thanks are due to the Film Studies departments at the University of Winchester and the University of Southampton for encouraging my academic ambitions. Without their enthusiasm and confidence this project, and many other works, would not have been undertaken. The bulk of research and writing took place between the spring of 2019 and 2021, and I owe fathomless gratitude to my parents and my brother for their loving support at this difficult time, as well as a lot of very useful proofreading.

Immeasurable thanks are also due to K. J. Donnelly for his tireless confidence and support throughout my studies thus far. His work as a teacher, researcher and mentor has been a vital source of inspiration and encouragement. I would also like to thank the many other academics, colleagues and artists who contributed to my professional development during this project or shared their valuable experience and perspectives: Louis Bayman, Tim Bergfelder, Amanda Bitouche, Ann Bingham, David Bretherton, William Brown, Sofia Bull, Aude Campmas, Helen Carmichael, Ruby Cheung, Shelley Cobb, Malcolm Cook, Maohui Deng, David Dennen, Alison Dickens, James Fenwick, Gábor Gergely, Tomi Gomory, Michael Hammond, Erik Hedling, Emma Hills, Karen Hockley, Katie Holdway, Gemma Holgate, John Izod, Fryderyk Kwiatkowski, Huw Jones, Dominic Lash, Claire Le Foll, Daniel Lentz, Karl Magee, Matt Melia, Mandy Merck, Maria Pramaggiore, Paolo Saporito, Mario Slugan, David Sorfa, Veronica Spencer, Tracy Storey, Paul Taberham, Jaap Verheul, Lucy Watson, Zack White and Michael Williams.

Were it not for the Covid-19 pandemic, this list of acknowledgements would undoubtedly be longer; but that only makes the connections that I did manage to foster or maintain at this time all the more meaningful. Thank you, all!

Introduction

Carl Schmitt's *Political Romanticism* (1919) contains the following accusation:

> Adam Müller... succumbed to the influence of heterogeneous impressions.... He always had looked for the nature of things in a sphere different from the one to which they belonged, and thus he shifted from one domain to another.... Having surrendered to the impression of the most immediate reality...
>
> [Romantics such as he] clothe affect with philosophical and scientific raiments and words rich in associations, collecting the material for this from the literature of the entire world, from all peoples, ages, and cultures. In consequence, the momentary impression of an enormous richness results. Entire worlds seem to be conquered.[1]

Perhaps Schmitt is right. And perhaps his accusations apply to film, and Film Studies, as well. Historically, film has been able to profit from its multimedia inheritance and pro-filmic brigandry by proclaiming that these features form part of its artistic significance. But if the Romantic artist, critic or film really does treat the object of their impressions not as a thing existing 'for itself', but, rather, as the indifferent *occasio* for their own individual world-creation, as Schmitt claims, then perhaps every instance of scholarly appropriation might be contaminated by the ravenous egoism of the 'Romantic spirit'. Maybe this very capacity for bloating – a voracious absorption of all that comes across its path – is a sign that Romanticism must be consigned to the scholarly ash heap, or rejected as a thoroughly unhelpful explanatory tool, as Karl Popper demanded of all irrefutable theories.[2] Yet, to borrow a metaphor from Isiah Berlin, the scholarly field of Romanticism is a 'wild wood';[3] who knows what strange and surprising things we might encounter along the way? Romanticism's scandalous affinity with inappropriate relations, paradox, inconsistency and dilettantism is perhaps a bad example for academic practice. But through all the confusion, it

---

[1] Carl Schmitt, *Political Romanticism*, 1919 (Brunswick and London: Transaction Publishers, 2011), 90, 107.
[2] See Karl Popper, *The Logic of Scientific Discovery*, 1935 (London and New York: Routledge, 2002), 17–20.
[3] Isiah Berlin, *The Roots of Romanticism*, 1965, ed. Henry Hardy (London: Pimlico, 2000), 100.

does impart one very valuable lesson. It asks us to question the nature of truth itself, our own desire to grasp it and how we go about our search.

It is a matter of explanation. Who is to say what belongs to one domain rather than another? For better or worse, Romanticism questions the very prescriptivism that is implicit in Schmitt's remark: the authoritarian desire to order schematic constructs and relations in terms of judgements of appropriateness and their realization in language. The kind of 'dilettante' and indecisive Romanticism criticized by Schmitt gains a positive moral value when we attempt to understand it in relation to its opposite: absolute decisions, glorification of action in the abstract, positivist epistemologies and those certain distinctions between 'friend' and 'foe' that led Carl Schmitt himself – critic of Romanticism and member of the Nazi Party – into the irrational world of fascism, the apotheosis of Romanticism's darker imperatives.[4] The contemporary relevance of this concept stems from its oldest clichés: paradox and contradiction, shock and excess and the questioning of norms and traditions, which inevitably follows such discontinuity. Proceeding by fits and starts, contemporary critical discourse is capable of recognizing the survival and pertinence of Romanticism in the world today, as well as the special relationship it shares with audiovisual media. Jacques Rancière has recently shown how film inherited the dream of the Blue Flower (*Blaue Blume*), becoming the art that most fully strives for a New Mythology capable of emancipating humanity from social inequality, assembled from scraps wrenched not only from the culture of the past but also from the naked surface of the world. Building upon such premises, this book offers a fresh perspective from which to examine this Romantic matrix – one that raises and connects some of the most important questions in aesthetics, politics and philosophy.

The aspect of Romanticism I want to address is complex and somewhat idiosyncratic. In a sense, it is a philosophy of action inscribed in the difference between two conceptual poles – a Dark pole and a Light pole – which might be profitably understood in reference to a contrast between 'cinema' and 'film'.[5] Rhetorically speaking, cinema's Romanticism is rooted in action. It includes those dynamic heroic figures who decisively embark upon great adventures; fascinating stories invested with unity, rhetoric and engaging style; dramatic narratives of conquering willpower, striving for communal or individual totality.

---

[4] For an informative critique of Carl Schmitt's philosophy and his relation to National Socialism, see Georg Lukács, *The Destruction of Reason*, 1954 (Delhi: Aakar Books, 2017), 652–61, 840–52.
[5] A table of comparative terms is provided in the Appendix. It charts some useful relationships and distinctions that may aid the reader in following my broadly dualistic interpretation of Romanticism, film and other concepts.

Film's Romanticism, however, lies in action's negation. It is found in those moments that interrupt the story; in the character who doesn't know what to do next; in the excess which reminds the viewer that they are experiencing a fiction. If 'cinema', understood in such terms, is the primary active guarantor of entertainment and economic capital, then the resistance created by 'film' marks an oppositional aesthetic truth-content. We will see later how this distinction also broadly corresponds to aspects of Rancière's theory of the 'regimes of art'. As I understand it, a more nuanced understanding of film's Romanticism derives from these dual powers – Dark and Light – which are enabled by the poetics of modern art itself.

The theoretical chapters in Part One of this book will explain how the Dark Romanticism of 'cinema' finds its progenitor in Fichte's *The Vocation of Man* (1799), which, like the Hollywood director, calls for 'action' before all else. It also shares this dynamism with the capitalist entrepreneur who masterfully chases the standard of quantity in profit margins, and the Nazi propagandist who imposes their will over non-Aryan races with undaunted conviction. The Light Romanticism of faltering 'film', however, will find expression in the artist who suffers impotence in their effort to produce the perfect work, the daydreamer torn between two competing thoughts and the immobile figures in the paintings of C. D. Friedrich who appear fixated by remote and sublime spectacles (Figure 1).

Obviously, such an interpretation of Romanticism requires a great deal of explanation, and this can best be accomplished by developing the argument

Figure 1 Immobile figures in *Mondaufgang am Meer* (*Moonrise Over the Sea*, 1822) by C. D. Friedrich. Reproduced by permission, Alte Nationalgalerie, Berlin.

throughout this book. Yet, the opposition of stillness and movement underlying the basic schema is, needless to say, somewhat familiar territory for Film Studies. Figures such as Deleuze and Bazin have long valorized immobile moments in film as emblems of an oppositional aesthetic set defiantly against that capitalistic ideology epitomized by the Hollywood dream factory. The Romantic approach opened by the work of Rancière, however, gives us opportunity to explore a new path and a new selection of subjects, and allows these debates to be broadened and enriched. For reasons that will become clear, this kind of filmic inactivity will not be sought in the work of Ozu or De Sica, but, rather, in films directed by those curious 'Romantic' artists, Arthur Penn and Lindsay Anderson. The historical overview of Romanticism that I provide before the filmic case study analyses in Part Two will explain why the idea of 'critique', and, more particularly, the critique of capitalism as a socio-economic and cultural development, is so vital to this approach. The films of Penn and Anderson – which often display a highly critical attitude towards ideas associated with capitalism and its values of economic rationality, individual agency and proactive morality – make suggestive use of a certain passivity that, I will argue, is more richly understood in reference to Romantic critical philosophy.

To jump ahead, it is worth emphasizing that this argument rests upon the belief that positive moral value is attached, or should be attached, to the idea of *negation*: the rejection of totality in all its forms. The guiding conviction is the idea that morality and freedom demand, not affirmation, positivity and the highest Good, but, rather, the affective revelation (not the resolution) of incoherence, falsity and suffering in our experience of both art and the world around us, even to the point of self-negation.

This approach to Romanticism will involve us in some surprisingly familiar debates. In the last thirty years, it has been relatively common to find connections drawn between Romanticism and more contemporary theoretical developments such as postmodernism, post-structuralism and deconstruction – those various 'isms' and their critico-ethico-rational problematics, which Richard J. Bernstein grouped together as the 'new constellation', populated by figures such as Foucault, Rorty, Derrida and Habermas.[6] That fascination with rupture, Otherness, anti-foundationalism and plurality which characterizes much twentieth- century-philosophical thinking – themes that Bernstein calls

---

[6] Richard J. Bernstein, *The New Constellation: The Ethical-Political Horizons of Modernity/Postmodernity* (Cambridge: Polity Press, 1991), 50.

'central in our time'[7] – possesses a decidedly Romantic quality. In many of its forms, the goal of this 'critical philosophy' is negation: the fight against totality, the disclosure of reification, the demythologization of entrenched ideologies, what Morse Peckham called 'cultural transcendence', and even what I have called elsewhere the conjectural presentation of erased explanans.[8] This is what a certain kind of Romanticism has always done: the disenfranchisement of language which creates meaning and order through distinction and identity. Yet, this critical Romanticism also has a *doppelgänger* which endeavours to enthrone such a language. Where one undertakes the critique of totality, its Dark half strives to bring it about. It is the former's task to reveal the latter's violence, just as film's aesthetic moments of stillness negate the dynamic life of cinema. Following Rancière, I contend that this Janus-faced Romanticism is not only a method of enriching political interpretations of cinematic content, but also something rooted in the poetics of film itself.

Romanticism and film: Rancière's regimes of art and audiovisual explanation

Romanticism and film are difficult yet richly rewarding things to examine. They are domains of sensory and political significance that transcend all attempts at verbal reduction. Both concepts pull in opposing directions: towards total indeterminate fragmentation through the very logic of their form, and yet, due to the gravity of categorization, these fragments simultaneously fall together into the confounding idea of an intrinsic and totalizing 'essence'. In other words, 'Romanticism' and 'film' are both things; but they are things that bear the ineradicable scar of never being one thing in particular. Recent history has shown how both Romantic Studies and Film Studies are undergoing a crisis of identity, struggling to draw boundaries around subjects that have traditionally accommodated an impetuous desire to do away with boundaries altogether. Romanticism and film share an oscillating ontology of presence and absence: darkness and light, the shot and the cut, sacred and profane, the sign and the

---

[7] Ibid., 57.
[8] 'Explanans' being, as I like to use the term, those interpreted secondary aspects of an explanation that it is necessary to take for granted in order to render that explanation intelligible and relevant to any given situation; see Will Kitchen, *Romanticism and Film: Franz Liszt and Audio-Visual Explanation* (London and New York: Bloomsbury Academic, 2020), 9. On Peckham and 'cultural transcendence', see note 31.

signified, the correct and the incorrect. Film theory through Eisenstein, Bazin, Metz and Deleuze has been aware of this slippage of categories, but its Romantic aspects did not fully emerge until the recent work of Jacques Rancière. Before we proceed, therefore, it is worth restating this historical and theoretical context, much of which was also outlined in my previous book *Romanticism and Film: Franz Liszt and Audio-Visual Explanation* (2020).[9]

Film is not one medium – one art form – and does not articulate the same set of essential properties across all of its products. Neither is this non-essentialism enough to distinguish it from other media in the modern era. Novels and symphonies participate in the same sense of distraction – the same wandering between correct ways of doing things, which define the products of what Rancière calls 'the aesthetic regime of art'.[10] Romanticism, in part, means exactly this multimedia imperative: boundaryless-ness in the face of an emancipated autonomy of artistic production. Modern, postmodern, *avant-garde* and Romantic art all mean the same thing, in these terms: a critical discipline of production and reception that questions the appropriateness of categorical pronouncements.

The theoretical ground opened by Rancière's work on 'regimes of art' (to be explained in greater detail in what follows) broadly accommodates other critiques of postmodernist thought, including the work of Morse Peckham, Alex Callinicos, Nikolas Kompridis and others. These theorists broadly refute the idea of a qualitative break at the dawn of the 'postmodern' era, and find the experiences, ideas and approaches supposedly characteristic of this postmodern world already emergent within 'the long nineteenth century'. Romantics like Novalis, Liszt and Wagner advocated the mixing of the arts, thinking that combined aesthetic effects provided greater philosophical insights into the higher regions of truth.[11] In his writings on art, Schelling describes this formal emancipation in a particularly filmic register: 'Contrasts and mixtures of subject matter are painted that are necessary in the romantic poem – and one can say in the strictest sense that they are *painted*, since everything in him is living colour, a moving impetuous painting in which the outlines sometimes disappear

---

[9] The introduction and opening chapters of *Romanticism and Film* also contain reflections on methods of textual interpretation that might help to frame the case study analyses presented later in this book.

[10] Jacques Rancière, *The Politics of Aesthetics*, 2000, ed. Gabriel Rockhill (London: Bloomsbury, 2017), 15–25.

[11] See Novalis, *Logological Fragments I*, c1798, in *Philosophical Writings*, ed. Margaret Mahony Stoljar, 47–66 (Albany: State University of New York, 1997), § 50, 58; see Kitchen, *Romanticism and Film*, 56.

entirely, sometimes emerge in stark emphasis.'[12] Rancière saw this 'impetuous painting' and named it the progenitor of film, whilst placing particular emphasis on the impetuosity. The stark disappearances and emergences of 'modern' art (i.e., art created during the period of modernity following the development of the broadly Romantic 'aesthetic regime') allegorize the vagaries of political representation itself. Emancipation from artistic form also carries with it the possible emancipation of society, for reasons that occupy the history of post-Kantian aesthetics. After Beethoven, Friedrich and Paganini, art is no longer bound by rules of appropriateness, and these rules, as critical philosophical aesthetics would later re-emphasize, are the accusatory ghost of *doxa*. It is for this reason that Romanticism has remained a potent and illuminating explanatory tool for cultural commentators who seek to understand the mutual dynamics of art and social critique.

A very important cultural ideal was born towards the end of the eighteenth century: faith in art as the one force capable of healing a dirempted modern subject. Western civilization was being traumatized by the chaotic revolutions and alarming philosophies that sprang from the Enlightenment, and it was hoped that art would become the new religion to save a humanity that was quickly losing faith in the metaphysical certainties, values and other organizing structures provided by religion, monarchy and positivist empirical rationalism. Art must strive to unite the 'subjective' and 'objective' – and, by extension, reason and nature, individual and society – which Kant's Transcendental Idealism and the murderous 'Terror' of the French Revolution had helped to split apart. The aesthetic regime, or the 'Romantic' idea, begins at this historical moment. It was the birth of the modern meaning of the word 'art' as something much more than τέχνη (*technē*), and as something more akin to ἔρως (*éros*) or δαίμων (*daímōn*) – some sublime apparition that promises to reveal a kind of truth beyond the power of language. It encourages the creative spirit to strive for the 'Absolute', or some perpetually deferred ideal. Fascinated by a respect for a mysterious objective reality, the new art often credited insignificant objects with their own power of muted speech. These turbulent circumstances marked the ascendency of the aesthetic regime in art.

The development of this new regime is usefully understood to be synonymous with what Adorno identifies in *Aesthetic Theory* (1970) as the moment of art's

---

[12] Friedrich Wilhelm Joseph Schelling, *The Philosophy of Art*, 1802–1803 (Minneapolis: University of Minnesota Press, 1989), 228.

'spiritualization' – its appropriation of the features characteristic of Kant's natural sublime, or the development of autonomous expressivity over the principle of mimesis.[13] Through the presentation of its own objectivity, the modern artwork makes the poignant declaration: "if only" – one that is untranslatable into ordinary language.[14] The utopian desire inherent to this claim is always thwarted by the constructed, historical, empirical and therefore bounded, nature of the work itself. Every artwork has its conservative aspect, not only, as Adorno suggests, in its fated contribution to the economic system of production, distribution and the compartmentalization of the social totality into separate and reciprocal domains of work and leisure, but also in what we will see described as the Rancièrian 'dialectic' of regimes: 'aesthetic' and 'representative'.[15] This is the dynamic I have taken the liberty of conscripting into the schema of Light and Dark Romanticism. We will see its form already present in Schiller's *Letters on the Aesthetic Education of Man* (1795) and Schelling's *System of Transcendental Idealism* (1800). It synthesizes Light and Dark by articulating free aesthetic cognition as a product of contextualizing explanation by an artist.

Although this new meaning given to the idea of 'art' followed from the Age of Revolution, its effects are alive and well today, being inherent to the form of cinema as well as audiovisual media in general. Figures such as Beethoven, Flaubert, Wagner, Barnum and Méliès have all played their role, passed the torch and helped to shape a world of modern aesthetics, which is explicable according to innumerable conflicts between ideas of art and entertainment, individual and society, explanation and freedom. What makes film particularly special, according to Rancière, is the unprecedented extent to which its aesthetic and technological functioning exemplifies this Romantic poetics. In *Film Fables* (2001), he suggests that the camera's disinterested mechanical reproduction of a genuine objective world is married to, and perpetually thwarted by, the filmmaker's interested selection and arrangement of captured images into a subjective and ideologically determined expression. It is in this way that film becomes the perfect embodiment of that perpetual Romantic striving after the 'Absolute' – that great promise and hope which was left hanging over the final pages of Schelling's *System of Transcendental Idealism*.[16]

---

[13] Theodor W. Adorno, *Aesthetic Theory*, 1970 (London and New York: Bloomsbury, 2017), 99–106.
[14] Ibid., 145.
[15] Ibid., 319.
[16] Jacques Rancière, *Film Fables*, 2001 (London and New York: Bloomsbury, 2016), 9; Friedrich Wilhelm Joseph Schelling, *System of Transcendental Idealism*, 1800 (Charlottesville: The University Press of Virginia, 2001), 219–36. It is perhaps interesting to note, considering the presence of

Rancière was right to suggest that film echoes Novalis' pronouncement that 'everything speaks':

> Everything we experience is a communication. Thus the world is indeed a communication – a revelation of the spirit. The age has passed when the spirit of God could be understood. The meaning of the world is lost. We have stopped at the letter. As a result of the appearance we have lost that which is appearing.[17]

It is important to recognize the sense of loss in Novalis' words, for it helps to reveal the specific truth that is sought through Rancière's own comparison. The sadness or poignancy that results from Novalis' elegiac pronouncement of a fallen world echoes Roland Barthes' notion of the photographic 'punctum'[18] – a wounding testimony from the borderland of presence and absence. Like Novalis, Rancière and Barthes, Adorno also accentuates such painful fragments, seeing them to bear an ill-defined 'truth' that forcefully negates the ideology of social totality: 'Artworks become eloquent with wordless gesture . . . they reveal themselves as the wounds of society . . . the socially critical zones of artworks are those where it hurts; where in their expression, historically determined, the untruth of the social situation comes to light.'[19]

As a pivotal phenomenon in the history of modern art, film exemplifies this development of aesthetic 'self-consciousness'. The unbiased objectivity of the camera, as Rancière puts it, records things in the world 'as they come into being, in a state of waves and vibrations, before they can be qualified as intelligible objects'.[20] Our attention is guided by the camera, capturing the immediate and autonomous presence of pro-filmic reality which is simultaneously conscripted into a tailored fiction. After assigning such elements a functional role, often dependent upon the logic of cause and effect – an 'explanation' for their inclusion – the artistic work then leaves them to their own expression of being. Typically, texts will oscillate between these poles of gravitation when a narrative is interrupted, and the film is distracted from its broader function of telling stories – stringing along plots with the assistance of images and sounds which

---

Adorno in the following chapters, that Rancière's conviction after Schelling also echoes a fragment of Adorno's *Aesthetic Theory* in which the dialectic function of cinematic montage displays a perfect oscillation between the intentioned construction of editing and the pure mechanical capturing of unintentioned reality of the shot; Adorno, *Aesthetic Theory*, 211.

[17] Novalis, *Logological Fragments II*, c1798, in *Philosophical Writings*, ed. Margaret Mahony Stoljar, 67–84 (Albany: State University of New York, 1997), 54, 81.
[18] Roland Barthes, *Camera Lucida*, 1980 (London: Vintage Books, 2000), 25–7.
[19] Adorno, *Aesthetic Theory*, 323.
[20] Rancière, *Film Fables*, 2.

invite attention to fly past what the camera is uniquely gifted with the ability to dwell upon. The interrupting image retains something of the power of the punctum, which it uses to expose a haunting presence of pro-filmic autonomy – an arrangement of sensory experience that refuses the act of explanation in becoming part of an artistic product. This is the distinction between what Rancière calls the 'aesthetic' and 'representative' regimes.[21] Read the other way, the objectivity of 'film' is curtailed by its constant and institutionally determined need to become 'cinema'.

Armed with the power to fulfil the Romantic dream of aesthetic autonomy, film returns ever again to the logic of the representative regime through the act of telling stories. It arranges fragments of a world standing for itself (puncta) into sequences containing intelligible actions, explanations, networks of causes and effects (stadia).[22] As Adorno puts it, 'the process of artistic production is precisely that of according importance to something' as things worth seeing, things which mean something, or demand certain responses, whereas Kantian disinterestedness would have artistic experience reject all such demands.'[23] For

---

[21] Jacques Rancière, *The Intervals of Cinema* (London and New York: Verso, 2014), 37.

[22] Rancière's approach to film seems in many respects to echo that of Jean-François Lyotard, particularly with regard to the conceptualization of both politics and aesthetics as a process of *mise-en-scène* – save with a pertinent addition in Rancière of the Romantic idea. In 'Acinemas' (1973), and other works, Lyotard also describes a process of partially authored directions and orderings at work in the audiovisual text which spill over into the 'real' world of spectatorship, defining the norms and responses; see Jean-François Lyotard, *Acinemas: Lyotard's Philosophy of Film*, ed. Graham Jones and Ashley Woodward (Edinburgh: Edinburgh University Press, 2017), 38–9. The 'subjective' dimension of the cinematic product suggested by Rancière is comparable to Lyotard's idea of the 'exclusion of movements'; Lyotard, *Acinemas*, 33; the authored film presents a series of excisions which curtail the presence of freedom through the conventions of representational form, against which 'the idea of a sovereign film' stands as a regulative opposite of free and unauthored representation; Lyotard, *Acinemas*, 65–9. For Lyotard, film is to be understood in reference to a tension between two poles: 'immobility and excessive movement'; the inherently transgressive aura of the aesthetic domain, as a non-functional play of movements (lights, colours, sounds) existing 'for themselves', meets the need for such movements to be ordered, limited, cut off and arranged into forms, narratives and commodities; Lyotard, *Acinemas*, 35. Despite Lyotard's problematic tone of ideological absolutism – recalling the 'ideal reader' fallacy that dogged contemporary Screen Theory – this description of *mise-en-scène* as a 'general process touching all fields of activity', when purged of this tone, is very much in tune with Rancière's aesthetic-political sensibilities; Lyotard, *Acinemas*, 38. If we are to curb the political pessimism of Lyotard's idea – that the 'exclusion of movements' '*eliminates all* impulsional movement, real or unreal, which will not lend itself to reduplication, all movement which would escape identification, recognition and the mnesic fixation' – with the Rancièrian idea that Romantic aesthetic indeterminacy always renders such orderings non-conceptual and non-binding, then we are quite close to the idea that I outlined in *Romanticism and Film*: of film as audiovisual explanation – as an imposition upon making sense, pulled out of shape by sovereign moments of limited autonomy, a movement that contains no immanence of success; Lyotard, *Acinemas*, 38; italics added.

[23] Adorno, *Aesthetic Theory*, 205.

all its promises of freedom, Romanticism's poetic schema never escapes the shameful shadow of violence in the form of the artist's explanation as expression.[24]

We can summarize Rancière's film theory with the following schema. The subjective expression of the filmmaker is wedded to the supposedly objective revelation of the camera, and the aesthetic object thus produced is caught between two Romantic tendencies, Dark and Light, dialectically realizing an aporetic condition:

1. The expression of the filmmaker presents 'cinema': stories, logic, order and ideology. It obeys the Dark Apollonian drive, as opposed to the Dionysian; enacts the placement of things in front of a camera as an intrinsic valuation of them as 'things worth seeing'. In this way, cinema presents us with *explanations* – interpersonal impositions upon making sense.[25] It actualizes an ostensibly 'real' world through a frame that includes and excludes; its content results from choices made by interested individuals. This, in Rancière's terms, marks its commitment to the representative regime of art: the arrangement of sensory elements as a rational and meaningful 'action', framed for consumption, and fit to be assigned a functional economic role. This effect, akin to Barthes' stadium, is cinema's explanatory tendency, based on interpersonal power relations: the Dark, subjective Romanticism of 'cinema'.

2. 'Film', on the other hand, thrives in the immediate presentation of an honest and free pro-filmic reality: an objectivity whose discontinuities and particularities refuse to be assimilated into the grand representation of the cinematic 'text'. It marks the alluring disorder of things that 'do not fit' – the Light Dionysian, as opposed to the Apollonian, drive. This experience of autonomy stands-in for Barthes' punctum: that which 'stings' because it is invested with its own incomprehensible power of speech, as Novalis wrote, and resists the pull of meaning. This is film's tendency towards freedom, based upon aesthetic disinterestedness: the Light, 'objective' Romanticism of 'film'.

These antithetical forces create a perpetual movement of political possibility. Moments free from functionality (2) are drawn back in (1). The world becomes

---

[24] The whole issue is encapsulated in the problematic statement made in the 'Oldest Program for a System of German Idealism' (c1795): 'Posey . . . becomes again what it was in the beginning – *the educator of humanity*'; Friedrich Hölderlin, (et al.), 'The Oldest Program for a System of German Idealism', c1795, in *Essays and Letters*, 341–2 (London: Penguin, 2009), 342.
[25] See Kitchen, *Romanticism and Film*, 7–14.

explained, but only by slippery and ambiguous means. This dialectical movement captures the richer application of terms such as 'the aesthetic regime' and 'audiovisual explanation', as continual processes of self-critiquing dependency. This is the place of the modern 'artwork': between indeterminacy ('art') and commitment ('work') – between Light and Dark.

Rancière's film theory emphasizes the political aspects of this dualistic Romanticism. The dialectic of regimes also operates between cinema's social function as 'mere' entertainment, and film's potential to foster genuine political change. Like many philosophers in the critical tradition, Rancière finds the political power of film to lie in its ability to bring about a kind of Schillerian 'aesthetic education', in allowing the mute speech of filmic representations – 'the splendour of the significant' or 'the wisdom of the surface' brought out by the aesthetic regime – to help us 'see things from another angle'.[26] The idea of freedom, which underlies this concept, is the capacity of the text's meaning to overstep the intentions of production. The audiovisual explanations of cinema can be received in multiple ways, and every attempt to translate their meanings is only ever an interpretation in terms of what I have called 'risky archeological analysis'.[27] Thanks to the 'objective' nature of the film camera (and it is, of course, merely a rhetorical gesture to state that the mechanical apparatus of film is 'objective' – it remains a process of representation, whether the method of light transference and indexing be chemical, digital or otherwise), cinema's Romantic dialectic is more developed than in other forms of media, and therefore more likely to foster the creation of new and interesting explanations of the world its texts claim to represent.

From Lumière to Netflix, the process of building narratives from audiovisual elements restages that eternal Romantic striving to unify the objective revelation of an autonomous pro-filmic reality and the subjective expression of the filmmaker. Individual texts can play with the limits of explanation, radicalizing the unstable ground between statements of moral normativity and the unmediated ground of individual response. We will see an illustrative example of where this kind of dynamic can lead in one of the central case studies analysed in this book, when the director of *O Lucky Man!* (1973), Lindsay Anderson himself, steps into the diegesis and slaps his protagonist with a copy of the script (Figure 2). Whilst the subjectivity, which creates narrative order and meaning, reveals itself

---

[26] Rancière, *The Intervals of Cinema*, 125.
[27] See Kitchen, *Romanticism and Film*, 14–17.

Figure 2 The artist (Lindsay Anderson) reveals the violence of artistic expression in *O Lucky Man!* (1973).

as a coercive force, our Everyman 'hero' has a moment of profound revelation, articulated as an explicit refusal to act – a refusal to forfeit a subtle degree of freedom by forming a willing part of the fiction. By radicalizing such moments of stasis, which playfully (or obstinately) resist the pull of totality inherent to artistic expression itself, films can slip between conditional and unconditional, objective and subjective – a slippage which, as critical philosophy demonstrates, can evoke potent political forces.

Rethinking Romantic critique in Film Studies

Working from these theoretical premises, this book offers an attempt to enrich the idea of Romanticism in politico-cultural analysis. In Film Studies, the word 'Romanticism' has long been the victim of simplification, often being used to frame a basic Left/Right distinction without much room for complex dialectics. Michael Ryan and Douglas Kellner in *Camera Politica* (1988), for example, occasionally employ 'Romantic' as a decidedly conservative schema corresponding neatly with the general cultural and ideological timbre of late-twentieth-century American Republicanism. Films such as *Star Wars* (1977) and the Lucas/Spielberg productions of the 1980s certainly position nominally 'Romantic' concepts of nature, authenticity, individuality, freedom and irrationality within narratives that can be read to validate Reaganite conservative political agendas, as Ryan and Kellner suggest.[28] This limited, but by no means

---

[28] Michael Ryan and Douglas Kellner, *Camera Politica: The Politics and Ideology of Contemporary Hollywood Film* (Bloomington and Indianapolis: Indiana University Press, 1988), 11.

false, understanding of Romanticism situates the concept as an arch enemy of all film analysis inspired by Marx, Adorno, Althusser, Foucault and many a progressive theory of cultural politics. This book seeks to resituate Romanticism in a more ambiguous relation to such approaches.

The hypothesis that every text is fundamentally political[29] – or that every instance of language and audiovisual production is an ideological act of explanation – sits at the very core of the current schematization of Romantic philosophy. The accommodation of philosophical notions of negation and freedom into narrative analysis can be more easily grasped in reference to an understanding of Romanticism as something that blends aesthetics and politics, in Rancière's terms, into a continuum of evaluative sensory and social experience. The essentially antagonistic relation between social classes – described by Fredric Jameson as the '*langue*' against which the individual text stands as an instance of '*parole*'[30] – here becomes one based on a more Romantic conflict (one which has traditionally been invalidated by Marxist notions of critical value) between the individual (the Romantic genius, poet, artist, as well as the capitalist entrepreneur) and the social totality. One of the significant advantages this offers over an approach such as Jameson's is the devaluation of collective, utopian moments. Rather than positive political ideology, a nominally 'Romantic' approach needs to give special consideration to the relational impasse between the individual and the communal totality, the subjective and the objective, and how the traumas and passions of the isolated subject create spaces for what Morse Peckham calls 'cultural transcendence': the negation of dominant social values, which have been unmasked as incoherent ideologies.[31]

This correspondence between ideological criticism and a Romantic approach to film analysis will also lead to a thickening of our theoretical engagements with the texts themselves; for, as already suggested, the idea of Romanticism hitherto employed by political criticism has often cut analysis rather short. For example,

---

[29] As asserted, for example, in Fredric Jameson's *The Political Unconscious*, 1981 (London and New York: Routledge, 2002).

[30] Jameson, *The Political Unconscious*, 70.

[31] The cultural theorist and philosopher Morse Peckham – who spent his life grappling with 'Romanticism' in an attempt to find an explanation that did justice to the far-reaching implications of the concept – coined the term 'cultural transcendence' to delineate his field of study. Romanticism implies the presence and negotiation of cultural transcendence; Morse Peckham, *Romanticism and Ideology* (Hanover and London: Wesleyan University Press, 1995), xiii. Peckham's explanation of Romanticism seems to accommodate the work of a diverse but not exhaustive range of Romantic schemas, bringing it within the scope of related aspects of critical theory, philosophical hermeneutics and critical rationalism. Elsewhere I have called cultural transcendence Romanticism's 'principle of agency'; see Kitchen, *Romanticism and Film*, 24–7.

like Robin Wood, Ryan and Kellner recognize an aura of Romanticism in the generic hybridity of Arthur Penn's *Bonnie and Clyde* (1967), in addition to the text's valuation of passionate and 'authentic' lived experience, expressive camera work, symbolic use of colour and framing, episodic narrative structure and so forth.[32] Such pronouncements have often seemed to lead to an inconsequential schematism of themes and formal tropes. In such terms, 'Romanticism' provides a mere stepping stone for critics who want to get from thematic and formal elements of films to the real political meat of their analysis, whatever it may be. This reductive approach to Romanticism has often rendered it a mere rhetorical structure in discourse, and robbed it of a richer interpretive potential, such as Rancière's schema provides.

Political film analysis over the last forty years – such as the work of Wood, Ryan, Kellner, Robert P. Kolker and Robert B. Ray – demonstrates that many texts can be read to value individuality, nature, passion and idealism without this necessary revealing anything decisive about their political or social meaning. The rhetorical malleability of these concepts, their openness to appropriation by (what are interpreted to be) broadly Left-wing and Right-wing narratives, should dissuade us from basing any representational concept of Romanticism upon their presence in any particular film. From this perspective, we will see that it is possible to refute criticisms that target a text's failure to offer any more 'positive' programme for revolutionary praxis. It is somewhat surprising that critics as well versed in critical theory as Ryan and Kellner should wish to see films end with possible 'images of success' in order to secure their political progressiveness.[33] The negatively valued 'immaturity' they detect in *Bonnie and Clyde* – 'more Marx brothers than Marx'[34] – demonstrates a need for a rejuvenation and deepening of Romanticism as both a political and a philosophical concept.

Yes, both Penn's and Lindsay Anderson's films, chosen for special consideration in this book, contain elements that may contradict their political intentions, as Ryan and Kellner interpret them;[35] but it is precisely this element of ambiguity or failure – a sense that a film is not in complete control of itself, or that the implied filmmaker is offering an imperfect expression, in which it is less a than straightforward matter to credit the film with meeting its own criteria for success, let alone orient one's values and sympathies – that is what perhaps

---

[32] Ryan and Kellner, *Camera Politica*, 21.
[33] Ibid., 23.
[34] Ibid.
[35] Ibid., 26–7.

makes these films more 'Romantic' than *Midnight Cowboy* (1969) or *They Shoot Horses, Don't They?* (1969), films that Ryan and Kellner praise for being more holistic, and therefore 'successful' in their critique of capitalist society.[36]

Throughout this book we will return to the seemingly paradoxical idea that 'failure is success' – that failure, like suffering, stillness and doubt, is a more valuable political category than success, affirmation or happiness.[37] To understand these films we must explore the philosophical and historical roots of the idea that negation – and its various filmic realizations – is on the side of freedom, as a philosophical category. Part One will situate film's Romanticism within a history of critical philosophy, ranging from Kantian epistemology to Frankfurt School critical theory, after having first understood why the films of Arthur Penn and Lindsay Anderson provide some of the most interesting ways of developing the vital and fascinating questions that arise from this history. The subsequent case study chapters presented in Part Two apply the underlying Romantic schema to selected film texts, and illuminate some of the most interesting, complex and neglected cinematic productions of the twentieth century.

Let us rethink what we mean by Romanticism, then, and allow it to find a new voice in political film analysis. Beyond reductive conceptualizations, exciting new meanings are being found for this concept. Where once cinema was deemed to herald a new era of technological modernism, we are now rediscovering the fact that it was also the culmination of a long Romantic dream. The developing field of 'film-philosophy' opened by the work of Cavell, Deleuze and others – one that provides a counterpoint to the theorizing and explicative methods of the naturalistic school of cognitive and behavioural psychology associated with David Bordwell, Noël Carroll, Greg Currie, Murray Smith et al. – has also been called 'romantic' by Robert Sinnerbrink.[38] There is much to be found by way of similarity between film-philosophy's willingness to treat film texts as objective progenitors of new and world-disclosing philosophical knowledge on behalf of those who experience them, and the historically Romantic faith in art to bring about the 'aesthetic education' of humanity to an elevated moral and political condition. Yet, the tensions inherent to this faith, as Rancière has shown, allow film to meet this goal only halfway, as a thwarted fable.

---

[36] Ibid., 26.
[37] The validation of this idea is nowhere more plainly apparent than in Darwinian evolutionary theory or critical rationalism's evolutionary epistemology; both of these conceptual frameworks can be adequately represented by the schema of 'trial and error'.
[38] Robert Sinnerbrink, *New Philosophies of Film: Thinking Images* (London and New York: Continuum International Publishing Group, 2011), 2–8.

Part One

1

No way out

Romanticism in the films of Arthur Penn and Lindsay Anderson

We now understand the need for a thorough reconsideration of the relationship between Romanticism and film, and also the need to remain alert to the variety of issues that such a reconsideration must raise. In addition to the idea, outlined in the preceding introduction, that film itself is a Romantic phenomenon, we can now forward the hypothesis that certain films can evoke 'more Romantic' critical concerns than others. The key to this argument lies in the idea of inaction: those moments of peculiar cinematic stasis associated with art cinema, already familiar to us from the work of Ozu, De Sica, Visconti and many a representative of that discursive Other to Hollywood dynamism which exemplifies Deleuze's idea of the 'time image'. The various moments of stillness to be found in such texts have often been read to contain a certain emancipatory potential (Figure 3).[1] The static qualities of their form and content supposedly serve to make time itself a subject, halting the flowing cause-and-effect structure of narrative, and, along with it, the ideologies that uphold the social totality. Products of Rancière's aesthetic regime, this kind of cinematic immobility short-circuits the mechanisms of explanation and power to create a liberating space of indeterminacy that symbolizes the possibility of social freedom.[2]

We occasionally find something comparable in the films of Arthur Penn and Lindsay Anderson, although differently inflected – something perhaps more complexly attuned to the Romantic poetics of film. The indeterminacy between the popular, artistic, realistic and allegorical modes of cinematic representation makes

---

[1] See Gilles Deleuze, *Cinema 2: The Time-Image*, 1985 (London and New York: Continuum, 2005), 1–23.
[2] Yet, as we saw in the introduction, this halting is always, as Rancière says, 'thwarted'. The representative regime will assert itself and subsume these autonomous, Dionysian, 'utopian' fissures within the totalizing pull of the Apollonian desire for order and continuity.

Figure 3 The rain scene from *Ladri di biciclette* (*Bicycle Thieves*, 1948).

their own articulations of cinematic inaction part of a distinct family of political critique. The approach I have adopted assumes that the films' inherent sense of 'failure' – reflected in the fact that they are not typically seen as canonical, 'successful' or even very coherent critical texts – may be one of their most interesting aspects.

There are always questions to be asked about the methods used to interpret any cultural product, as well as the value of the interpretations produced. Perhaps Paul Ricœur put it best when he compared the dynamic social life of a text to an ongoing trial by jury: authors, critics, academics and other readers bring their own testimonies to bear, and we never arrive at any final verdict except by a kind of institutionalized violence.[3] Absolute relativism is avoidable, however, through employment of the critical hermeneutic method: rational discussion, or 'trial and error', as Karl Popper so often put it. For better or worse, although certain people are in superior positions to judge what others say about texts by virtue of vocation, ability, privilege and luck, no one is above criticism. The critical dialectic between statement and dissent formalizes one of the most illuminating aspects of the Romantic schema – one perched at the divide between subjective and objective commitment, or between what is meaningful and what is meaningless; between tyrants and freedom fighters;

---

[3] Paul Ricœur, 'The Model of the Text: Meaningful Action Considered as a Text', 1971, in *Hermeneutics and the Human Sciences,* ed. John B. Thompson, 159–83 (Cambridge: Cambridge University Press, 2016), 177.

between morality and expediency; between heroes and villains. Few films seem to evidence this process more richly than those directed by Arthur Penn and by Lindsay Anderson, the contemporaneous 'auteurs' behind those iconic artefacts of late 1960s countercultural cinema *Bonnie and Clyde* (1967) and *If....* (1968). Their works reveal a consistency of thematic interests and values that seems to restage the irresolvable dialogue between tradition and innovation, history and myth or freedom and oppression, that has lain at the heart of modern critical philosophy since at least the time of the German Idealists.

At first glance, Penn and Anderson may seem a strange pairing, but it takes only a little reflection to find their significant connections. They were both Left-leaning 'intellectual' filmmakers, reluctant to embrace the revolutionary ideals of the 1968 generation, which their early work seemed to endorse. Outsiders in the film industry, their roots were in documentary, television and the 'serious' theatre, to which they periodically returned throughout their sporadic careers. The importance their works seem to attach to ideas of passion, individuality, generic hybridity, rebellion, anti-realism, a certain distrust of principles associated with the capitalist economy and a formal playfulness that pushes the representative paradigms of classical narrative cinema – all this may bring the word 'Romantic' quickly to mind.

There are several potential approaches to the Romanticism of Penn and Anderson. We could find it in the films' aesthetic discontinuity, expressionistic excess, unconventional framing, ambiguous character motivations, self-consciously allegorical moments and a lack of 'realistic' psychological depth to characters. All such elements correspond to the nineteenth-century fascination with the darkly sensational, the affective surface and the multimedia spectacle. But, as suggested previously, these developments only accentuate the surface-level Romanticism(s) of film more generally. If there is something more richly 'Romantic' about certain films, it is not to be found by analysing the poetics of a historically specific post-classicism in narrative cinema. Bearing in mind Carl Schmitt's warning, we need to remain alert to the slippery value of Romanticism as a critical concept, and its tendency to subsume such an expansive variety of practices, tropes and aesthetic practices that its overzealous application can completely dilute its truth-content. We need to prefer an explanation that asks more of this discursive formation. It is necessary to investigate what is more revealingly 'Romantic' about these directors' works, beyond the more obvious points of reference.

We can begin with the fact that Penn and Anderson were industry outsiders. Throughout their careers, they refused to 'play the game' inscribed by the dominant cinematic cultural economy. In effect, their work displays a strong tendency towards anti-capitalism, something which we have seen situated within the development of modern audiovisual aesthetics. As part-time film directors, they both matured outside of the mainstream industry and experienced considerable periods of absence from behind the camera. They would make films periodically, and often as the result of some pressing personal need to return to such work.[4] After crowning successes early in their careers, their subsequent projects began to alienate audiences and critics, inflecting their overall attitude towards concepts such as work, wealth and success. Yet, they were never radically *avant-garde* filmmakers, and the films they completed often had potential for wide audience appeal. Their unusual careers recall Adorno's comment about the more specific radicality of part-time artists, or those who refuse to take part in the routine production of marketable commodities, either by choice or by accident.[5]

As we saw in the introductory discussion of Rancière, just as the desire for totality conflicts with the desire for difference in the counterpoint of artistic regimes, so too does the economic role of cinema come into conflict with the Romantic poetics of film. In the films of Penn and Anderson, the tensions of art in the age of mass technological reproduction meet within the texts themselves as part of a general and multifaceted critique of capitalism. The political and philosophical complexities of these encounters will be illuminated throughout this book. Although merely epitomizing something to be found to a greater or lesser extent in many works of art, the films of both Penn and Anderson can first of all be interrogated from this productive tension within the poetics of film itself: between the desire for anti-capitalistic critical autonomy as works of art, and a capitalistic ethos inscribed in the commercial and explanatory logic of narrative cinema production – between 'art' and 'art-work'.

Arthur Penn's Romanticism

As Robin Wood affirmed, '"complexity" and "ambivalence" are words one can hardly escape from in talking about Penn'.[6] His films emerged during a crucial

---

[4] For example, Penn made *Night Moves* (1975) as an attempt to break the stultifying effect of personal crises he experienced during the early 1970s, and Anderson was finally convinced to work on *O Lucky Man!* (1973) through the intervention of Malcolm McDowell and David Sherwin. On Penn's experiences, see Michel Ciment, 'Interview with Arthur Penn', in *Arthur Penn: Interviews*, ed. Michael Chaiken and Paul Cronin, 151–61 (Jackson: University Press of Mississippi, 2008), 152.
[5] Adorno, *Aesthetic Theory*, 313.
[6] Robin Wood, *Arthur Penn*, new edition (Detroit: Wayne State University Press, 2014), 8.

period of transition for Hollywood cinema, and, like many of his contemporaries, their thematic and ideological content makes them distinguishable from the output of the classical period. Hollywood has been very efficient at assimilating formal and thematic innovations that once may have possessed a genuinely disruptive potential, yet it seems hard to completely agree with Robert B. Ray's conclusion that the 'Left' movies of Hollywood's countercultural era simply continue to 'glorify the old myths' and ideological structures that were prevalent during the classical period, despite their various appropriations from the European *avant-garde*.[7] Sympathetic criminals and unsympathetic lawmen; violence treated as shocking, painful and sometimes divorced from a predictable and ideologically explicative logic of cause and effect; a penetrative and entertaining critique of patriarchal authority, framed within narratives that consistently refuse the comfort of a 'happy ending' – Penn's films are suffused with such elements. They are characteristic of a new, ideologically confrontational period for Western filmmaking, and an industrial climate ready and willing to profit from the high tide of European art cinema and the imported vogue for auteurism. Robin Wood called Penn the heir to John Ford – a cinematic exponent and (de)constructor of the American myth.[8] Films such as *The Miracle Worker* (1962), *Mickey One* (1965), and *The Chase* (1966) and *Bonnie and Clyde* evoke a profound disillusionment with mid-century US culture. Although later works such as *Alice's Restaurant* (1969), *Night Moves* (1975), *The Missouri Breaks* (1976) and *Four Friends* (1981) reflect the failure of the 1960s counterculture, they also continue a pattern of thematic interests and ambiguous ascription of representational values that maintain the critical force evident in the earlier works.

In his book on Penn, Wood makes a passing comment that is perhaps truer than he knew. The critic makes brief and superficial reference to the English Romantic literary tradition, encompassing (in Wood's definition) the work of writers such as Blake, Keats, Yeats and Lawrence.[9] Like these authors, Wood explains, Penn's films seem to value concepts that have a schematic relevance to that more generalized Romanticism which includes valuation of feeling, nature, spontaneity and intuition. The young and dynamic protagonists of *Bonnie and Clyde*, for example, appear to behave according to seemingly 'freer' and more 'human' impulses than those operant in the society around them: passion, physicality and a flesh-and-

---

[7] Robert B. Ray, *A Certain Tendency of the Hollywood Cinema, 1930–1980* (Princeton: Princeton University Press, 1985), 17, 323, passim.
[8] Wood, *Arthur Penn*, 165.
[9] Ibid., 58, 148.

blood authenticity. Character development in the films is often fragmented and volatile, sometimes revelling in inconsistency. For instance, there is an alarming arbitrariness in the violence with which the eponymous protagonist of *Mickey One* (Warren Beatty) accuses his romantic partner (Alexandra Stewart) of innocently betraying him to his creditors: 'You're a slut with a snake in your mouth', he says, before screaming in her face the single word: 'Die!' This violence is all the more affective because Mickey is given no reason to disbelieve the innocence of her motives. Volatility such as this is often called 'postmodern', but, as Morse Peckham has shown, the idea that personality is necessarily incoherent was chiefly a Romantic discovery. The common interpretive paradigm that can be projected onto most of Penn's films roughly corresponds to the Miltonian 'fall of man' from a state of innocence, as divided and incoherent protagonists struggle to make sense of, and survive within, an unfriendly world beset with tempting utopian dreams and corrupting social influences.

The value of identifying such 'Romantic' themes is always dubious, of course; but what is more interesting is the way these tropes are consistently articulated alongside narratives that support a more specific allegorical meaning – one corresponding to the place of the individual within the modern capitalist economic system, and their struggle to escape, or at least maintain a critical distance from, that system. As the director's biographer Nat Segaloff notes, Penn 'matured in an era when politics were much clearer: "Labor was good, capital was bad"'.[10] He considered Reaganite 'selfishness' to have 'severed the moral obligation that unites us all'.[11] His cultural image accommodates more than a simple opposition to mainstream film production practices; it also maintains a certain hostility against the financial criteria for success and failure dominant in Hollywood. Penn often claimed that it was characteristic of him to 'struggle against the establishment', and particularly against the reviled studio system.[12] 'Money-making ... doesn't interest me in the slightest', he said, even considering himself fortunate to have been fired by Burt Lancaster whilst directing *The Train* (1965), a popular film which would have helped to make his career more financially rewarding, to the detriment, he believed, of his artistic integrity.[13]

---

[10] Cited in Nat Segaloff, *Arthur Penn: American Director*, 2nd edition (Sarasota: Bear Manor Media, 2020), 184.

[11] Cited in Paolo Mereghetti, 'America has Changed', 1990, in *Arthur Penn: Interviews*, ed. Michael Chaiken and Paul Cronin, 172–5 (Jackson: University Press of Mississippi, 2008), 173.

[12] Richard Combs, 'Arthur Penn', 1981, in *Arthur Penn: Interviews*, ed. Michael Chaiken and Paul Cronin, 133–45 (Jackson: University Press of Mississippi, 2008), 139.

[13] Cited in Mereghetti, 'America has Changed', 175; Michael Chaikin and Paul Cronin, 'A Summing Up', 2007, in *Arthur Penn: Interviews*, ed. Michael Chaiken and Paul Cronin, 200–13 (Jackson: University

Nevertheless, despite this personal anti-capitalistic prejudice, Penn's films reflect the complications inherent to the demythologizing of such simplistic ideologies as 'Labor good, Capital bad' (*sic.*); 'We are part of a generation which knows there are no solutions', he said.[14] It is the tension between moral commitment to anti-capitalistic ideals of authenticity and the refusal to allow any other ideology to unproblematically run its utopian course that contributes, according to the current interpretation, a considerable part of Penn's political Romanticism, as well as his affinity with Lindsay Anderson. Time and again, Penn's films tell that ambiguously political story so common to Romantic culture: that of an individual, or group of individuals, whose ideal of personal freedom is confronted by an oppressive social system that engineers their destruction as the only alternative to assimilation. In the case study chapters in Part Two we will see how this Romantic struggle is articulated as the necessity to choose between total violent destruction and the contamination of the principle of freedom by adopting the cruelties and unjust violence of the oppressor. Any kind of revolution (symbolic or otherwise) that might redress the balance of power in more favourable, 'humanist', terms can be secured only at the cost of relinquishing the moral superiority of that oppositional position. This Romantic theme is extremely revealing for Penn's oeuvre. The sense of push and pull – a tragic drama of irreconcilable forces which finds explosive expression throughout the narratives; the profound awareness of similarities between a cherished and humane ideal and the very worst of evils; the painful necessity to choose between action and inaction in the face of historical expediency; and the sense of guilt implicit in the very act of decision itself – we must understand how all this can be called 'Romantic' in a much richer sense of the word.

Lindsay Anderson's Romanticism

There is no shortage of references to Romanticism in Lindsay Anderson's films, essays and critical commentaries.[15] In the secondary literature, too, figures such

---

Press of Mississippi, 2008), 205. Such after the fact recontextualizations of 'failure' are always to be taken with a grain of salt, of course.

[14] Penn cited in Segaloff, *Arthur Penn*, 207; *sic*.

[15] See Lindsay Anderson, 'How *If*.... Came About', in *Never Apologize: The Collected Writings*, ed. Paul Ryan, 108–11 (London: Plexus, 2004), 108; Lindsay Anderson, 'School to Screen', in *Never Apologize: The Collected Writings*, ed. Paul Ryan, 112–15 (London: Plexus, 2004), 113; Lindsay Anderson, 'Notes for a Preface', in *Never Apologize: The Collected Writings*, ed. Paul Ryan, 120–3 (London: Plexus, 2004), 123.

as Blake are not uncommon points of comparison.[16] British cinema criticism more generally has attracted a malleable image of 'Romanticism', most notable in Powell and Pressburger, Olivier, Reed, Gainsborough, Hammer, Russell, Greenaway and Jarman.[17] But, again, there are particular reasons for claiming Anderson to be 'more Romantic' than many of his fellow creatives.

We can begin with the obvious subjective attitudes displayed by Anderson as a critic and artist. He was passionately interested in political, social and cultural questions, and his writings evidence an insightful, moralistic and often polemical attitude towards many issues that encompass both politics and aesthetics. Anderson's attraction to the Brechtian 'alienation' effect (*Verfremdungseffekt*) – a confrontational dialectic of naturalistic and expressionistic elements designed to undermine the ideologically charged realism of audiovisual representation – typifies his opposition to mainstream cultural practice.[18] Anderson's works declare themselves to be enacting art's intimate relationship with the empirical concerns of the historical present. He lamented the lack of 'urgency, moral passion and imaginative concern a film needs if it is to move mountains' in the majority of contemporary cinematic products; such an aspiration is, Anderson declares, 'the highest function of art'.[19] As with Penn's own cultural image, an aura of Romantic passion is interwoven with critical invective against dominant social forms. This inclination was strong enough to convince scholar Erik Hedling that 'Anderson's primary aim' as a creative individual 'was the deconstruction of "commercial" and "bourgeois" values'.[20] Only by pursuing quasi-Brechtian aesthetics, and turning a critical, even 'bitter', eye on the modern world around him, could Anderson reputedly 'live by' his 'convictions' both as a public figure and as a filmmaker.[21]

Most often, Romanticism finds expression in an expansive discourse of oppositional passion, which has greater depths than are perhaps at first

---

[16] See Elizabeth Sussex, *Lindsay Anderson* (London: Movie Magazine Ltd., 1969), 6, 14.
[17] See for example Peter Wollen, 'The Last New Wave: Modernism in the British Films of the Thatcher Era', in *Fires Were Started: British Cinema and Thatcherism*, ed. Lester D. Friedman, 30–44 (London: Wallflower Press, 1993), 34–7.
[18] Erik Hedling, *Lindsay Anderson: Maverick Film-Maker* (London and Washington: Cassell, 1998), 63–6.
[19] Lindsay Anderson, 'British Cinema: The Historical Imperative', 1984, in *Never Apologize: The Collected Writings*, ed. Paul Ryan, 390–7 (London: Plexus, 2004), 397.
[20] Hedling, *Lindsay Anderson*, 76.
[21] Lindsay Anderson, 'Get Out and Push!', 1957, in *Never Apologize: The Collected Writings*, ed. Paul Ryan, 233–51 (London: Plexus, 2004), 251; John Izod, et al., *Lindsay Anderson: Cinema Authorship* (Manchester: Manchester University Press, 2012), 149. Although I have selected these particular directors as a reading strategy and grouping technique, this book will not treat authorial intention as a privileged source of meaning.

Figure 4 Mick Travis (Malcolm McDowell) during the climactic school shooting from *If....* (1968).

apparent. Anderson himself stated that the band of student Crusaders in *If....* 'are very, I suppose fatally, romantic'; like *Bonnie and Clyde*, the pessimistic and conflicted violence that erupts in the final scene dramatizes, in Anderson's own words, society's violent retribution against 'the man who says "No"' (Figure 4).[22] Anderson's politico-aesthetic efforts were intended to articulate a sense of sincerity concerning important concepts such as 'Love', 'Duty', 'Freedom' – concepts that he saw denigrated by prominent intellectuals in contemporary Britain.[23] Unafraid to confront such big words, Anderson's films are set to be interpreted as grand and unapologetic allegories about pressing human concerns. If Mick Travis' journey in *If....*, continued throughout *O Lucky Man!* (1973) and *Britannia Hospital* (1982), is '"about" anything' at all, Anderson wrote, then it is about 'freedom'.[24] The idea of freedom, which we will attempt to explore in the films selected for analysis, abhors the false hypostasis of social distinction, all mythologizing of judgements regarding classical totality and all narrative elements that condone a conservative ideological catharsis. Yet, it manages to vent this passion only in problematical form.

As the 1956 manifesto for Free Cinema proclaimed, Anderson was also suspicious of 'perfection' – that hallmark of classicism. Any film displaying untarnished technical sheen evokes a distrust comparable to the Frankfurt School's attitude towards the products of the culture industry. 'Perfect' films could be 'a sort of drug', Anderson wrote, and can prompt a lack of critical

---

[22] Anderson, 'Notes for a Preface', 123.
[23] Anderson, 'Get Out and Push!', 250.
[24] Anderson, 'Notes for a Preface', 123.

reflection among their audience.²⁵ Adorno claimed something very similar when he critiqued the illusory processes of realism or spectacle that make some artworks appear to be self-producing. 'Phantasmagoria' was his name for this ideologically mystifying effect.²⁶ It resulted from erasing the presence of human agency behind a work's inherently politicized constitution. Given this preference for artworks that declare their constructed and ideological nature, it is hardly surprising that Anderson and Adorno were initially attracted to Brechtian aesthetics. For Anderson, 'authentic' art opposed the dominant conditions of production and reception that were imposed by its economic context: 'I suppose if you want to become a professional filmmaker, it would be wise for you to adapt your work to your market. If you want to become what I call a film artist, you're apt to go the other way.'²⁷ This is why he posited an antagonism between the higher artistic principles and the popular notion of 'success' represented by mainstream culture.²⁸ Value, it seems, is to be more broadly inscribed in what is categorically oppositional. Comforting and familiar things are not to be trusted. This attitude is encapsulated in a scene from *Is That All There Is?* (1992), during which Anderson explains that he reads the conservative publication *The Daily Telegraph* because he expects to disagree with it. He dismisses the prospect of reading a more liberal newspaper. There seems to be no value in reading editorials that will fail to arouse his critical faculties.

When Anderson writes of the 'true' artist speaking in a language that is wholly 'unfamiliar' and being unafraid to court charges of crudeness and subtlety, we recognize his intimate connection to the Romantic aesthetic, which similarly privileges the destruction of classical paradigms and categories of taste, unity and value.²⁹ For Erik Hedling, bricolage – a broad and 'overlapping aesthetic . . . with little bits of everything in it' – is a characteristically 'Andersonian' style.³⁰ We have already seen how the Romantics legitimated a new aesthetics of boundaryless-ness, and how Rancière situated this drive as the underlying poetics of cinema itself. With this focus on the films of Penn and Anderson we are now beginning

---

[25] Lindsay Anderson, 'The Film Artist – Freedom and Responsibility!', in *Never Apologize: The Collected Writings*, ed. Paul Ryan, 210–14 (London: Plexus, 2004), 213.
[26] Adorno, *Aesthetic Theory*, 141–2; Theodor Adorno, *In Search of Wagner*, 1952 (London and New York: Verso, 1991), 85–96.
[27] Cited in Scott Stewart and Lester Friedman, 'An Interview with Lindsay Anderson', in *Film Criticism*, Vol. 16/1–2, 4–17 (1991–92): 17.
[28] Lindsay Anderson, *The Diaries*, ed. Paul Sutton (London: Methuen, 2004), 401.
[29] Anderson, 'The Film Artist', 214.
[30] Hedling, *Lindsay Anderson*, 131.

to explore the potential for certain aspects of aesthetic content and form to become malleable variables of artistic production within, and intensifying, a general schema of film's Romanticism.

It is worth noting, before we move on, that there are 'Romantic' readings of Lindsay Anderson's cultural image whose methods are less significant for our purposes. Frank Cunningham wrote an essay entitled 'Lindsay Anderson's *O Lucky Man!* and the Romantic Tradition' (1974), which, although highlighting the relevance of the aesthetic, thematic and even philosophical connections between the titular elements, offers an argument resting on a limited and ultimately redundant concept of Romanticism.[31] Employing the early writings of Morse Peckham (writings which, in fact, Peckham later refuted), Cunningham begins with the particularly unhelpful definition of Romanticism as 'that mode of perceiving reality that celebrates man's unique significance in terms of his potential for enduring . . . in a cosmos that is seen as continually expanding, dynamic, and thus purposive'.[32] In this sense, what makes the protagonist 'Romantic' is simply his journey – supposedly like Coleridge's Ancient Mariner – from problematic self-absorption and an enthrallment with externally imposed worldviews to a freer condition of self-determination by escaping 'the prison of the self'.[33] By refusing, finally, to subjugate his cognition to the systems of other social entities, Mick Travis 'triumphs over stasis' and brings about a utopian condition in the final dance, which ends the film.[34] Cunningham's 'Romantic' reading reduces the film to an ultimately affirmative celebration of the dynamic world presented in the diegesis, making the metalanguage complicit in the horrors and injustices perpetrated throughout the narrative, and robbing the text of its critical potential. It is ultimately conservative readings of our chosen films' 'Romanticism', such as this, that I will attempt to complicate in the following chapters.

A multifaceted Romanticism creates productive tensions within both directors' works. One such tension develops between the desire for oppositional, critical art, and the need for popular appeal. Despite their post-classical excesses, the films of both Penn and Anderson are not 'hermetic intellectual exercises', and can appeal to a broader audience than a considerable proportion

---

[31] Frank R. Cunningham, 'Lindsay Anderson's *O Lucky Man!* and the Romantic Tradition', in *Literature/Film Quarterly*, Vol. 2/3 (1974): 256–61.
[32] Ibid., 256.
[33] Ibid.
[34] Ibid., 261.

of similarly 'political' filmmaking influenced by the mid-century *avant-garde*.[35] Both filmmakers' works, although standing on the border of the mainstream, encounter the fundamental economic necessity to appeal to an audience. As Anderson said, 'you can't engage your audience purely intellectually because that's not what they are there for. They're there to feel, to laugh and to enjoy themselves.'[36] More than the superficially Romantic synthesis between methods of popular appeal and the intention to bring about a Schillerian aesthetic education of humanity, this tendency towards problematic reception is distinctly thematic. Anderson intended to induce his audience to 'think'[37] – to simulate them into finding their own ideas to negate the problematic and damaged world reflected in his films' allegorical mirrors. This desire is easily relatable to the typically Romantic faith in the capacity of the non-specialized public to interpret and direct social reality – the desire to trust an emancipated social body with the capacity to direct human political, moral and philosophical development. Yet, as we saw in the introduction, and will continue to bear in mind throughout this book, such a Romantic desire is also burdened with an aura of authoritarianism, which needs to be worked through. The promise of aesthetic freedom is only ever precariously established.

No way out

As noted, the films of both Penn and Anderson have been criticized for offering, in their representations of social problems and injustices, no positive programme for improvement. Their narratives end in chaos, violence and disillusion, leaving no room for an optimistic alternative – no 'solution' to the problems they address.

Colin MacCabe, for example, criticized *O Lucky Man!* for its failure to properly realize the productive Marxism of Brechtian aesthetics, and for merely allowing the spectator to enjoy the satire from a privileged and elevated position.[38] Erik Hedling has confirmed that the 'lack of a clearly defined political stance in

---

[35] Gary Crowdus and Richard Porton, 'The Importance of a Singular Guiding Vision: An Interview with Arthur Penn', in *Cinéaste*, Vol. 20/2, 4–16 (1993): 5.

[36] Lindsay Anderson, 'Stripping the Veils Away', 1973, in *Never Apologize: The Collected Writings*, ed. Paul Ryan, 129–36 (London: Plexus, 2004), 136.

[37] Lindsay Anderson, '*Britannia Hospital*', 1994, in *Never Apologize: The Collected Writings*, ed. Paul Ryan, 148–59 (London: Plexus, 2004), 157.

[38] Colin MacCabe, 'Realism and the Cinema: Notes on some Brechtian Theses', 1974, in *Tracking the Signifier – Theoretical Essays: Film Linguistics, Literature*, 33–57 (Minneapolis: University of Minnesota Press, 1985), 56–7.

Anderson's films has ... become a prevailing target for their reception in Britain', leading to their faltering canonization.³⁹ Anderson's role as a public figure 'was that of a scathing social critic; he was not directly a propagandist for radical change';⁴⁰ and, indeed, his films often go out of their way to suggest that radical, revolutionary action can be destructive, ineffectual and easily misguided. In *If...., O Lucky Man!* and *Britannia Hospital*, rebellious characters, fired with a passion to assert their individual freedom, to mitigate the unhappy condition of others or to overturn a corrupt situation, are consistently thwarted in their efforts and meet with destruction, disillusionment or bewilderment. Anderson replies to his detractors by saying: 'The criticism has been made of my films ... that "they only show what is: they should show what ought to be – and how this can be achieved".'⁴¹ This is a criticism that Anderson is right not to take very seriously, and it is important that we understand why.

Critics such as Robert Kolker, in turn, have read a similar pessimism in Penn's films and their relation to 1960s counterculture. *Alice's Restaurant* and *Four Friends* doubt the possibility of progressive social change in ways that leave the texts themselves open to accusations of conservatism (Figure 5). The counterculture was, the films seem to say, a crucible of 'wasted energy' – a misguided moment of opportunity that fizzled out without aim or ultimate benefit.⁴² The social totality in Penn's films often remains imposing, unrepresentable and completely beyond the control and comprehension of individuals, despite their best efforts to

Figure 5 Ray (James Broderick) struggles to preserve the moribund spirit of the counterculture in *Alice's Restaurant* (1969).

---

³⁹ Hedling, *Lindsay Anderson*, 123.
⁴⁰ Ibid., 75.
⁴¹ Anderson, 'The Film Artist', 213.
⁴² Robert Kolker, *A Cinema of Loneliness*, 4th edition (Oxford: Oxford University Press, 2011), 57.

succeed. As we will see, this threatening absence is paradigmatically represented in *Mickey One* by the diegetic vacuum characterizing the unseen criminal/capitalistic underworld.

Penn was accused of producing a 'dangerous' film in *Bonnie and Clyde* because it supposedly encouraged violent rebellion without any 'positive ideology, or program'; an accusation that Penn countered by saying: 'I don't believe that there is revolt without a program which will emerge from it . . . a revolt comes out (of) a social condition. I don't think it comes out of abstract goal definition, and an attempt to achieve these goals.'[43] Anderson voiced similar ideas on revolutionary praxis, which are also reflected in his films: 'I don't think that revolution is the solution because revolution almost always, historically speaking, results in the substitution of one elite for another, of a different kind of power structure.'[44] I believe this to be the very point on which it becomes possible to read their films in reference to Romantic critical philosophy.

Aside from the historical variations in interpretation, part of the reason it is hard to attribute to Penn's and Anderson's films a decidedly Left-wing or Right-wing perspective results from this primarily *critical* attitude towards the holistic object of social satire. The kind of Romanticism that matters here is to be found in the completeness of the negating images which the opening pages of this chapter first evoked – the cinematic disavowal of action, whether it be in the form of social injustice or revolutionary praxis. It is an idea that, as we will see, involves us in a complex history of post-Kantian philosophy.

For now, the essential point is the refusal on the part of these films to unproblematically affirm their content. No preferential treatment is given to any positive political ideology. The lack of sympathy evidenced towards Left-wing perspectives and revolutionary praxis, and the criticism from Left-wing interpretations, which sometimes follows, distracts from the overriding determination, on the part of the films, not to ascribe a privileged valuation to any perspective whatsoever. The sense of confusion, disorientation and dissatisfaction that recurs in these texts is dependent upon this Romantic commitment to non-commitment.[45] "What ought to be" is defined in opposition to the negative valuation of what exists, as represented in the films. The presentation of an unjust state of affairs speaks in favour of an unthinkable better

---

[43] Wood, *Arthur Penn*, 149.
[44] E. Rampell and Lenny Rubenstein, 'Revolution is the Opium of the Intellectuals: An Interview with Lindsay Anderson', *Cinéaste*, Vol. 12/4, 36–8 (1983): 36.
[45] This phrase was coined by Morse Peckham in *Explanation and Power: The Control of Human Behaviour* (New York: The Seabury Press, 1979), 282.

condition, which is nothing save the negation of an abhorrent positive. There can be no positivity – that is the point.

It is worth exploring how this element brings Penn and Anderson into direct conflict with the kind of critical practice championed by Brecht. It is also something we must ultimately see embedded – if we are to fully appreciate its meaning – in a long tradition of critical philosophy extending through Kant, the Early German Romantics, Popper and Adorno.

One of the ways of understanding what this book attempts to accomplish is to imagine a space of correspondence between cinematic moments of Romantic passivity, inaction and indecision, and Adorno's attitude of 'non-participation (*nicht-mitmachen*)', along with the tensions and problematic results that can be associated with such positions, both narrative and philosophical.[46] As is well known, Adorno believed that explicitly political critique in the work of art was a lesser form of emancipatory action than those offered by purely formal innovation. Since all form – for both philosophy and art – contains the imprint of social history, there is no need to progress beyond the pure domain of the medium itself to critically engage with the categories of social life.[47] Penn and Anderson, however, adopt explicitly political themes in their work. The aforementioned determination, based upon Adorno's wider Aesthetic Theory, does not invalidate the correlation between critical philosophy and narratives of explicit political critique. As Susan Buck-Morss usefully summarizes, Adorno's thought does not exclude the potential for a genuinely referential narrative procedure; a polemical work 'could indeed be positively valued, so long as its intent was limited to critical negativity, the exposure of society's contradictions, without any pretension that . . . [art] could resolve them.'[48] Brecht came close to this method of negative aesthetics, but as soon as a work expressed any form of solidarity with a particular oppressed class or group, it fell victim to the pull of totality.[49] This refutes the criticism that commentators such as MacCabe and Kolker levelled against films such as *O Lucky Man!* and *Alice's Restaurant*. It was precisely the films' refusal to admit of any privileged ideology, which, although it might work to distinguish them from Brecht (the subject of MacCabe's critique), actually brings them closer to Adorno. By refusing to offer any legitimate vision of 'a way out', or a

---

[46] On 'non-participation', see Susan Buck-Morss, *The Origin of Negative Dialectics: Theodor W. Adorno, Walter Benjamin, and the Frankfurt Institute* (New York: The Free Press, 1977), 31.
[47] Genuine 'art' for Adorno is revolutionary on account of its historical relation to form; see Chapter 2; Adorno, *Aesthetic Theory*, passim; see also Buck-Morss, *The Origin of Negative Dialectics*, 35.
[48] Buck-Morss, *The Origin of Negative Dialectics*, 40.
[49] Ibid.

sympathetic perspective containing a meaning that lives beyond the screen, Penn and Anderson avoid the philosophical trap identified by Adorno.

These films are not Marxist, capitalist, anarchist, nationalist or anti-nationalist. Their attitude disavows any kind of ideological particularization, and (not dissimilar to Dostoevsky's Underground Man)[50] seemingly refuses even to credit the premises upon which they build their metanarrational perspectives with any kind of transcendental authority. As we will come to understand, the suspicion of being able to dispense with social injustice, hypocrisy and violence in the interests of pursuing the broadest of creative goals is as alive and productive in these films as is the suspicion of being able to do without the fictive and normative categories of thought in Adorno's *Negative Dialectics* (1966). The anguish, disorientation and irony that hangs over these works is fuelled by a Romantic passion which does not allow for untrammelled moments of hope, glory or comfort. Indeed, it is the prerogative of satire more broadly to adopt this kind of negative aesthetics and refuse to imagine unproblematic solutions to the allegorical situations it represents.

Satire and allegory as Romantic modes

The concept of satire is fundamentally linked to the allegorical. As aesthetic and political modes, they both proclaim to uncover a hidden 'truth' behind social reality. Although dating back to classical antiquity, these artistic modes characterize a nominally Romantic process. Being inherently 'open' modes of discourse – 'unruly, various, "open to whatever men do" (as Juvenal said)'[51] – satire and allegory traditionally enact a scandalous slippage between the comic and the tragic, the sacred and the profane. Being what Schelling called a 'double genre', satire is emblematic of Romantic boundaryless-ness.[52] Like allegory, in which things take on a 'true' identity that is not their own, the law of satire was thought to be inscribed in its name, '*satura*', 'full'/'a mixture' or '*satyr*', the breaking of boundaries between human and animal.[53] In the Kantian mode of thought

---

[50] The nameless protagonist of *Notes from Underground* (1864), who will return in the following chapters.
[51] Dustin Griffin, *Satire: A Critical Reintroduction* (Lexington: University Press of Kentucky, 1994), 4.
[52] Schelling, *The Philosophy of Art*, 226. Schelling makes no claim about this himself.
[53] Gilbert Highet notes that the Latin root 'satura' makes the Greek derivation from 'satyr' a scholarly misinterpretation, albeit a useful one; see Gilbert Highet, *The Anatomy of Satire* (Princeton: Princeton University Press, 1962), 231–2.

so valuable to critical philosophy, this latter association explicitly politicizes the space between appearances and things-in-themselves: human experiences as they are, and human experiences as they claim to be. The picaresque literary form exemplifies allegorical satire's desire to unmask and ridicule social conventions, ideologies and *doxa*. In Bakhtin's words: 'A reformulation and loosening up of all these high symbols and positions, their radical re-accentuation, takes place in an atmosphere of gay deception.'[54] The exaggerated and animalistic behaviours of characters (and even the direct conflation of human and non-human in *O Lucky Man!*'s infamous pig scene) finds its crudity validated, and its critical edge sharpened, by the oldest of cultural techniques: 'the ontology of beasts apes the age-old, always newly repossessed bestiality of men.'[55] Satire's critical effect takes the form of naming totality as ideology, that very same process which, in the dual realm of art and political analysis, has been given a host of names ranging from 'aesthetic education' in the heritage of Schiller to 'demythologization' in that of Roland Barthes. Allegory, too, sharpens an audience's receptiveness to the historical and ideological context of aesthetic experience, as Walter Benjamin suggested.[56] The allegorical mode, when read through the lens of Brecht's epic theatre, performs a similar *Verfremdungseffekt*, interrupting the classical paradigm of narrative action and encouraging spectators to reinterpret the social context of the text's reception and the conventions that allow it to have meaning. The political motivation for this allegorical effect is, in some respects, the same as for the satirical: the affective representation of a world that is somehow offensive – a social reality containing an elusive evil.

The satirico-allegorical approach, therefore, provides another way of understanding why some films can be thought of as more Romantic than others.[57] Undoubtedly, the generic groundwork here is stronger in the case of Lindsay Anderson. In addition to his often-noted inheritance from Brecht, critical discourse has frequently made comparisons between his work and that

---

[54] M. M. Bakhtin, *The Dialogic Imagination: Four Essays*, 1975 (Austin: University of Texas Press, 1996), 408.
[55] Theodor W. Adorno, *Negative Dialectics*, 1966 (New York: The Continuum International Publishing Group, 2007), 348.
[56] Walter Benjamin, *The Origin of German Tragic Drama*, 1963 (London and New York: Verso, 2009), 45; see also Daniel Mourenza, *Walter Benjamin and the Aesthetics of Film* (Amsterdam: Amsterdam University Press, 2020), 160–1.
[57] It is worth noting, with Benjamin (although he meant it in a different way), that 'the technique of Romanticism leads in a number of respects to the realm and emblematics of allegory'; Benjamin, *The Origin of German Tragic Drama*, 188.

of Voltaire, Kafka, Bunyan and Swift.[58] Yet, although Arthur Penn's own work has often been too distanced from the idea of the comic and the literary (and also characterized as too specifically 'American') to encourage similar parallels, both directors' works can be illuminated if we consider their association with the satirico-allegorical mode.

Anderson's fluid inheritance from Brechtian aesthetics is well known.[59] In spite of the aforementioned distinction, which attracted the attention of Colin MacCabe, his filmmaking choices outwardly correspond to Brecht's aesthetic strategy, minus the Marxist inclination to foster revolutionary praxis.[60] Influenced by theorist Karl Korsch, Brechtian methods entail a rejection of coherent realism, unity, empathy, illusion and action in favour of a deconstructive and hybridized approach to fiction that encourages an audience to critically reflect upon an allegory of historical conditions.[61] Rather than empathizing with a protagonist, or being allowed to 'forget' themselves and enter into a fictional world, an audience is called upon to cognitively interrogate the representation, and supposedly learns 'to be astonished at the circumstances within which . . . [the protagonist] has his being'.[62] Stories and logical relationships can momentarily break down, revealing 'dysfunctional' spaces suggesting something as yet unthought (Figure 6). Any reasonable interpretation of such scenes must recognize and respect their aura of unfathomability.

The desire to break the spell of totality in this way often becomes synonymous with a kind of stillness or inactivity, as the interruption of fiction's inherent dynamism becomes reflective of a contradictory reality, serving to reveal and demystify its determining ideologies.[63] Brecht championed the disrupting shock effect, the inharmonious montage – a textual practice capable of bringing things to a standstill – as a spur to critical reflection.[64] In its emphasis on disrupting a smooth running surface – a regularity of dynamic movement, which, by its

---

[58] Izod, et al., *Lindsay Anderson*, 231; Hedling, *Lindsay Anderson*, 113–14; Anderson, 'Stripping the Veils Away', 129.

[59] All three of the Mick Travis films were linked with Brechtian aesthetics in Anderson's published commentaries; see Anderson, 'Notes for a Preface', 121; Anderson, 'Stripping the Veils Away', 129; Anderson, '*Britannia Hospital*', 155.

[60] See also Izod, et al., *Lindsay Anderson*, 98–9, 151.

[61] See Douglas Kellner, 'Brecht's Marxist Aesthetic: The Korsch Connection', in *Bertolt Brecht: Political Theory and Literary Practice*, ed. Betty Nance Weber and Hubert Heinen, 29–42 (Manchester: Manchester University Press, 1980), 31–4.

[62] Walter Benjamin, 'What is Epic Theatre?' (second version), 1939, in *Understanding Brecht*, 15–22 (London: NLB, 1973), 18.

[63] Ibid.

[64] Ibid., 18–19; Walter Benjamin, 'What is Epic Theatre?' (first version), 1966, in *Understanding Brecht*, 1–13 (London: NLB, 1973), 3, 12.

Figure 6 The enigmatic science cabinet scene from *If. . . .* (1968) – one of the film's various moments of Brechtian 'interruption'.

mythic symbolism of continuity, equates to the world 'going on' as it should – the satirico-allegorical mode rearticulates the essentially democratic impetus of Rancière's aesthetic regime. The meaningful stillness brought about by such excesses enables the world to be seen from a more disinterested, and seemingly 'more objective', point of view, and the impossibility of determinate interpretation hints at the impetuous political realization that 'any person, any object, any relationship can mean absolutely anything else'.[65] This move towards objectivity is due to the illusory powers of art, of course, and can be maintained only as a moral form of 'aesthetic education' when it is articulated as an explicit negation of action. Otherwise, the idea that the bridge between subject and object has been overcome reverts the aesthetic experience to ideology.

Like Novalis' 'everything speaks', the moment of shocking stillness where detail becomes divorced from the whole brings with it a potent and elegiac refutation of the false totality.[66] This aesthetic mode entails a kind of discipline on the part of the creative or interpretive subject. The oscillation between subjective meaning and objective autonomy turns the work into a dialectic of self-critique. The detail becomes both unimportant for the artist's communication of a grand and determining Idea (such as a critique of capitalism), and, simultaneously, able to articulate its own corrective through the unbounded aura of meanings that its puncta can take upon themselves due to the poetics of the aesthetic regime. The satirico-allegorical mode is imposed upon the raw material, like any other narrative fiction, by an operation of the representative regime; yet, the aesthetic commitment to interrupting – thwarting – this operation with

---

[65] Benjamin, *The Origin of German Tragic Drama*, 175.
[66] Novalis, *Logological Fragments II*, § 54, 81.

disturbing and anti-cathartic fragments and intrusions, based upon this very mode itself, returns the text to a Romantic condition of ambiguous oscillation between artistic explanation and aesthetic freedom.

The need to consciously interrupt the fiction with a device that shatters the hypothetically comforting surface of the text leads to another significant Romantic concept shared with satire and allegory. Benjamin also notes that 'heavy-handedness, which has been attributed either to lack of talent on the part of the artist or lack of insight on the part of the patrol, is essential to allegory'.[67] The crudities and simplicities of the satirico-allegorical mode – the brashness of their interruptions – are also, perhaps, responsible for why Penn and Anderson are occasionally open to criticism as 'unsubtle' and 'crude' directors, lacking the cultural cache of more 'tasteful' auteurs such as an Ozu or a Visconti. This 'heavy-handedness' is also, needless to say, a significant part of the Romantic aesthetic schema. It operates in the idea of 'going-too-far' that is necessary for cultural transcendence, validated in the figure of the genius and returned to a scandalous cultural position in the figure of the virtuoso. It is of primary importance to the demythologizing impetus of the *avant-garde*, of course, that the creator be de-idealized – that the artist's role as an ideological figure be not forgotten through phantasmagorical effects. This was 'the first commandment of the epic theatre', as Benjamin put it.[68] In these terms, Anderson's on-screen appearance at the end of *O Lucky Man!* is an emblematic Brechtian gesture, exposing the self-proclaimed 'artist' behind the text. This gesture of the *enfant terrible* finds an appropriate double, and a political justification, in Rancière's pedagogical theory: that the one who teaches shall be the first object of knowledge[69] – that the one who creates for aesthetic cognition shall be the thing created and understood. In each case the desire (inevitably thwarted, yet brought into the light as a result) is to demythologize the phantasmagorical element in social and cultural life, and to turn the audience of interested individuals, as Brecht and Benjamin put it, into a collective of emancipated 'experts'.[70]

But where Brecht's aesthetic practice aimed to encourage productive revolutionary praxis on the part of its audience, the films of Penn and Anderson land upon a different result. Inspired by the political theorizing of Korsch, epic theatre was allied with the typically Romantic idea that the artist should

---

[67] Benjamin, *The Origin of German Tragic Drama*, 187.
[68] Benjamin, 'What is Epic Theatre?' (first version), 11.
[69] See Jacques Rancière, *The Ignorant Schoolmaster: Five Lessons in Intellectual Emancipation*, 1987 (Stanford: Stanford University Press, 1991), passim.
[70] Benjamin, 'What is Epic Theatre?' (second version), 15–16.

practice 'radical pedagogy', striving (in this case) to awaken their audience to class consciousness and the need for revolutionary praxis.[71] Yet, these films seem to be aware (whether or not the filmmakers themselves are) of the aporia that is inherent to the Romantic dream of aesthetic education: that tension in modern art between freedom and explanation I have already explored. The rhetoric becomes, instead, in its refusal to affirm any positive action, an exercise in totalizing self-critique – a negation that refuses to become a positive – as Adorno would ask of all thought and art that is truly emancipating.

Anderson said: 'In a sense to be a satirist you have to be a frustrated romantic.'[72] What such a comment lets slip is the significant possibility that Romanticism is itself intimately connected with the idea of frustration – the impulse behind Adorno's *nicht-mitmachen*. This gives an additional significance to Penn's and Anderson's shared sense of pessimism; the feeling most acute in many of their works is that of always already being defeated. In the iconic final scenes of *If....* and *Bonnie and Clyde*, filmic sympathies are only problematically allied with the protagonists in their hopeless stand against an authority that unleashes an overwhelming violence upon dissidents (Figure 7). The ambiguity of the heroes' own violence creates at least two positions for spectators. First, a space of critical distancing; repulsed by the indiscriminate violence of the rebels and the accidental victims of the bank robberies, viewers learn to reorganize their sympathies in reference to a textual objectivity that comprises a confusing and oppressive social cosmos. Secondly, the films create an opportunity to submit to

Figure 7 The violent death of Clyde Barrow (Warren Beatty) during the final scene of *Bonnie and Clyde* (1967).

---

[71] Kellner, 'Brecht's Marxist Aesthetic', 34.
[72] Anderson cited in Izod, et al., *Lindsay Anderson*, 228.

the cathartic spectacle of violence and the desire for change, which it radicalizes into a moment of thrilling and emancipatory terror.

This vision of Romantic freedom wrestling with nightmarish blood and purification becomes ever more problematic as the careers of Penn and Anderson progress. It leads from images of acquiescence and disappointment (*Mickey One*, *The Missouri Breaks* and *O Lucky Man!*) to nostalgic escape and the spectre of totalitarianism (*Four Friends* and *Britannia Hospital*), whilst, in the general concept of Romanticism, it leads straight from Schiller and Hölderlin through Marx and Wagner to the gates at Auschwitz. It may be the case that 'true satirists', true Romantics, desire to sweep away a false social totality. But they also know that by so doing they open a space for the New that can be viscerally appalling and cripplingly unjust.

A Romantic phenomenology of capitalism

Rancière's focus on the emancipatory detail points the way to something more than the dialectic of authored and unauthorized images as the origin of film's Romanticism – cinema's supposed fulfilment of Schelling's *System of Transcendental Idealism*. The extraneous detail that resists the pull of totality, standing for the objectivity of a pro-filmic reality beyond the command of the filmmaker, is also motivated by an authored choice regarding categories of inclusion and exclusion. It is a choice that, in the cases of Penn and Anderson, turns upon the presence and absence of painful elements of human experience under capitalism, and, as Adorno's *Aesthetic Theory* so effectively explains, the failure of art to live up to its own utopian ambitions.

Perhaps Robin Wood's comment about Penn's sense of visceral physicality is relevant here.[73] The powerful sensory impression made by these cinematic depictions of brutality and pain – the affective nature of their violence – suggests a particular alertness to the minutiae of human suffering along with its causes. The import of Rancière's explanation of Romantic film art is most keenly felt in those fleeting yet haunting images of poverty and pain, when the camera lingers on things that we, the viewers following a story, don't necessarily need to think about, that have no particular narrative function, and that we might otherwise ignore or pass over quickly, as we do when going about our lives. The films of

---

[73] Wood, *Arthur Penn*, 1–10.

Penn and Anderson show us characters with expressive and highly individual faces, like gargoyles or medieval paintings, perhaps reminding us of the cinema of Pasolini, Eisenstein or Dryer. They give a fervent, human expression to the injustices of the represented political worlds and their various interconnected tensions, power struggles and abstractions. The rawness of pro-filmic reality is co-opted to craft allegorical fables of political injustice, and an idealism fatally bound to the authoritarianism of the filmmaking process itself. Yet, more often than not, they interrupt the story, evoking that divide between 'cinematic' action and 'filmic' stillness. Like Adorno's metaphor of the 'firework' – which represents aesthetic truth-content as a mysterious and fleeting 'apparition'[74] – a suffering humanity emerges when it is least expected, bringing the narrative dynamism of cinema to a standstill and creating a momentary moral illumination that seems to demand an indeterminate response.

To illustrate, we might jump ahead and consider a moment from *Mickey One*. Whilst exploring an indoor amusement arcade, Mickey momentarily contemplates the possibility of using facial surgery to avoid his underworld creditors. He stands before a two-way mirror (presumably a security observation portal) and squashes his nose into a new shape. An old man with a craggy visage and misshapen nose appears beside him and, brushing his thinning hair, appears to momentarily contemplate his own reflection (Figure 8). Mickey's attention is fixed on the new arrival, and the diegetic soundtrack becomes

Figure 8 A strange encounter – Mickey (Warren Beatty) and a visitor at the arcade. *Mickey One* (1965).

---

[74] Adorno, *Aesthetic Theory*, 112.

muted, accentuating the intensity of the visual field. The event fascinates both Mickey and the camera for several seconds – longer than its content seems to demand in relation to the narrative. The response to such an image on the part of both protagonist and spectator, and even the film itself, seems to be a still and pregnant – nothing. Things grind to a halt.

A third figure, the watcher at the edge of the frame, accentuates the image's almost Brechtian effect of 'display'. The scene does not 'say' anything in particular, and does not invite any particular response. Yet, there is, in the conjunction of represented elements, a significant contrast between the material conditions of two fictional subjects. The old man's clothes, appearance and facial characteristics invite the not unreasonable conclusion that he is poor; we cannot easily imagine him being the man in the opening montage of *Mickey One* – our same protagonist, played by the handsome Warren Beatty – who drove sports cars and romanced beautiful women. Mickey has only to remove his fingers to correct the temporary disfigurement experimentally applied to his own nose.

In the difference between the beautiful protagonist who plays with alternative experiences of lived existence and this unfortunate yet quite 'normal' man, who wanders into and out of the fiction after a few seemingly incidental seconds, like an innocent passer-by in a documentary – between these two worlds lies the politicized condition of art's guilt. Art's play with materials, guided by a validating ideal of beauty, order and movement, runs up against the moral imperative to render unto aesthetic experience the tragedy of 'meaningless' ordinary life and its empirical conditions. Like Adorno's firework, the aesthetic experience claims a material objectivity and truth-content irreducible to any form of translation, yet burns itself out in appearance.[75] The mute stillness that permeates this scene becomes an acknowledgement that 'saying' anything at all – articulating the material as a functional element under the representative regime of art, transcending its ephemeral ontology as apparition – would be a kind of lowering. Yet, this is precisely what we find ourselves doing when we read the violence marking the old man's face as a meaningful sign, perhaps anticipating Mickey's entanglements with the mob. Through the act of assigning a determinate meaning, the firework burns out.

Penn and Anderson are by no means alone, of course, in making films that interrupt their narratives with the unwelcome detail, which, like Barthes' 'reality

---

[75] Ibid.

effect', marks the presence of the aesthetic regime.⁷⁶ Yet, the technique forms part of a multifaceted and politically motivated programme of anti-capitalist Romantic aesthetics. To find a productive critical potential in the representation of painful details is to stand against the totalizing pull of narrative function and refute the positivistic, and 'positively' inclined, cultural ethos, which functions as the work's historical present. The affinity between opposites, the power of montage to reveal what is hidden, the negative dialectic of the categories that creates a space for something New – all this 'filmic' material stands at the heart of the Romantic aesthetic schema, and is to be found prefaced in the writings of Hölderlin:

> Purity can only be represented in impurity and if you try to render fineness without coarseness it will appear entirely unnatural and incongruous ... beauty, when it appears in reality, necessarily assumes a form from the circumstances in which it emerges which is not natural to it and which only becomes its natural form when it is taken together with the very conditions which necessarily give it the form it has ... Nothing fine, then, can be represented without coarseness; and for this reason I shall always tell myself, when I encounter coarseness in the world: you need it just as much as a potter does clay, therefore embrace it and don't reject it or shrink from it.⁷⁷

Adorno would have agreed with this, as much as it chimes with the films of Penn and Anderson. Such perspectives seek value in what is insufferable, disorderly and blunt.

The 'truth' revealed in representations of intrusive and functionless suffering can be thought of as a kind of moral imperative against totality and its associated capitalist ideology. They are what cannot be allowed, for example, in adverts. The affective powers of the television charity appeal, for example, result from their breaking of this unwritten rule that determines the content of the commercial interests which surround them. Perhaps it was for this very reason that Anderson inserted images of starving children into the supermarket scene from *Is That All There Is?* (Figure 9). A sober documentary montage of shoppers in a London market is counterpointed with intrusive silent shots of malnourished Third

---

⁷⁶ Rancière rereads Barthes' famous concept, seeing it not as a marker of bourgeois ideology presenting certain ordinary things as the legitimating surface of a natural and mythologized sensory order, but, rather, as the emancipation, to a state of cognitive significance, of fictional elements that sever the old categorical determinations of unity and totality; see Jacques Rancière, *The Lost Thread: The Democracy of Modern Fiction*, 2014 (London and New York: Bloomsbury: 2017), 3–25.
⁷⁷ Friedrich Hölderlin, Letter 58, To Christian Ludwig Neuffer, 12 November 1798, in *Essays and Letters*, 108–10 (London: Penguin, 2009), 109–10.

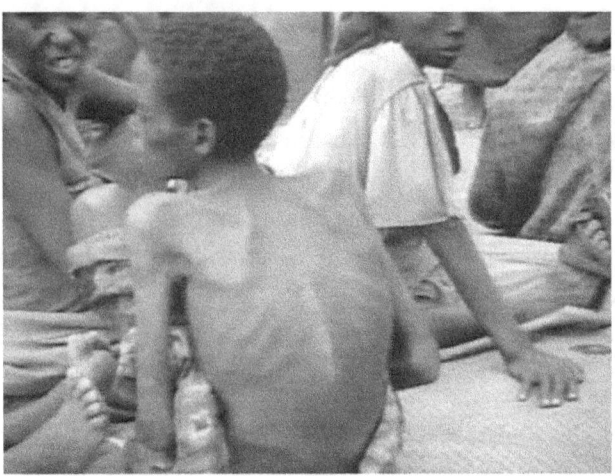

Figure 9 Intrusive images of poverty during the supermarket sequence in *Is That All There Is?* (1992).

World communities. Such representations contain the spectre of their opposite: joy and fulfilment, as an accusation over its absence. If, as Adorno phrased it, the pain of aesthetic experience contains the hope for a perfect world, then the stilled images of injustice and pain to be found in such films may (depending on interpretive disposition) impart a moral demand for action and response, which the texts themselves insist can never be unproblematically fulfilled.[78]

The camera's ability to interrupt a story and linger on things with the immobility of contemplation creates the effect of a poignant embrace. This wounding paralysis inflects the Romantic 'seeing anew' with a kind of love – an aesthetic that is drawn to painful things which fall outside of totality, whether it is represented by form, narrative or society. As Adorno writes: 'Things congeal as fragments of that which was subjugated; to rescue it means to love things . . . happiness would lie in the fact that the alien, in the proximity it is granted, remains what is distant and different, beyond the heterogeneous and beyond that which is one's own.'[79] The objective eye of the camera germinates an uncanny affective response that cannot be reduced to the expression of any filmmaking individual, cannot be denied to possess an objective content, and is all the more politically potent for it. If Adorno is right, what is crystallized in such moments – which disregard the distinction between form and content

[78] See Adorno, *Aesthetic Theory*, 74, 145, passim.
[79] Adorno, *Negative Dialectics*, 191.

– is the objective condition of society: the capitalistic world through which categories, aesthetic forms and reception practices circulate.

Such emergent elements resist the pull of totality and therefore have a critical and potentially emancipating effect, yes; but, as Rancière's dialectic theory of film shows, the process is always thwarted. The totality must be there in the end. What I will call the 'false endings' offered by each of the case study films, therefore – *Mickey One*'s final transcendence of its existential dilemma, the Elizabethan jig at the end of *O Lucky Man!*, the quasi-generic parting of the ways at the end of *The Missouri Breaks* and the sublime yet faltering vision of post-humanity at the end of *Britannia Hospital* – these false endings illustrate the fatal effect of the emancipating detail on the wider scope of narrative totality. In each case, the film and the filmmaker, like the Romantic innovator described by Morse Peckham, 'snatches intellectual and personality triumph from failure, but the result embodied a ruinous incoherence'.[80] Like the philosopher described by Adorno who aims to lose the argument, but 'in such a way as to (also) convict their opponent of untruth', their critical content emerges from a negative dialectic.[81] We will see all these endings perform, in different ways, their own self-critique through their very failure *as* endings. They give us fleeting access to the Romantic truth that – to borrow another insight from Peckham – success equals failure and failure equals success.

This is not just narrative cinema with rough edges. It is an incitement to reflection – a daydreaming camera that interrupts to underscore and innervate a critical representation of an offensive world. In the films of Penn and Anderson we see worlds troubled by conflict and injustice, carefully constructed diegeses that push against the bounds of classical representation, and, in the process, expose their nature as fiction. They do not isolate and differentiate themselves by adopting too obscurely the labels of 'art cinema'. They are made for entertainment, and yet, they do something else besides. They play a dangerous game between 'realism' and 'modernism' – amuse, horrify and frustrate their audiences. They strive to find a balance between the aesthetic critique of social reality and popular cinema, to perform the impossible and perpetually thwarted task of integrating the aesthetic and representative regimes. We are free to pay for a cinema ticket, Blu-ray or subscription and enjoy these texts as movies,

---

[80] Morse Peckham, *Victorian Revolutionaries: Speculations on Some Heroes of a Culture Crisis*, 1970 (Piscataway: Transaction Publishers, 2010), 110.
[81] Theodor W. Adorno, *Minima Moralia: Reflections from a Damaged Life*, 1951 (London and New York: Verso, 1987), 70.

and yet they make us aware of being shown worlds that are dark and distorted allegories of our own, striving to expose and make us feel the pain, delusion and injustice they both contain. The tensions resulting from the ways this dual task is realized makes up what is both so vital and interesting in these works, as well as what is so liable to be classified as aberration, pretension or failure. Robert Kolker is right to say that such films 'are interrogations of failure'.[82] Their vitality as works of audiovisual media turns on the fact that although no one 'wins' – neither diegetic characters nor the filmmakers themselves – the visions of failure that remain cast a dark shadow over the social relations, ideologies and maxims for activity which make up a world other than it should be.

These films are 'more Romantic' because in moments of inaction they objectify the tension inherent to modern art itself: the aesthetic rejection of the authoritarian act, meeting with the moral imperative to 'do something' because things in the world are bad and could be better. Allegorical satire forms the essential modality for a poetics of, and about, distortion, in form and content – the lie against the lie of totality – an emancipatory phenomenology of capitalism. Saying nothing positive, they assert, along with the tradition of critical philosophy to be explored in the following chapters, that an impossibly pure negation, even to the point of self-negation, is the only moral path for the true Romantic rebel.

---

[82] Kolker, *A Cinema of Loneliness*, 58.

2

Romanticism after Auschwitz
The tradition of critical philosophy

As a growing body of literature is coming to acknowledge, our modern interpretations of Romanticism can easily align certain aspects of this infamously slippery concept with fields that, according to traditional discourse, lie well outside its proper boundaries. In this chapter I will explore a number of these relationships in some detail and formulate explanatory constructs that will underlie the textual analysis presented in the following chapters.

Romanticism is to be understood here as a concept that possesses a certain continuity with aspects of twentieth-century culture and philosophy. The key hypothesis maintains that Romanticism is a revealing rhetorical synonym for a schema of ideas, values and behaviours that found itself of vital importance to the development of modernity. Terms such as 'modernism' and 'postmodernism' name various aspects of a continuous and developing Romanticism, which we are still experiencing. Key forebears of this position include Jacques Rancière, Morse Peckham, Michael Löey, Robert Sayre, Andrew Bowie, Elizabeth Millán-Zaibert and Nikolas Kompridis. In most cases, I have outlined their relevance to my own approach elsewhere, although their arguments will arise again, where appropriate, in what follows.[1]

I believe that the idea of Romanticism also overlaps with, among other things, the critical theory of the Frankfurt School and the critical rationalism of Karl Popper and Hans Albert, as well as certain contemporary formations of post-Althusserian Marxism. These philosophical developments are all related to a Kantian realist epistemological tradition, and a specific genus of Romantic culture – one associated with the work of Novalis, Schlegel and Hölderlin – which thereafter matured via Schiller's *Aesthetic Education* and Marx's concept of alien-

---

[1] Kitchen, *Romanticism and Film*, 21–39.

ation. The underlying themes of this Romantic critical philosophy are the essential points to grasp if we are to undertake my proposed filmic interpretations.

One of the most significant new voices in this field is Nikolas Kompridis, who has done much to reconcile what Jürgen Habermas famously called 'the philosophical discourse of modernity' (or, alternatively, what Richard Bernstein called 'the new constellation') with a more expansive approach to Romanticism as a critical concept. His *Critique and Disclosure* (2011) leaves few doubts about the Romantic trajectory of certain tendencies in modern continental philosophy, which, at first glance, could not seem further away from the world of Schiller and Novalis. Much like Peckham, Kompridis decisively concludes that critique and Romantic thinking are virtually one and the same form of philosophical or behavioural practice.[2] The essential object of this critique is the concept of *totality* – a self-perpetuating ideological system of socio-epistemological order. Ideas such as capitalism, class and positivism align with this concept of totality, which has, as its *telos*, the idea of a closed and unified system of categorical relations and value distinctions, such as quantity over quality, action over inaction, decision over indecision and so forth. The question remains how critical philosophy's flight from this idea of totality can be reconciled with a moral principle, or, more practically, a principle of agency. How can philosophy find a role for itself in a world that has become suspicious of the shadow of normativism, which supposedly lurks within the cultural schema of critique itself? Romanticism remerges here as a figure that is able to fill a gap in critical discourse, reminding us all the more forcefully of the patchwork structures which make up all our explanatory schemes, philosophies and languages, and the need to avoid treating them as timeless, universal and true.[3] The critical philosophies of the Kantian realist tradition, as we will see, contain a kind of Romanticism that recent scholarship has been at pains to reappraise.[4]

Romanticism thrives in the moment of seeing anew – like *Mickey One* (1965), when the old man joined the protagonist at the mirror. To witness the emergence

---

[2] Nikolas Kompridis, *Critique and Disclosure: Critical Theory between Past and Future* (Cambridge and London: The MIT Press, 2011), 274–80.

[3] Ibid., 254–62.

[4] It is now possible to dismantle the misconceptions maintaining fictive divisions within the rationalist Left. As we will see, it does not take much to recognize the fundamental points of agreement between Popper and Adorno, for example, despite the infamous controversy over the *Positivmusstreit* of 1961/1996, when Habermas contributed to a fatal rift between the two anti-positivist camps over what was essentially a matter of methodology; see Steve Fuller, 'Karl Popper and the Reconstitution of the Rationalist Left', in *Karl Popper: A Centenary Assessment, Volume III – Science*, 2006, ed. Ian Jarvie, Karl Milford and David Miller, 181–96 (Milton Keynes: College Publications, 2015), passim.

of the New is to value the prospect of an uncertain and painful infinite. The process of 'disruption' – as something that interrupts movement – is something we have already seen inscribed within the poetics of film itself. This encounter with a perplexing Other, which marks all critical thought, has a considerable heritage in Romanticism, and will form a vital theme in the following selective history of critical philosophy.

This is, admittedly, a complicated programme of interpretation. By pursuing it, I will be at variance with many traditional approaches.[5] Before I attempt to explain a 'Romanticism' sympathetic to a perspective such as Adorno's and relate it back to the study of film, however, there are several interrelated topics which it is necessary to illuminate by briefly tracing their development since the end of the Enlightenment. These topics include certain conceptions of truth and freedom, and the growth of modern capitalism and aesthetics. In the first part of this chapter, these themes will merge as I outline, in roughly chronological order, key theories and approaches within this history. By the end of this chapter, I will have introduced the idea of 'Romantic inaction' as a paradigm to aid my selected filmic case studies.

The critical path

The term *critical philosophy*, as I use it, designates a tradition of intellectual practice in modern European philosophy which extends from Kant through the Early German Romantics to the critical rationalists, critical theory and beyond. It begins with the Transcendental Aesthetic in the opening section of Kant's *Critique of Pure Reason* (1781), where a distinction is asserted between the 'subjective' and the 'objective', or between 'appearances' and 'things-in-themselves'.[6] In the subjective experience of time and space (what Kant calls a 'synthetic a priori'), we create an unbridgeable gap between the 'real' world (objective truth) and the world of illusionary appearances. Despite a surface level similarity with older Greek concepts, such as the famous story of Plato's cave, this rendering of spatiotemporal experience as synthetic a priori entails

---

[5] M. H. Abrams, Frank Kermode and Northrop Frye, for example, will have little part to play in the following analysis, and the kind of interpretations of Romanticism offered by critics such as Isiah Berlin sometimes overstep an important distinction, which I will attempt to make between Light and Dark aspects of this concept.

[6] Immanuel Kant, *Critique of Pure Reason*, 1781 (Indianapolis and Cambridge: Hackett Publishing Company, 1996), A 42–3, B 59–60, 94–5.

that there is no possibility of standing up, leaving the fireside and transcending the illusion.

A certain idea of truth and freedom results from this position. Truth is real, but it remains external to the knowing subject and can never be fully known. This is what is meant by Kantian 'realism'. But faced with this boundless ignorance, the subject is nevertheless 'free' because they can choose to adopt a 'moral' position.[7] Kant characterized this choice very clearly, as one between a 'dogmatic' and a 'critical' attitude.[8] Where dogmatic, or positivistic, thinking assumes the manifest nature of truth and equates appearances with things-in-themselves, critical thinking understands the structure that presents itself to the comprehending faculty as knowledge to be a cognitive framework, and not an aspect of the object itself. The concept becomes merely a regulative form for the application of reason in the face of an ultimately unknowable reality.[9] If truth is always hidden, then what appears to be true is merely a subjective construct resulting from a falsely positivistic ascription of objective value to appearance. Freedom, therefore, is given here, in the Kantian realist tradition, a fundamental derivation in the idea of critique. Because we can never equate the world of appearances with things-in-themselves, critical philosophy retains the belief that freedom means, first of all, the moral obligation to negate the truth-content of what is immediately given to experience.

This Kantian realism negates positivism and empiricism, yet these principles were of vital importance to the contemporaneous European Enlightenment and stimulated the development of modern capitalism. The new autonomy ascribed to the rational individual revolutionized Western culture by facilitating the emancipation of the subject from the dogmas of religion, mythology and superstition, whilst, by the same token, fortifying the capitalist ideology of competition. Among the complex social transformations brought about by the partial dissolution of organized religion and feudalism in Europe around the time

---

[7] Immanuel Kant, 'What is Enlightenment?', 1784, in *Political Writings*, 54–60 (Cambridge: Cambridge University Press, 2000), 54–5.
[8] Immanuel Kant, *Critique of Judgement*, 1790 (Indianapolis and Cambridge: Hackett Publishing Company, 1987), § 74, 277; see also Kant, *Critique of Pure Reason*, A 238–9, B 298, 306.
[9] However – and this is an essential point – subsequent continental philosophy through to Heidegger struggled with the necessity of reconciling this Kantian idea of subjectivity with the question that it implied over reality's objective existence; Lukács has shown (albeit with a selective, although often convincing, Marxist bias) how this struggle can be understood as essentially one between a persistent and malleable subjective idealism (Schelling, Kierkegaard, Schopenhauer, Simmel, Nietzsche, Heidegger, fascist philosophy) and a 'dialectical' materialism (Marx) that retains the firm ground of a realist conception of social and economic reality; Lukács, *The Destruction of Reason*, passim. The cultural image of philosophical Romanticism, I will argue, straddles this ambiguity between the subjective and objective basis of knowledge, in the form of a Light and a Dark attitude.

of Kantian philosophy, the principles of positivism and empiricism were being verified ever anew by advances in science, trade and industry. There was fostered a vigorous climate of faith in *quantification* as the prerogative of knowledge and social action: calculation, measurement, observation and inductive reasoning. The figure of the flourishing rational entrepreneur in the late eighteenth and early nineteenth century testified to the triumph of positivistic economic rationality, despite Kant's assertion that positivist empiricism was utterly groundless as a means of comprehending and manipulating the world.[10] Which is not to say, of course, that such manipulation was therefore beyond human capability; there was plenty of evidence to the contrary. The Transcendental Aesthetic entails, rather, a *moral* rejection of the ontological validity of positivism and empiricism – a rejection of their false claim to truth, when actions citing positivist foundations are, in fact, relying upon an unconscious pragmatism.

Enlightenment rationalism and Kantian critique thus provided the antagonistic poles of a dialectical construct that became central to the development of critical philosophy. Romanticism, in turn, would radicalize the idea of critique inherent to the Kantian programme whilst rejecting the secularized principles of religious morality that Kant offered as the solution to modernity's diremped subjectivity. A free subject estranged from reality could be only problematically reliant upon its own faculties when it came to intersubjective social responsibility. The French Revolution lit a fire under a great philosophical effort to base human morality on a stable foundation. The systems of Fichte, Hegel, Schelling and the Early German Romantics resulted from this effort, and, a century and a half later, fascism would ultimately provide a similar stimulus for Popper, Hayek, Adorno, Horkheimer and other heirs of Kantian realism.

Aesthetics flourished in the nineteenth century as a powerful alternative method of organizing modernity's grasp of knowledge, truth and morality. One telling explanation for this was to be found in the primacy of the unknowable objective reality within the critical tradition. The same kind of subjective individualism that had been galvanized by the American and French Revolutions during the contemporary stages of capitalist development was, by its very problematization in the Kantian system, flung back upon a need to acknowledge, and seriously reconsider, the role which the objective – or 'the

---

[10] For a simple definition of economic rationality, see Georg Lukács, *History and Class Consciousness: Studies in Marxist Dialectics*, 1923 (Cambridge, MA: The MIT Press, 1988), 88; for a sustained analysis, see André Gorz, *Critique of Economic Reason*, 1988 (New York and London: Verso, 1989), passim.

unknown' – played in human life. As Adorno explains, the historical development of 'individualism has indeed weakened the objectifying power of the mind, its capacity for insight into objectivity . . . but it has also equipped the mind with a discriminating sense that strengthened its experience of the object'.[11] In contrast to the dogma of quantification, which underlies modern capitalism, the critical attitude supports a contrasting notion of *qualitative* understanding that is bound up with the development of Romantic aesthetics. If modern capitalism saw the 'useful' emerge as a distinct criterion of positive value, then aesthetics, in turn, must place this category at the opposite extreme to artistic value, as in Kant's famous notion of 'disinterestedness' in the *Critique of Judgement* (1790). It is this very distance from capitalistic utility, pragmatism and action that has oriented the aesthetic object in the critical philosophical tradition.

Novalis, Schlegel and Hölderlin attempted to do justice to the notion of Kantian realism by transforming the search for understanding into an infinite and unending quest based upon aesthetic experience. According to scholar Manfred Frank, the most characteristic idea upheld by these Early German Romantics is 'anti-foundationalism', or a belief in the impossibility of grounding knowledge on first principles – things that are universal, true, eternal and knowable.[12] For the Romantics, there are no first principles, only regulative ideas that stand and fall within the process of history.[13] As Schlegel put it: 'Our philosophy does not begin with a first principle . . . From an unlikely and modest beginning – doubt regarding the "thing" which, to some degree shows itself in all thoughtful people . . . – our philosophy will develop.'[14] Subjective knowledge is qualitatively distinct from objective truth, and the idea of 'absolute knowledge' is replaced with that of 'absolute "not knowing"'.[15] All thought takes place within the influence of conditions, and, since there are no primary conditions for knowledge, everything we know is dependent upon some other piece of knowledge being taken for granted. To justify something according to any ground becomes a deception – to cut short a process of infinite regress. Long before Popper and Hans Albert developed the outline of an 'evolutionary

---

[11] Adorno, *Negative Dialectics*, 42.
[12] Manfred Frank, *The Philosophical Foundations of Early German Romanticism* (Albany: State University of New York Press, 2004), 23. Fichte, for example, held that knowledge must proceed from such first principles; see Johann Gottlieb Fichte, *The Vocation of the Scholar*, 1794, in *The Popular Works of Johann Gottlieb Fichte, Vol. 1*, 149–205. Bristol: Thoemmes Press, 1999), 195.
[13] See Novalis, *Fichte Studies, 1795–96* (Cambridge: Cambridge University Press, 2003), § 472, 152; § 566, 168.
[14] Cited in Frank, *The Philosophical Foundations of Early German Romanticism*, 202.
[15] Ibid., 56.

epistemology', the Romantics reached the analogous conclusion that the ideal of knowledge eludes the grasp of any scientific system, no matter how pure its methodology. Hölderlin exemplifies this conviction:

> I have always believed that for its knowledge as for its actions mankind needed an infinite progress, an unbounded time, in order to approach the boundless ideal; I called the opinion that science could be completed or was completed at a particular time scientific quietism; there will always be error, whether it contents itself with an individually determined boundary or simply denies a boundary that is in fact there, even though it ought not to be.[16]

Novalis put it even more bluntly: 'error is the necessary instrument of truth. With error I make truth.'[17] Since truth becomes graspable only in a negative form, the business of philosophy as the search for truth then becomes, again, a discipline of critique: the negation of affirmation – the inquiry into falsehood. Positivity becomes suspect, according to its structural relationship with the corresponding idea of truth. This Romantic perpetual striving after an ultimately unknowable reality becomes one of the most significant tenets of critical philosophy.

The Romantic paradox

We are now approaching a central issue, which has already been outlined in the introduction, and I am finally able to situate it within a richer historical context: the aporetic tension between freedom and explanation in modern aesthetics.

Schelling's *System of Transcendental Idealism* (1800) argued that art could progress beyond science as a means of cognition, allowing us to access that which were not reducible to empirical language.[18] If humanity was to benefit from such a possibility, however, now that the authority of religion had been undermined, there needed to be instilled a discipline that would innervate humanity. A new religion, or 'New Mythology', was needed.[19] A religion headed by 'artist-priests' – a shade of the modern post-Kantian notion of the 'genius' as a cultural type – who would strive to bring about the 'aesthetic education'

---

[16] Friedrich Hölderlin, 'Hermocrates to Cephalus', in *Essays and Letters* (London: Penguin Books, 2009), 233. [1795].
[17] Novalis, *General Draft*, c.1799, in *Philosophical Writings*, ed. Margaret Mahony Stoljar, 121–36 (Albany: State University of New York, 1997), § 29, 130.
[18] Schelling, *System of Transcendental Idealism*, 219–36.
[19] Hölderlin, 'The Oldest Program for a System of German Idealism', 341–2.

of modern subjectivity, commonly modelled on a lost Golden Age represented by Greek antiquity. Schiller's *Letters on the Aesthetic Education of Man* (1795) is perhaps the paradigm expression of this desire, to which many subsequent Romantics such as Liszt and Wagner implicitly adhered.[20] The Romantic imperative for boundaryless-ness endows science, art, religion and philosophy with the potential to combine as a single discourse. Artist-priests, as limited historical individuals, produce works that have as their goal 'the education of the earth'[21] – the emancipation of humanity through the power of free aesthetic experience.

But herein lies that great paradox which, as we know, cuts right to the heart of cinema. For if art was now to be defined in reference to its confounding otherworldly disinterestedness, then other new and powerful forces were rapidly gaining authority to decide what was and was not worthy of earthly interest. Nineteenth-century European philosophy had not been entirely concerned with an aesthetic programme of moral rejuvenation, for Kantian critique also led down more materialistic pathways. Alongside Romanticism and its dream of a New Mythology, modern capitalism had also been gaining ground and attracting its own critical attention. Like Romanticism, Marxism emerged from German Idealism, and more particularly from the writings of Hegel and Schiller. Kant's own 'What is Enlightenment?' (1784) neatly illustrates the sense of anxiety concerning the supposed 'immaturity' and unfreedom of the people under a rising capitalist social system – an anxiety that would soon be allied with a critique of the principles of empirical calculation and positivism associated with that economic system.[22] Despite Kant's warning and the Romantics' utopian dreams, a harmful capitalist rationalism was flourishing.

Economic rationality possesses a vast explanatory power. There are few things in life that cannot be accounted for in terms of their monetary value. As Franco Moretti put it: 'the market mechanism is . . . praised . . . as the system best adapted to discover the connection that links the most disparate human activities; to assign a meaning even to the most negligible and insignificant things.'[23] The market is able to give those who ascribe value to its mechanism a formidable instrument to make sense of anything they might encounter. Yet, if the

---

[20] Friedrich Schiller, *On the Aesthetic Education of Man*, 1795 (London: Penguin Books, 2016), § 6, 18.
[21] Novalis, *Miscellaneous Observations*, c.1798, in *Philosophical Writings*, ed. Margaret Mahony Stoljar, 23–46 (Albany: State University of New York, 1997), § 32, 28.
[22] Kant, 'What is Enlightenment?', 54.
[23] Franco Moretti, *The Way of the World: The* Bildungsroman *in European Culture* (London and New York: Verso, 1987), 25.

scientific rationalization of social institutions had increased their effectiveness at governing the social life of individual subjects, and if Enlightenment positivism could decide the 'objectively' best ways of arranging human conduct according to quantitative calculation and efficiency, then human freedom to think, argue, innovate and choose – a moral ideal shared by Kant and the Romantics alike – became problematically situated.

The voracious positivism of economic rationality would soon become critical philosophy's most persistent antagonist.[24] New voices came to the aid of the nostalgic and organicist Romantics in their (conflicted and often paradoxical) struggle against capitalism. Thanks to the Enlightenment, a veil had been lifted from the historical conditions of social reality, and Marx and Engels put the concept of ideology centre stage. Knowledge was now recognized (but certainly not by all) as a fictional construct that is subject to the development of various historical ideological relationships: relationships between social authority, and the standards of legitimacy and hypostasis, which are enforced and maintained on a changeable historical basis. Marxism revealed, not that knowledge is power, exactly, but, rather, that knowledge is a condition of power – that knowledge is shaped by it. Certain groups of people had more power than others, but the naturalness of this state of affairs was becoming increasingly questionable. Self-awareness grew on the part of a humanity divided by more than just the sterile and separated institutions and mechanisms of religion, culture and state, which made Schiller and his followers hark back to the ideal of a unified Greek condition. Modern humanity was now seen to be divided by economic worries, exploitation, distinctions, power struggles and state apparatus, which, through appeal to the new Gods of economic rationality – maximum attainment of ends and efficiency of means – meticulously planned for the profitable division of jobs, groups and classes. Feudal lords and priests had lost much of their power, but ideology found new targets for critique in emergent and transforming social groups made up of employers, traders, exploiters and politicians: those who had become the new rulers of a fast-globalizing world increasingly emancipated from the idea of autocratic rule based on non-economic capital.

If, as Romantics no less than Marxists began to point out, modern society was becoming dominated by the quantitative standard of value, then art –

---

[24] Few Romantics attacked the tyranny of quantity more forcefully than Carlyle: 'Cash never yet paid one man fully his deserts to another; nor could it, nor can it, now or henceforth to the end of the world'; Thomas Carlyle, *The Works of Thomas Carlyle, Vol 10 – Past and Present*, 1843 (Cambridge: Cambridge University Press, 2010), 189.

for the first time endowed with its modern (post-Kantian) anti-pragmatic meaning under the aesthetic regime – simultaneously becomes increasingly sensitive to the qualitative nature of things, coming to stand in ultimate antithesis to the quantitative concerns of the everyday world. Thanks to its categorical indeterminacy, art was still perhaps the one place where the tyranny of quantitative explanation could be resisted. But here emerges that great paradox we encountered in the introduction to this book: art's great aporia – a guilty condition between freedom and explanation. Romanticism stands problematically between the ideal of its own aesthetic condition, defined in opposition to economic rationality, and the desire for art to enact some kind of practical change in the empirical social and political world – a New Mythology of aesthetic education. Art's usefulness returns as its own uncanny embarrassment.

Yet, to understand the force of resistance that critical philosophy mustered against capitalism in the field of aesthetics, we must first look at the work of the critical rationalists. This will help us understand how the Romantic interest in art and unknowable objectivity, which critical theory rearticulated in its own way, was strengthened by contemporary responses to some of positivism's (and Romanticism's) most nightmarish excesses.

Romanticism after Auschwitz

The structural similarities between the theories of Marx, Darwin and Freud demonstrate quite clearly one simple idea of knowledge that is significant for critical philosophy. Peckham phrases it in the following terms: 'Inadequacy is the source of the principle of growth.... Success is to be founded on a necessary and eternal failure.'[25] The critical rationalism associated with Karl Popper, F. A. Hayek and Hans Albert comprises one of the most productive tributaries of this philosophical imperative. The Kantian rejection of first principles, absolute knowledge, positivism, empiricism and pragmatic subjective reason has perhaps yet to find a stronger realization than the arguments presented in books such as *The Logic of Scientific Discovery* (1937), *The Road to Serfdom* (1944), *Conjectures and Refutations* (1963) and *Treatise on Critical Reason* (1968). The Romantic imperative for negation and reciprocal interrogation of certainties as the source

---

[25] Morse Peckham, 'The Problem of the Nineteenth Century', 1955, in *The Triumph of Romanticism*, 87–104. (Columbia: University of South Carolina Press, 1970), 103.

of knowledge and progress finds an unlikely ally in Popper's philosophy of science, Albert's epistemology and Hayek's political theory. The dramatic surface differences between figures such as Popper, Novalis, Hayek, Schlegel, Adorno and Hölderlin should not prevent us from seeing the interesting points of agreement between them.

At the heart of critical rationalism lies 'falsificationalism', or the idea that any proposition that makes a claim to truth can only be empirically disproved, never proved.[26] This is a direct contravention of classical empiricism, which holds that knowledge is verified by appealing to observation of sources. Popper advocated the seemingly counterintuitive belief (derived, as he often admitted, from Xenophanes) that we cannot find the truth by looking at the facts; human knowledge is conjectural, and no source of knowledge has ultimate authority.[27] The critical rationalists were in complete agreement with their Frankfurt School contemporaries in believing that the idea of pure reason – a subjective potential for knowledge completely independent of all history and society – is an ideological mystification.[28] Truth here has a negative character; it is something we can know only through an experience of falling short.[29] Knowledge we may claim to possess is nothing more than a provisional conjecture, which is subject to criticism, refutation or revision.

Critical rationalism holds that human knowledge processes by the negation of falsehoods, not the accumulation of truths; not the search for certainty, but the search for contradiction – uncertainty.[30] Rather than stockpiling proven 'facts', we must attempt to discover truth by making 'risky predictions' – statements that transcend our current knowledge whilst being structurally falsifiable, that is, subjected to tests which are logically capable of disproving the statements – if we are to practise a moral pursuit of ultimately unknowable truths:

> The process of learning, or the growth of subjective knowledge, is always fundamentally the same. It is imaginative criticism. This is how we transcend our local and temporal environment by trying to think of circumstances beyond

---

[26] The core statements regarding Popper's rejection of inductive reasoning, Plato and Hegel, as well as some useful introductory remarks, can be found in Popper, *The Logic of Scientific Discovery*, 3–26 and 57–73. See also Karl Popper, *Objective Knowledge: An Evolutionary Approach* (Oxford: The Clarendon Press, 1979), 29–30.
[27] Karl Popper, *Conjectures and Refutations: The Growth of Scientific Knowledge*, 1963 (London and New York: Routledge, 2002), 32.
[28] Hans Albert, *Treatise on Critical Reason*, 1968 (Princeton: Princeton University Press, 1985), 116.
[29] Ibid., 40.
[30] Ibid., 56. Albert went so far as to call critical rationalism a non-Hegelian dialectical method – a revealing statement, which suggests the strong correspondence between Popper and Adorno; Ibid., 57.

our experience; by criticising the universality of, or the structural necessity, of what may, to us, appear (or what philosophers may describe) as 'given' or as 'habit'; by trying to find, construct, invent, new situations – that is, test situations, critical situations; and by trying to locate, detect, and challenge our prejudices and habitual assumptions.[31]

So the growth of scientific knowledge is a process of evolutionary 'dialectics' (although Popper disliked that term). Negation – criticism of manifest experience – is the essential point. Based on his rejection of Platonic idealism and Hegelian historicism, what Popper calls 'imaginative criticism' corresponds quite neatly with the Romantic schema of cultural transcendence described by Peckham: the rejection of existing explanatory constructs as a method of social progress. This emphasis on negation over any positive dialectical synthesis – a result of maintaining the Kantian thing-in-itself – is enough to distinguish critical rationalism from the naïve pragmatism it superficially resembles.

The idea that failure is a source of value becomes more profound than a simple acknowledgement of the progressive force of Darwinian evolution. For if the schema of 'trial and error' implies a dialectic of productive growth that corresponds to capitalistic notions of success (in, for example, Thatcherite and Reaganite economic policy), then Romanticism can also choose to radicalize the negative character of evolutionary epistemology. Rather than seeing failure, pain and suffering as an impetus to action and change, critical philosophy also displays a tendency to endow such experiences with an insular and self-contained value; again, as Peckham expresses it: 'The flower of value must be plucked not on the sunny mountaintop, but in the very abyss. . . . The worship of sorrow is divine', for it endows with truth everything that rejects the false gods of totality, success and even the inevitability of 'progress'.[32]

This tendency to valorize error, desolation and pain, without recourse to ideals concerning a higher Good to which they merely stand as a functional impetus, is a potent illustration of the kind of Romanticism we also find in Adorno. If pleasure is an intense experience of subjectivity, then pain tends to reach out beyond the self towards the wider reality of objectivity. If *éros* is an isolating

---

[31] Popper, *Objective Knowledge*, 148.
[32] Morse Peckham, 'Toward a Theory of Romanticism II: Reconsiderations', 1960, in *The Triumph of Romanticism*, 27–35 (Columbia: University of South Carolina Press, 1970), 33. This idea is also powerfully evoked in Joseph P. Lawrence's commentary on Schelling's *The Ages of the World* (1811), a text which shares with the tradition of critical philosophy a belief in the value of self-negating thought and passive suffering over practical results and affirmation; see Joseph P. Lawrence, 'Translator's Introduction: The Ecstasy of Freedom', 2019, in *The Ages of the World*, 1811, Friedrich Wilhelm Joseph Schelling (Albany: State University of New York Press, 2019), 1–52, passim.

thing, then suffering demands witnesses – demands a bearing-witness, which goes hand-in-hand with the demand for truth. As Adorno writes: 'The need to lend a voice to suffering is a condition of all truth. For suffering is objectivity that weighs upon the subject.'[33] Although Auschwitz was most frequently on Adorno's mind during the development of this perspective, the source of suffering that attracts critical philosophy today, as it has done since the days of Schiller, is capitalism: one of critical (or Light) Romanticism's most persistent antagonists.

Romantic anti-capitalism

Like other forms of critical philosophy, the thought characteristic of the Frankfurt School is also born of failure. Adorno and Horkheimer were acutely conscious of the failure of orthodox Marxism to realize the demise of capitalism, the disastrous development of Russian and Chinese state communism and the nightmarish failure of Romantic unboundedness that fuelled both the triumph of global capitalist enterprise and the ovens at Auschwitz. Popper and Hayek had shown that positivistic statements were inherent to the Marxist historicism of socialist state planning, and how they lead to a totalitarianism which is just as bad as that which it was hoped they would overthrow. For post-war twentieth-century philosophy, failure must become again the moral ally of truth, just as it had been for the Romantics a century before. That dialectics after Hegel should never come to a rest in higher unity – never find a 'home' – is indicative of its Romantic heritage.[34] As Horkheimer stated: 'We in contrast (to Marx) are Romantics.'[35]

---

[33] Adorno, *Negative Dialectics*, 17–18, 365; also 'Someone who has been offended . . . (or) who is rebuffed becomes human . . . (–) he who has lost love'; Adorno, *Minima Moralia*, 164. Adorno even went so far as to say that running, as opposed to walking, is a sign of negative truth in its 'archaic power' as a symbol of violence and compulsion; 'someone running after a bus unwittingly bears witness to past terror'; Adorno, *Minima Moralia*, 102.

[34] The Romanticism of critical theory is not a novel observation, of course. Lucio Colletti and Jürgen Habermas, for example, pick out a few 'Romantic' tendencies in Marcuse, Adorno and Horkheimer; see Lucio Colletti, *From Rousseau to Lenin*, 1969 (London: NLB, 1972), 139–40; Jürgen Habermas, *The Philosophical Discourse of Modernity*, 1985 (Cambridge: Polity Press, 1998), 187. Habermas wedded these perspectives to that nominally Romantic desire for a new religion, an unspoilt past, free from the corruption of capitalist principles of rationality, or a new 'beginning to philosophy'; Habermas, *The Philosophical Discourse of Modernity*, 122–3, 134–5. Nikolas Kompridis has recently developed this explanatory paradigm – one which legitimates the 'Romanticism' of critical theory itself – to a more sustained degree.

[35] Theodor W. Adorno and Max Horkheimer, *Towards a New Manifesto*, 1989 (London and New York: Verso, 2019), 59.

Adorno was more committed to the Kantian tradition than his famous response to Hegel would at first suggest. As he writes in *Negative Dialectics* (1966): 'Entity is not immediate . . . it is only through the concept', which is inherently an abstraction.[36] Consequently, the appearance of reality advocated by the dominant economic system is mere ideology. Authentic philosophical behaviour then becomes, once again, wholly negative in character, and, rather than progressing towards a higher totality, the search for truth becomes a non-teleological programme of negation.

This Romantic trope was evident in critical theory from the earliest stages. As Horkheimer proclaimed: 'Every part of the theory (critical theory) presupposes the critique of the existing order. . . . Conformism . . . betrays the very essence of thought.'[37] By championing the category of objectivity as marking those revelations of fresh thought implied by the idea of theory itself, the critical theorists follow the critical rationalists in bringing together various Romantic principles of value – critique, the New, emancipation, boundaryless-ness – under a new banner. Truth and freedom are to be found on the side of the negative: error, falsehood, suffering, wrongs – all things associated with the experience of *weltschmerz* ('world-weariness'). Ideas of eternal peace, universal Truth and the highest Good are discounted, for throughout history they have often brought about their opposites according to the actions of those who were willing to realize them by any means necessary. 'The thinker,' Horkheimer says – the rational individual who values and seeks freedom – 'must constantly be beginning anew', enlisting untrustworthy but necessary historical categories in a continual process of self-critique.[38] Conforming to the existing order, by contrast, means playing along with capitalism – a system with little time for pain and suffering (as the supermarket scene from *Is That All There Is?* [1992] reveals), or the confounding realm of objective reality.

For critical theory, as for Romanticism and the rest of critical philosophy, capitalism can easily represent the greatest 'wrong' or the most potent cause of unfreedom. 'The (modern) economy,' as Horkheimer put it, 'is the first source

---

[36] Adorno, *Negative Dialectics*, 153.
[37] Max Horkheimer, 'Traditional and Critical Theory', 1937, in *Critical Theory: Selected Essays*, 1968, 188–243 (Lexington, NY: The Continuum Publishing Company, 2002), 229, 243.
[38] Ibid., 234. There are numerous similar statements in Adorno's writings; see for example Adorno, *Minima Moralia*, 124–6. There are also many obvious similarities between critical theory and critical rationalism; for example, consider Horkheimer's Popperian comment: 'True theory is more critical than affirmative'; Horkheimer, 'Traditional and Critical Theory', 242.

of wretchedness.'³⁹ The Frankfurt School thinkers directed their philosophical diatribes against a newly 'cultured' conception of capitalism, one functioning according to a regime of positivity which was sometimes pathological in its intensity. As Adorno stated: 'I know that everything is false so long as the world is as it is'; the desired 'open' condition for philosophy must begin with a general idea of 'the perversity of things', or the underlying ontological fragility of all epistemological certainties associated with consciousness.⁴⁰ The enemy was, accordingly, those ideas of affirmation, bold decision, quantitative morality and the making of confident pronouncements concerning competing products, services and pleasures, upon which this 'first source of wretchedness' had, since the days of the Enlightenment, thrived and used to undermine freedom.

Critical theory's attacks on economic rationality, consumer culture and market economics highlight the great ambiguous tension between Romanticism and capitalism. Both concepts share a fascination with the disruptive New, the latter preferring one that does not negate the given, but, rather, reiterates it in ever changing and emergent forms: in the drive towards more efficient, useful and profitable forms of social relationships; in the logic of fashion; and the fetishization of 'the latest thing' on the market.⁴¹ The idea of Romantic anti-capitalism (familiar from the writings of Sismondi, Carlyle, Blake, Wordsworth, Keats, Coleridge, Ruskin, Morris and others) remains relevant to these debates, despite the complications created by conflicting interpretations and historical variations.⁴² As is well known, Marx also recognized something 'anti-Romantic' in capitalism's ability to reduce human dependency upon myth and superstition. Yet, this transcending of irrational belief revealed itself, as Adorno and Horkheimer often professed, to be capable of a radical and destructive reversal. Alex Callinicos has suggested that Marx's antagonistic positioning of

---

[39] Horkheimer, 'Traditional and Critical Theory', 249.
[40] Adorno and Horkheimer, *Towards a New Manifesto*, 68; Theodor W. Adorno, *Lectures on Negative Dialectics*, 1965–1966 (Cambridge: Polity Press, 2008), 122.
[41] For an interpretation of capitalism that emphasizes this (Romantic) innovative aspect, see the work of Jospeh Schumpeter, or, more particularly, Richard Bronk. For example, the Romantic desire for cultural transcendence is reflected in the malleable image of innovation and 'creative destruction' famously described by Schumpeter in *Capitalism, Socialism and Democracy*, 1943 (London and New York: Routledge, 2010), 74–5, 117, passim. See also Richard Bronk, *The Romantic Economist: Imagination in Economics* (Cambridge: Cambridge University Press, 2009), passim.
[42] On anti-capitalism and related themes in English Romantic poetry, see John McVeagh, *Tradefull Merchants: The Portrayal of the Capitalist in Literature* (London: Routledge and Kegan Paul, Ltd., 1981), 101–27; E. P. Thompson, *William Morris: Romantic to Revolutionary*, 1955 (New York: Pantheon Books, 1976), 18, passim; Catherine Gallagher, 'The Romantics and the Political Economists', in *The Cambridge History of English Romantic Literature*, ed. James Chandler, 71–100 (Cambridge: Cambridge University Press, 2009), passim.

capitalism and Romanticism provides a rhetorical background for the eventual transcendence of this dichotomy in the Hegelian theory of class struggle and the socialist state.[43] Nevertheless, the original opposition is highly suggestive. The twentieth-century critical reception of the English Romantic poets demonstrates that a highly ambivalent antithesis can be maintained between the idea of bourgeois capitalism and Romantic aesthetics; as Marx evocatively noted in the *Grundrisse* (1857–8): 'the latter will accompany it (the former) as legitimate antithesis up to its blessed end.'[44]

This ambiguity is part of the reason why I have attempted to develop, in the next chapter, what I believe to be a useful distinction between Light and Dark Romanticism, which has already been cited in the opening discussion of film poetics. Against traditional readings of Romantic anti-capitalism, I believe it is unnecessary to consider this opposition in terms of a nostalgic valuation of pre-capitalist worlds.[45] In *Romanticism Against the Tide of Modernity* (2001), Michael Löwy and Robert Sayre maintain that the critical force of Romanticism is dependent upon a backward-looking value system: 'a critique of modernity... in the name of values and ideals drawn from the past.'[46] However, the significant point for Romanticism, in terms of its critical relation to the spirit of capitalism, is not, in my reading, this nostalgic and 'utopian' relation to the past, but, rather, the nature of its relation to the present – the negation of what currently exists as the given state of affairs. This can be understood if we consider Novalis' assertion: 'The soul strives for what is new – even for what is old – in short, for something *different*.'[47] It is this formalized and de-historicized aspect that, I believe, makes Romanticism such a potent tendency within critical philosophy, and a fictive division between its Light and Dark aspects a useful explanatory construct.

---

[43] Alex Callinicos, *Against Postmodernism: A Marxist Critique* (Cambridge: Polity Press, 1989), 38.

[44] Karl Marx, *Grundrisse: Foundations of the Critique of Political Economy*, 1939 (London: Penguin Books, 1993), 162.

[45] Typically cited examples of this perspective, not always accurate, include several of the aforementioned Romantic writers, and their championing of feudalism, Medievalism, Orientalism and the ancient world. This approach is central to Lukács, for example, who adopts this line in his history of irrationalism in German philosophy, largely equating the term 'Romantic' with a reactionary political perspective: the nostalgic tendency, found in Nietzsche and others, to glorify a lost 'golden age' of political and cultural organization, typically serving the discursive needs of the German ruling classes and, later, the intellectual bourgeoise, in the ideological battle against socialism; Lukács, *The Destruction of Reason*, 341–2, 351, 730–2.

[46] Michael Löwy and Robert Sayre, *Romanticism Against the Tide of Modernity* (Durham and London: Duke University Press, 2001), 17. Löwy also provides an extensive historical overview of nineteenth-century Romantic anti-capitalism in his book on Lukács; see Michael Löwy, *Georg Lukács – From Romanticism to Bolshevism*, 1976 (London: NLB, 1979), 15–90.

[47] Novalis, *Last Fragments*, c.1799–1800, in *Philosophical Writings*, ed. Margaret Mahony Stoljar, 153–65 (Albany: State University of New York, 1997), § 20, 157.

Negation and freedom

Romanticism and modern capitalism are both consequences of the European Enlightenment, and share more than a historical association. Adorno's approach pursues the Romantic critique of capitalist economy whilst extending a fundamentally aesthetic conception of truth and knowledge through negation. As a Kantian realist, he claims the primacy of the objective over epistemological concepts, but only to the extent that the former is ultimately unknowable: 'no object is wholly known .... Truth is objective ... it falls into no man's lap.'[48] This critical realist conception of truth echoes not only Popper, but also Schlegel.[49] The positivistic idea that someone can grasp something true and manipulate reality according to principles for action is ultimately an ideological mystification. It takes a fundamentally violent and authoritarian attitude towards reality, but its violence is difficult to expose because of the monopoly it possesses over practical action.

Adorno's philosophy can be interpreted as a Romantic procedure of ironic paradox. Diametrically opposed concepts are clashed together in order to find meaning in their opposites, revealing the processes of reification that sustain social reality. What such a philosophy demonstrates is the fictive relation between concept and reality – a fictive relationship that is, nevertheless, still necessary for thought. In the face of a reality riddled with tensions and antagonisms, dialectics must forsake the Hegelian synthesis in identity. 'Non-identity' – the crux of negative dialectics[50] – posits the unbridgeable distance between concept and reality, which all language accomplishes by force.[51] Consequently, Adorno's contradictions, ambiguous explanations and rhetorical strategies, which blur the boundary between philosophy and poetry, are all distinctly thematic. His method results from what is easily understood to be a nominally 'Romantic' approach to philosophical thinking. Adorno opts for a critical and aesthetic conception

---

[48] Adorno, *Negative Dialectics*, 14, 41.
[49] See Friedrich Schlegel, 'On Incomprehensibility', 1800, in *Theory as Practice: A Critical Anthology of Early German Romantic Writings*, ed. Jochen Schulte-Sasse, et al., 118–28 (Minneapolis: University of Minnesota Press, 1997), 122.
[50] A useful interpretation of Adorno's negative dialectics, without this Romantic tint, can be found in Buck-Morss, *The Origin of Negative Dialectics*, 58, 63.
[51] Yet, in another sense, negative dialectics is truly 'linguistic', because of the acknowledgement that language shares with all thinking the 'symbolic' effect identified by Barthes. The unavoidable plurality of meanings that can be taken from signs opens the idea of dialectics – dialogue – to a non-identificatory conception. Adorno explores this issue under the heading of dialectics as 'constellation'; Adorno, *Negative Dialectics*, 162–3. See also Roland Barthes, *Criticism and Truth*, 1966 (London and New York: Continuum, 2007).

of philosophy based on a quasi-Romantic conception of imaginative and non-identical cognition: 'Dialectics – literally: language as the organon of thought – would mean to attempt a critical rescue of the rhetorical element, a mutual approximation of thing and expression, to the point where the difference fades.'[52] Adorno claims that this is not a positivistic and identarian dissolution, however, but, rather, a poetic (Romantic) conviction that understanding comes about through infinite indeterminacy – the pursuit of a moment in which language fails and becomes witness of a truth it does not claim to subsume by identifying with the concept, for 'the utmost distance alone would be proximity'.[53] As with critical rationalism, 'the saving principle' is to be found, not in synthesis, but in the 'antithesis alone'.[54]

Such convictions are strikingly similar to those found in the writings of the Early German Romantics. Hölderlin objected to positivism and the enthronement of subjective reason long before Adorno or Popper.[55] Like much philosophy, old truths are here rediscovered in new times, and critical philosophy continues to find truth in the category of the Romantic infinite rather than totality[56] – a open infinity evoked by the ideas of striving, *Sehnsucht* and 'homesickness' celebrated by Hölderlin, Schlegel and Novalis.[57] The most valuable things for the development of knowledge are not meaningful unities, coherent forms and achieved goals, but, rather, those wounding puncta that refuse to be subsumed by totality – the old men with broken noses. They are the extraneous elements that fall outside the category, the theory or the narrative structure, being encountered as a confounding and painful excess. Painful experiences, even neuroses, have

---

[52] Adorno, *Negative Dialectics*, 56.
[53] Ibid., 57. In *Minima Moralia* Adorno summarizes this aspect in a particularly evocative way: 'Dialectical reason is, when set against the dominant mode of reason, unreason: only in encompassing and cancelling this mode does it become itself reasonable ... once it has recognized the ruling universal order and its productions as sick ... then it can see as healing cells only what appears by the standards of that order, as itself sick, eccentric, paranoia – indeed, "mad"; and it is true today as in the middle ages that only fools tell their masters the truth'; Adorno, *Minima Moralia*, 72–3.
[54] Adorno, *Minima Moralia*, 150.
[55] Friedrich Hölderlin, 'There is a Natural State ...', c.1794, in *Essays and Letters*, 227–8 (London: Penguin, 2009), 228.
[56] Adorno, *Negative Dialectics*, 13.
[57] It appears Adorno's philosophical lexicon was largely unprepared to acknowledge the Romantic character of his own tradition. He acknowledges Hölderlin's contribution to dialectics, but he does not ascribe the progressive features of his poetry to a more general concept of 'Romanticism'; see Theodor W. Adorno, 'Parataxis: On Hölderlin's Late Poetry', 1963, in *Notes to Literature, Volume Two*, ed. Rolf Tidemann, 109–49 (New York: Columbia University Press, 1992). Adorno also occasionally references Hölderlin concerning the goal of 'openness'; see Adorno, *Lectures on Negative Dialectics*, 116.

a profound truth-content, for they reveal the general incompatibility of the self with the wider 'healthy' totality of social life.[58]

As for freedom, this can be experienced only as the absent 'counter-image' to the suffering caused by socialization itself.[59] In its modern realization – as the freedom of trade, movement, opportunity and representation – the idea of freedom breeds a slippery and insidious opposite:

> The more freedom the subject – and the community of subjects – ascribes to itself, the greater its responsibility; and before this responsibility it must fail in a bourgeois life which in practice has never yet endowed a subject with the unabridged autonomy accorded to it in theory. Hence the subject must feel guilty.[60]

Every free subject who experiences poverty or material privation is confronted by the cruel judgement that their condition is a result of their own lack, be it of confidence, intelligence or luck. Under the logic of modern capitalist meritocracy, the 'free' political and labouring individual lives in a 'society that stimulates freedom without realizing it'.[61] Betrayed by an interpretation of freedom, which results from the era of democratic Enlightenment, the modern subject becomes complicit in legitimating their own material and political condition within the social totality, and this guilty experience is echoed by the aporetic condition of modern art under the aesthetic regime. Since totality will attempt to erase or absorb suffering as a marker of freedom, which exists only as potential, the moral idea of freedom becomes allied (for Romanticism) in negative experience. When a film like *Mickey One* stops to involve us in nothing but the spectacle of an old man looking into a mirror, therefore, or when *Is That All There Is?* shows us malnourished bodies – is this guilty stillness actually the closest we come to understanding what freedom means?

Before we return to art in more detail, it is worth noting that Adorno was not alone in all this. Other members of the Frankfurt School, such as Horkheimer and Herbert Marcuse, articulate these themes equally strongly. Here, too, philosophy largely equates with criticism, and criticism with freedom – thinking demands a negation of the existing world order, which contains an essential wrong.

---

[58] Contradiction, 'pain and negativity' are the 'moving forces of dialectical thinking'; Adorno, *Negative Dialectics*, 202, 222.
[59] Ibid., 223, 231.
[60] Ibid., 221.
[61] Ibid., 285.

The idea of a dirempted humanity – one removed from its 'natural' or 'best' condition – is, as we have seen, a familiar one for Romanticism. Kant's 'What is Enlightenment?', Schiller's *Aesthetic Education* and Novalis' fragments put it in different ways, but the formulation is roughly consistent: 'At present spirit is moving only here and there – when will the spirit move in *the whole*? When will humanity en masse itself begin to reflect?'[62] Every individual carries within themselves the potential for an ideal and fully 'human' moral constitution, thought Schiller.[63] There are persistent Schillerian tones resounding in subsequent Marxist assertions that 'the world is unfree; that is to say, man and nature exist in conditions of alienation, exist as "other than they are"'.[64] To comprehend reality as an objective autonomy – to hold this as a regulative ideal enabling the progress of knowledge – entails the rejection of social appearance: for 'rejection' is nothing less than 'the process of thought'.[65] As Marcuse writes in *One-Dimensional Man* (1964):

> the dialectic process involves . . . recognition and seizure of the liberating potentialities. . . . To the degree to which consciousness is determined by the exigencies and interests of the established society, it is "unfree"; . . . (since) the established society is irrational . . . consciousness becomes free . . . only in the struggle *against* the established society.[66]

This is, again, strikingly similar to that 'cultural transcendence' that Peckham believed to be the lynchpin of Romanticism[67] – the stringent subjective imperative, felt as an expression of a moral duty towards an objective reality, to oppose a false social hegemony. Marcuse's words echo not only Kant, Schiller and the derivation that became Marx's concept of alienation, but also Schlegel's claim that 'it is characteristic of humanity that it must raise itself above humanity'.[68] Again, the distinction between art and philosophy is obliterated in their common search for a New Mythology: '(a) *search* for an "authentic

---

[62] Novalis, *Miscellaneous Observations*, § 37, 29.
[63] Schiller, *Aesthetic Education*, § 4, 10.
[64] Herbert Marcuse, 'A Note on Dialectic', 1960, in *The Essential Frankfurt School Reader*, ed. Andrew Arato and Eike Gebhardt, 444–51 (New York: Continuum, 2002), 446.
[65] Marcuse, 'A Note on Dialectic', 446.
[66] Herbert Marcuse, *One-Dimensional Man: Studies in the Ideology of Advanced Industrial Society*, 1964 (London and New York: Routledge, 2010), 227.
[67] Peckham, *Romanticism and Ideology*, xix; see also Peckham, *Explanation and Power*, 272–82.
[68] Friedrich Schlegel, 'Ideas', 1800, in *Theory as Practice: A Critical Anthology of Early German Romantic Writings*, ed. Jochen Schulte-Sasse et al., 326–8 (Minneapolis: University of Minnesota Press, 1997), § 21, 327.

language" – the language of negation as the Great Refusal to accept the rules of a game in which the dice are loaded'.[69]

Like Jacques Rancière's work on cinema, critical theory unites the truth-content of the objective to a philosophical voice reminiscent of Novalis and Schlegel, emancipating thought through openness and indeterminacy, and striving for that authentically 'poetic' language which will never feel itself fully adequate to speak for what really is. Drawing on a Nietzschean heritage accentuated by Habermas, the idea of aesthetics championed by critical theory entails a kind of Dionysian loss of the self in the presence of this confounding objectivity, and the result is a potentially liberating unchaining of categories of thought and action, which keep the subject bound to prevailing ideologies.[70] In Marcuse's words: 'Art contains the rationality of negation. In its advanced positions, it is the Great Refusal – the protest against that which is.'[71] The incomplete, oppositional and objectifying quality of art is now the best hope for moral social development, set against the subjectivizing forces associated with capitalist quantity. Rancière's film theory, as we have seen, follows such viewpoints by advocating the power of art – despite the limitations placed upon it by the representative regime and the processes of commodification – to remain the one arena of cognition that has the potential to perform 'the great task of *thought*. . . . Naming the "things that are absent" . . . breaking the spell of the things that are'.[72] This 'naming' is also addressed in Adorno's *Aesthetic Theory* – a complex and fragmented work, which will be read here as a treatise on modern 'Romantic' art and its dialectic of regimes, as described by Rancière.

Art's guilt

The point of departure for Adorno's great posthumous work on aesthetics is Kant's neglect of the objectivity of artworks themselves. Adorno follows the Kantian theme of disinterestedness to the extent that the aesthetic object removes itself from the domain of pragmatic or teleological thought; but he makes a radical extension of Kant's theory of the natural sublime that ends up giving primacy to the category of the object, but only in memory of its

---

[69] Marcuse, 'A Note on Dialectic', 448.
[70] Habermas, *The Philosophical Discourse of Modernity*, 91–3; see also Callinicos, *Against Postmodernism*, 10.
[71] Marcuse, *One-Dimensional Man*, 66.
[72] Ibid., 71.

infinite incommensurability: 'Art reminds us . . . of an objectivity freed from the categorical structure'[73] – a remembrance of a possibility for truth that falls eternally outside what is thought, and which is always experienced as uncanny and confounding. For Adorno, this is the place of the aesthetic under modernity, specifically – a mode corresponding with the emergence of Rancière's aesthetic regime, and, as we have seen, the dialectic that gives film its Romantic poetics.[74]

Art's objectivity (what Adorno also calls its 'spirit') is what makes a work 'speak' – what makes it more than just an empirical thing whose meaning can be reduced to a verbal explanation.[75] It is in this way that Adorno essentially expands Kant's natural sublime over the entire domain of modern aesthetics: 'Nature is beautiful in that it appears to say more than it is. To wrest this more from that more's contingency, to gain control of its semblance . . . . This is the idea of art.'[76] The non-existing emerges in artworks as a 'revelation', which resists the subjectivizing pull of pragmatic thought.[77] The observing subject experiences an 'irruption of objectivity'; they lose themselves in the work's objectivity at the very moment when this sense of subjective experience is at its strongest.[78]

As suggested, it doesn't seem too great a leap to interpret what Adorno discusses as roughly corresponding to the Romantic poetics that interest Rancière.[79] The historical primacy of expression over mimesis transforms artworks into fleeting appearances of truth: 'Romanticism', Adorno admits, 'wanted to equate what appears in the apparition with the artistic. In doing so, it grasped something essential about art, yet narrowed it to a particular.'[80] The truth that appears in an artwork is an 'apparition' or vision, like the fleeting flash of a firework:

> They appear empirically yet are liberated from the burden of the empirical, which is the obligation of duration; they are a sign from heaven yet artificial, an ominous warning, a script that flashes up, vanishes, and indeed cannot be read for its meaning . . . everything in them becomes other.[81]

---

[73] Adorno, *Aesthetic Theory*, 435.
[74] Rancière, *The Politics of Aesthetics*, 15–25.
[75] Adorno, *Aesthetic Theory*, 120.
[76] Ibid., 109.
[77] Ibid., 115.
[78] Ibid., 332.
[79] Adorno himself discovered the core of his Aesthetic Theory – the 'alien' quality of aesthetic objectivity, the breaking of unity in form through a newfound 'freedom of negativity' – in Hölderlin's poetry; Adorno, 'Parataxis: On Hölderlin's Late Poetry', 112, 127.
[80] Adorno, *Aesthetic Theory*, 114–15.
[81] Ibid., 112.

Yet, this fleeting impression of truth is linked to an inherent sense of sadness, for the Absolute is grasped only in its absence: 'In each genuine artwork something appears that does not exist. . . . The unstillable longing in the face of beauty . . . is the longing for the fulfilment of what was promised.'[82] This mixing of presence and absence, truth and illusion, means that art becomes, in effect, Enlightenment's Other. Through a process of 'spiritualization' consequent upon the idea of Romanticism under the aesthetic regime, art converges with natural beauty to impart a sense of guilt over a subject increasingly sure of their ability to manipulate and master nature itself through pragmatic doctrines of 'proactive' rationality. For when confronted by natural beauty – a confounding intensity of the object – the subject experiences a sublime weakness of rational thought. Like objects of Kantian disinterestedness, nature is not 'perceived as an object of action.'[83] More than this, natural beauty appears to stand in opposition to human action in general, and this exposes, for Adorno, the characteristic of nature that is most like art.[84] The essential similarity between natural and artistic beauty lies in the strained and irresolvable relationship between the presentation of something that is both resolute in its self-sufficient meaning, as well as demanding an interpretation: 'Above all it is this double character of natural beauty that has been conferred upon art.'[85] The sublime ambiguity that natural beauty used to hold over subjects as a promise of both mortality and infinity is here adopted by art itself to define its concept. Art's 'spiritualization' – its appropriation of the natural sublime, or its 'Romanticization' – emancipates norms of reception, productive modalities and the notion of appropriate form, only at the cost of art then becoming aware of its inherent ideological problematic: between a truth-content that holds the spectator bound in deference to an unknowable truth (sharable only in its unknowability), and a promise of mastery over the boundless content of the work and its history via the subjunctivization of the sublime – as a facilitator of an understanding that invites meaning (sharable in its knowability). Here, again, we find that great paradox: the distinction between freedom and explanation – theoretical abstractions of the tension inherent to audiovisual media's own Janus-faced Romanticism: between 'film' and 'cinema', shot and cut, punctum and stadium, 'art' and 'artwork'.

---

[82] Ibid., 114.
[83] Ibid., 90.
[84] Ibid., 95.
[85] Ibid., 97.

Adorno's aesthetics serve to bind together art and Otherness in mutual incommensurability. The understood work reveals itself as an unanswered question, and even that which is given exhaustive hermeneutical analysis is not purged of a hidden mystery. Not only a totalizing interpretation, but even a 'fully *adequate* interpretation is a chimera'.[86] This sense of failure in modern (Romantic) aesthetics is of paramount importance; it is to be found not only in the work's social and historical realization (as the case study chapters will later make explicit) but also within its own poetics: 'Art cannot fulfil its concept. This strikes each and every one of its works, even the highest, with an ineluctable imperfectness that repudiates the idea of perfection toward which artworks must aspire.'[87] Artworks demand to be understood, and it is the qualitative distinctness of this demand that is more significant than any comprehension which might be found. Works have a gaze that they direct upon the subject[88] – a visage which marks their objectivity. Because what is true in art is always only indeterminate, that truth is also multiple, and the guiding essence of art – whether it be 'truth', 'beauty' or 'play' – will, as a result, always resist explanation. Its meaning overflows the bounds of the work in the ways described by both Kant's natural sublime and Hegel's Romantic form.[89] This is how art maintains its alliance with freedom: by resisting historically bounded meanings and ideological explanations.

Yet, despite this power, artworks do not have the capacity to actually impart knowledge of the Absolute. They are 'punished with a blindness', and, like the ill-fated protagonist of a children's morality tale, artworks both 'have the absolute and they do not have it'.[90] If the meaningfulness of a work is derived from its unity of form, but its meaning is not actual – for Adorno, the meaning of a work is what it will only ever conceal in itself – then 'all art is endowed with sadness; art greaves all the more, the more completely its successful unification suggests (a) meaning (which is absent), and the sadness is heightened by the feeling of "Oh, were it only so." Melancholy is the shadow of what . . . form strives to banish: mere existence'.[91] The "as if" stated by freedom's absence in *Negative Dialectics* corresponds to the "if only" imparted by the artwork in

---

[86] Ibid., 374.
[87] Ibid., 74.
[88] Ibid., 168.
[89] Georg Wilhelm Friedrich Hegel, *Introductory Lectures on Aesthetics*, 1820–1829 (London: Penguin Books, 2004), 82–8.
[90] Adorno, *Aesthetic Theory*, 182.
[91] Ibid., 145.

Aesthetic Theory.[92] Art's dynamic process is directed towards evoking a freedom that is absent. Paradox, melancholia, the conflation of past and future in the desire to create a perfect reality and being sadly reliant on past conditions, which are inherently unsuitable to right the present wrong of social existence – such schematic Romantic tropes are the distinctive effects that result from Adorno's objectification of aesthetic experience: 'Art desires what has not yet been, though everything that art is has already been.'[93] Adorno announces this in a typically poetic passage:

> Because for art, utopia – the yet-to-exist – is draped in black, it remains in all its mediations recollection; recollection of the possible in opposition to the actual that suppresses it; it is the imaginary reparation of the catastrophe of world history; it is freedom, which under the spell of necessity did not – and may not ever – come to pass .... Art is ever the broken promise of happiness.[94]

This idea of a 'broken promise' returns the critical cultural product under the Romantic aesthetic regime to its historical relation with social life and its constituent political and economic basis in capitalism, as well as evoking the familiar theme of guilt. Fascinated as it is by the disquiet caused by societal wrongs, 'What would art be', Adorno asks rhetorically, 'if it shook off the memory of accumulated suffering?'[95]

Despite Adorno's protestations, we cannot help but recognize the Romanticism of this schema. We now see how both *Negative Dialectics* and *Aesthetic Theory* facilitate 'Romantic' interpretations. The synergizing of philosophy, criticism and artistic practice in this 'secularization of melancholy' fulfils, in a sense, the dream of the Romantics who called for a New Mythology.[96] Adorno's rhetorical contradictions invite, just as much as they problematize, such a reading. His words on the objectifying power of art seem to echo Novalis when the latter writes: 'Poetry dissolves the being of others in its own.'[97] By this, Novalis appears to mean that in the experience of the work of art we encounter its Otherness as a synecdoche of the objective world. In art we encounter Otherness itself, and this power endows it with the greatest progressive potential. 'Through poetry there arises the highest sympathy and common activity, the most intimate

---

[92] Adorno, *Negative Dialectics*, 231; Adorno, *Aesthetic Theory*, 145.
[93] Adorno, *Aesthetic Theory*, 184.
[94] Ibid., 185.
[95] Ibid., 352.
[96] Theodor W. Adorno, *History and Freedom: Lectures, 1964–1965* (Cambridge: Polity Press, 2006), 134.
[97] Novalis, *Logological Fragments* 1, § 40, 56.

communion of the finite and the infinite', wrote Novalis.[98] Against the world as it is, art eulogizes a state of existence that is not.

Mere mimesis was anathema to Romanticism. Corresponding to Schelling's *System of Transcendental Idealism* (and film's derivation therefrom, according to Rancière), art is valued according to the surplus of meaning to be found within it – its transcendence of whatever the artist was aware of creating. As Kant expressed, long before Adorno took the next step, the concept of genius inherent to the subjective creation of works of art entails only a partial or occluded awareness on the part of the individual regarding the processes of expression.[99] This highlights an important distinction within Romanticism itself. By going beyond the realm of 'self-expression' and its reduction of works to a mere intellectual or emotional intentioned product of any individual artist – the photographic film image, through its mechanical relation to pro-filmic reality, containing more than the filmmaker was aware of putting into it – in this way, film (and, in analogous terms, art in general) calls out to the Absolute. Art's inability to completely break free of the objects and institutions of the empirical world – a world upon which it relies for its content and modes of reception – gives it the irresolvable character of the Romantic concept itself: an infinite striving to overturn the conditions of social reality, even as they sustain its privileged mode of enunciation and critique.

Towards Romantic inaction

Having provided a brief overview of these key themes in critical philosophy, we now have an outline of the schematic construct which will be the focus of the next chapter and will become the vital paradigm for the subsequent textual analyses: Light Romantic inaction.

Morse Peckham recognized the significance of inaction to Romanticism, or the necessary connection between the erosion of Enlightenment belief systems (premises for meaningful social participation) and the Romantic individual's experience of cultural transcendence by withdrawal from praxis.[100] The 'entry of the divine into the human' was predicted upon the 'gradual closing off of possible

---

[98] Ibid., § 25, 54.
[99] Kant, *Critique of Judgement*, § 46–7, 174–8.
[100] Peckham, *Victorian Revolutionaries*, 96–7.

routes of action to the point at which no action is possible'.[101] Peckham evokes this theme in order to explain the poetic style of Robert Browning, but we will also see it repeated in the films of Arthur Penn and Lindsay Anderson. Peckham's interpretation of Browning, Carlyle and others shows that Romanticism, long before Adorno and the guilt of Auschwitz entered the picture, was dealing with the metaphysical proposition that action can be based only on self-deception – that silence and stillness could be the first markers of truth. A problematic truth, certainly, but the only one that was untainted by compromise and the stain of pragmatism.

Old philosophical problems are enlightened by this perspective. To read, for example, Adorno's famous lecture 'Marginalia to Theory and Practice' (1969), in which the philosopher explains why he did not support the radical student movements at the end of the 1960s, is now to encounter a Romantic document.[102] Critical philosophy from Kant to Popper rejects revolutionary praxis for similar reasons to those Adorno describes: that the wholesale eradication of conventions, traditions and institutions, imperfect and often harmful though they may be, is no guarantee of ensuring a better future.[103] The isolated individual who refuses to participate in the world serves the betterment of humanity more faithfully than one who, by taking part, perpetuates indefinable and omniscient wrongs. Yet, 'no less infected is he who does nothing at all'; this aporia is a secularization of original sin.[104] As Adorno autobiographically acknowledged, 'the detached observer is as much entangled (in the material and ideological processes of the social world) as the active participant'.[105] The only advantage for the self-imposed exile is the nominal sense of freedom that results from acknowledgement of difference. The comforting sense of being 'superior' to a 'deluded' majority becomes a source of guilt, one reflected, for Adorno, in the aesthetic mode of experience. Yet, this temptation is never allowed to become fully realised in nihilistic isolation.[106] The central moral aporia of Adorno's philosophy concerns

---

[101] Ibid., 97.
[102] Theodor W. Adorno, 'Marginalia to Theory and Praxis', 1969, in *Critical Models: Interventions and Catchwords*, 259–78 (New York: Columbia University Press, 2005), 258–78. This is also true of the short radio lecture 'Registration' (1969), which echoes many of these ideas; Theodor W. Adorno, 'Resignation', 1969, in *Critical Models: Interventions and Catchwords*, 289–93 (New York: Columbia University Press, 2005), passim.
[103] Kant, 'What is Enlightenment?', 55; Popper, *Conjectures and Refutations*, 462–3.
[104] Adorno, *Negative Dialectics*, 243.
[105] Adorno, *Minima Moralia*, 26.
[106] As happened, for example, in the philosophy of Schopenhauer and Nietzsche, according to Lukács' interpretation; Lukács, *The Destruction of Reason*, 192–243, 309–95. See also the work of Edgar Saltus, who avoided a quietist nihilism by secularizing religious moral doctrine.

the 'aestheticisation' of individuality. It stands between the intolerability of quietism in the face of evil, and the need to respect objective truth through abstention of the will. No good exists 'that is not externalised in action', he writes; 'An absolute state of mind, devoid of all specific interventions, would be bound to deteriorate to absolute indifference, to inhumanity.'[107] This sense of neurosis – strongest felt, perhaps, in *Minima Moralia* (1951) – saves itself from elitist quietism and political estrangement by swamping its privilege in a dialectical engagement.[108] It is obsessed with a confounding objectivity characterized by pain and suffering, the central figures of which are the Holocaust, capitalism and the maxims and ideologies that sustain them both as an 'inevitable development' of Hegelian world spirit.

There are similar demons at play in the films of Arthur Penn and Lindsay Anderson, frustrating the subjective willpower of their protagonists. Aesthetic morality demands that things grind to a halt and think on the infinite, like Mickey before the mirror, or the tortured Romantic artist before their canvas. This is the tragic drama of cultural transcendence. The genius sitting in the ivory tower becomes a guilty paradigm of social progress, perpetually haunted by the spectre of what their lofty position has often meant to history. Torn between painful and poignant visions of the world as it is and the world as it might be, the subject realizes not only that all action is intolerable, but also that this intolerability is intolerable; and so the dialectic of reason and necessity is consummated in negativity, without a positive Hegelian synthesis. All first principles for action disappear except the conviction that there are none. With a final irony, the one who stands apart and says "No!" finds that they are then expected to inaugurate a new Golden Age for the betterment of all.

Conclusion

Adorno's re-Romanticization of aesthetics has been influential for critical philosophy. Sharing the characteristic aversion for positivistic pronouncements, recent philosophers such as Rancière continue to champion art as a means of creating emergent cognitive ruptures and dissonances in the fabric of sensorial

---

[107] Adorno, *Negative Dialectics*, 296.
[108] Although Adorno's moral philosophy is Kantian at its epistemological root, this essentially Marxist assertion is a primary distinction between the two positions; see Adorno, *Negative Dialectics*, 297.

experience under capitalism.¹⁰⁹ An art emancipated from the explanatory authority of the subjective artist and the cultural metaphysic of convention, explanation and marketization (for Rancière, the crux of cinema itself) is the most potent vehicle available for genuine critique in the modern world.

The goal of this kind of critique is, by necessity, to end the domination of the harmful principles of reason that uphold the capitalist economy – an end to which Romantics can direct themselves with a corresponding conviction that to affirm the existing conditions is worse than literally doing nothing. But there is nothing to guarantee that what this faith will enable or bring about will ultimately be better. When describing the prospects for a kind of 'universal brotherhood', Dostoevsky arrived at the same conclusion: 'What can we do then? We can do nothing; *it must be done of itself*, the solution must exist in nature', that is, it must come about independently of explanation – without any individual will imposing upon another.¹¹⁰ Art remains a way of ensuring that authoritarianism is kept free from emergent understandings to the greatest extent possible, even whilst allowing theory to maintain a critical hold on the ineradicable spectre of ideology.

Critical philosophy radicalizes Kantian realism to stress the fictive and ideological character of positivistic statements, and moral action becomes thinkable only in the realm of the isolated event divorced from context and consequences – the immediate and often emotional response to a perceived wrong. This results in the inability to rationalize any action by situating it in an ethical matrix of relationships and valuations that extends beyond the specificity of the singular event which demands action. The dominant maxims for conduct in the material world are determined by an all-embracing rage for totality: the capitalistic prioritization of quantity. If the critical attitude can countenance any authentic or moral attitude, then, it must be of the Romantic paradigm of negation through a prioritization of aesthetic quality. These questions will continue to occupy us in the following chapter, as we dig deeper into the philosophical implications of a Romanticized aesthetic of film art.

---

[109] Alain Badiou is another contemporary philosopher who might have contributed much to this current discussion. However, his complex philosophical system maintains distinct and equally complex relationships with both Romanticism and film, which, for the sake of brevity and focus, require separate discussion at a future date.

[110] Fyodor Dostoevsky, *Winter Notes on Summer Impressions*, 1863 (Richmond: Oneworld Classics Ltd., 2008), 69.

Critical philosophy recounts a fable of moral redemptionism: 'Philosophy is actually homesickness – the urge *to be everywhere at home*'[111] – to find, like film under the aesthetic regime, that 'everything speaks'; 'Not to conclude, not to affirm, but "to murmur", akin to the wind in the leaves'.[112] Transformed into a ghost of political praxis, morality can stand only as a static yet restless 'obsession' with what is wrong with the world – an obsession with those wounding puncta to which Barthes and Rancière pointed as the spirit of film.[113] Thanks to capitalism, humanity, like art in the age of mechanical reproduction, has strayed from what it might have been, and only what is already in the concept has the power of recall. But there is nowhere that we can really call home, after all the cultural transcendence, for Greece was always just a myth. The urge is all that remains.

---

[111] Novalis, *General Draft*, § 45, 135.
[112] Rancière, *The Lost Thread*, 88.
[113] 'Praxis appears in theory merely . . . as a blind spot, as an obsession with what is being criticized'; Adorno, 'Marginalia to Theory and Praxis', 278.

3

Empty infinities

Freedom and the doctrine of action

The previous chapters have shown that moral questions regarding social emancipation are reiterated by critical philosophy at the very point where Romanticism meets film. The opposing forces of free aesthetic cognition and artistic explanation – which, as Rancière suggests, create productive antagonisms between representative and aesthetic regimes – can be read to partly characterize the cultural status of both audiovisual media and the general concept of Romanticism. Before advancing to the textual analysis of selected films directed by Arthur Penn and Lindsay Anderson, this chapter will build upon the themes already introduced and explore a new interpretive paradigm based upon this dualistic idea of Romanticism.

Light and Dark Romanticism

The distinction between Light and Dark is an illustrative, although fictive and reductive, tendency in Romantic scholarship. Morse Peckham openly refuted this aspect of his own early work, yet his initial distinction between 'Positive' and 'Negative' Romanticism remains an interesting model to consider.[1] According to Peckham, the recognition of the incoherent nature of Enlightenment metaphysics can create a period of quasi-nihilistic disillusionment among certain Romantic individuals. The loss of faith in scientific explanation, order and totality creates a space of uncertainty and hesitation, and this Negative Romanticism preludes the Positive Romantic emancipation of action and agency created by the heightened valuation of free imagination. The realization that 'the

---

[1] Morse Peckham, 'Toward a Theory of Romanticism', 1950, in *The Triumph of Romanticism*, 3–26 (Columbia: University of South Carolina Press, 1970), 3–26.

universe is alive . . . (or that) it grows'² – and, consequently, that dynamic ideas of disorder and change become positive in relation to the overall processual and fictive nature of experienced reality – creates a profound sense of subjective elation, and rejuvenates the idea of freedom and agency leading to the critical programme of cultural transcendence.

Maintaining Peckham's later insistence that this dualistic schema is fundamentally insufficient to account for Romanticism in its entirety, we might suggest that the idea can be profitably revised if we merely identify two fictive 'poles'. If Positive Romanticism equates to Dark Romanticism, then Negative Romanticism equates to Light Romanticism. Yet, rather than seeing these constructs as quasi-teleological stages of a moral or epistemological 'evolution', moving from one condition to the other, it is more revealing to think about Light and Dark Romanticism as reciprocal nodes of gravitation within an apolitical formal structure.³

Cultural transcendence entails an unflagging rejection of the world as it exists. It targets that which holds back freedom, give it what name we might, according to our prejudices. Marx found it in capitalism; for Hitler, it was the Jews. The Romantic conviction that every limiting and determinate state must cease to exist makes no formal distinctions between 'good' and 'bad' conditions of reality – between elements that may by their removal lead to a utopian condition, or to a state of complete barbarism. Romanticism needs an enemy to critique, regardless of its identity. The distinction between Light and Dark Romanticisms is attuned to the fact that sometimes (as in the films of Arthur Penn and Lindsay Anderson) this critical impetus finds its object in a reflection of its own self. As the German Idealists knew all too well, unbounded freedom leads to chaos and terror.⁴ Similarly, Adorno's distaste for what he took to be 'Romanticism' retains the Kantian realization that 'a thinking which blithely begins afresh, heedless of the historic form of its problems, will so much more be their prey'.⁵ This kind of cultural transcendence is something apart from the Light Romanticism that goes into critical philosophy. The kind of Dark and proactive Romanticism critiqued by Kant, Adorno and Carl Schmitt leads through the idea of the supreme artistic 'auctor' to a condition of moral bankruptcy – from Wagner, through

---

² Ibid., 10.
³ For additional context, see the table of comparative terms in the Appendix.
⁴ See Georg Wilhelm Friedrich Hegel, *The Phenomenology of Spirit*, 1807 (Oxford: Oxford University Press, 1976), § 582–95, 355–63; also Lucien Goldmann, *Immanuel Kant*, 1967 (London: Verso, 2011), 120.
⁵ Adorno, *Negative Dialectics*, 17.

Nietzsche's superman to Auschwitz, and thence to Wall Street.⁶ As the previous chapter demonstrated, the rejection of this Dark aspect entails a denunciation of certainty and action. In this moment, cultural transcendence turns against itself. We find a self-negating negation of action.

There is much to unpack in this proposition. The remainder of this chapter will develop the essential ideas so as to provide conceptual foundations for the textual analyses presented in Part Two.

Hamlet and history

The subject who experiences an inactive condition of uncertainty is never comfortable. Light Romanticism finds non-participation untenable as a moral position because of the need to combat evil through decisive action. As Adorno states: 'there is no ... good that is not externalised in action. An absolute state of mind, devoid of all specific interventions, would be bound to deteriorate to absolute indifference, to inhumanity.'⁷ In other words, it is only by taking action that anything can be done to combat pain and suffering. Yet, morality can never make this leap from theory to praxis in unproblematic form.

Adorno often explained this philosophical problem in reference to *Hamlet* (c1601), that most famous of Shakespeare's plays, and one particularly important to the Romantics.⁸ The more the modern subject – allegorized in the Prince of Denmark – 'turns into a being-for-itself', or thinks upon its own condition in relation to an external world, 'the greater the distance it places between itself and the unbroken accord with a given order, (and) the less its will to action and its consciousness be one'.⁹ The existing order, again, is found to contain a determining evil or 'wrong' (the false sovereignty of Claudius/capitalism) that would be perpetuated only by affirmative participation. In Shakespeare's play, the will to act is secured only after a period of passive and painful introspection, and then only at a terrible price. Hamlet's revenge on behalf of his murdered father causes an uncontrollable and unpredictable sequence of devastating events. Things get out of hand, and Polonius, Gertrude and others die in error. The aesthetic category of tragedy exemplifies the aporia of modern moral

---

⁶ For more on the connections between capitalism, subjective reason and authoritarianism, see Lukács, *The Destruction of Reason*, 341–54, 394–5.
⁷ Adorno, *Negative Dialectics*, 296.
⁸ Adorno, 'Marginalia to Theory and Practice', 260; Adorno, *History and Freedom*, 213–36.
⁹ Adorno, *Negative Dialectics*, 228.

subjectivity, whereby action taken to combat evil causes a pervasive suffering of its own.[10]

These themes are familiar to many a student of Shakespeare, yet they have a particular relationship with the Romantic doctrine of action. The significance of *Hamlet* to the question of negation and freedom lies in the fact that the young prince is 'incapable of performing an action that he believes is right', and only capable of acting, finally, in a moment when an archaic force (the desire for revenge, which Adorno categorizes as irrational) breaks through the rationalism of modern subjectivity.[11] Hamlet encounters the old irrational category of 'spontaneity', and causes a level of diegetic disaster beyond that which any rational reflection might have anticipated.[12] To bridge the gap between theory and praxis (between 'To be, or not to be'), Hamlet must compromise his rationality and leap into the Dark. The demands made by historical circumstance – that 'something rotten' which characterizes the diegetic world – requires from Hamlet, as a free and moral being, some kind of corrective response. But he can honour this impulse only by betraying the 'good', which was, in negative form, the motive underlying his conduct. This problem is echoed in *Negative Dialectics* when Adorno writes: 'In decisionism, which strikes out reason in the passage to the act, the act is delivered to the automatism of domination; the reflected freedom to which it presumes comes to serve total unfreedom. We have been taught this lesson by Hitler's Reich', in addition to Shakespeare's most philosophical and most Romantic play.[13]

The conclusion that follows from Adorno's interpretation of *Hamlet* is that these moments of spontaneous action, which chaotically break through the false surface of the rationalized social world, become emblematic of both freedom's potential and its negation. The significance of Prince Hamlet to Romanticism is to be found in this narrativized tension between rationality and irrationality, inaction and action – freedom as both the Light power for critical reflection and the Dark potential for unbridled chaos resulting from action. Hamlet's Romanticism symbolizes the idea, central to all critical philosophy, that

---

[10] The 'hero' in both domains is forced into decisive motion by an acute and plaguing consciousness of the wrong inherent to the constitution of the existing social world: the regicide of Hamlet's father, and the ascendancy of modern capitalism. Claudius' rule, and the rule of the market, provide the 'necessary evil', or narrative antagonism and impetus to moral action on the part of the Romantic protagonist. The passive moment of hesitation through moral uncertainty – in the famous soliloquy – guarantees the ambiguity of any positive actions that suffering protagonists allow themselves to commit. The committal of such actions becomes a crime in itself, evoking a mirror image of the wrong it once idealistically hoped to annihilate.

[11] Adorno, *History and Freedom*, 213–36.

[12] Ibid., 234.

[13] Adorno, *Negative Dialectics*, 229.

'fallibility is an essential characteristic of all moral action . . . at the very point where we feel certain that we are doing the right thing and are acting in good faith, we often end up behaving quite wrongly'.[14] Yet, to sit back and do nothing is equally bad, because it is conducive to suffering and injustice.[15] In short, the competing demands of history and freedom turn every action into a tragedy. The critical mode that occupies Hamlet through most of the drama demonstrates the business of theory in remove from praxis: 'Contemplative conduct, the subjective correlate of logic, is the conduct that wills nothing. Conversely each act of the will breaks through the mechanical autarky of logic; this is what makes theory and practice antithetical.'[16] And yet, this positive valuation of theory goes hand-in hand with the realization that, more than language, all thought, too, is a species of violence.[17] The category – demanding, as it does in Adorno's philosophy, a perpetual moment of self-critique – is an inherently discriminating modality, yet without the 'coercive moment' that it provides, 'there could be no thinking'.[18]

'Practice is put off and cannot wait', and 'not even silence gets us out of the circle'.[19] There is no way out. Least of all in complete quietism. For the horrors of the real world left unchecked call upon a self-annihilating moral principle which demands that a wrong be combatted with another wrong. Lukács succinctly explains the intractable moral demand that history makes of the modern individual: 'the rational perception that has its origins here is twofold: perception of the objective task, and perception of one's own share in its execution . . . human reason – if humanity is not to come to grief – must take the initiative, neither leaving events to run their own immanent course nor permitting them to be swayed by criminal intentions.'[20] The objective suffering of the empirical world demands practical action, yet, for reasons inherent to the modern concept of freedom itself, reason balks.

Romanticism's hesitation to wholeheartedly embrace freedom, despite the moral accusation resulting from the processes of history, and the consequent turn to self-critique, is dramatized by negative dialectics' own reluctance to dispense with the historically and socially determined categories of epistemological ordering. Bearing in mind Kant's suspicion of unbounded Romantic

---

[14] Adorno, *History and Freedom*, 262.
[15] Ibid., 263.
[16] Adorno, *Negative Dialectics*, 230.
[17] Ibid., 233.
[18] Ibid.
[19] Ibid., 245, 367.
[20] Lukács, *The Destruction of Reason*, 850.

freedom, critical theory develops from the painful realization that critique is dependent upon the very social conditions that it rejects. Because 'entity is not immediate . . . it is only through the concept', we should, therefore, 'begin with the concept'.[21] Horkheimer writes that criticism which doesn't begin with the concepts available for discourse 'seems to have the ground taken out from under it'.[22] The essential point for profitable and legitimate analysis is that the concepts themselves become the focus of criticism, first and last. Like Romantic agents of cultural transcendence, critics stand on the shoulders of the social and democratic institutions that have ensured their present level of freedom and (with an intransigent yet guilty 'ingratitude' for traditions) shout downwards. To valorize them, instead, would be, under the auspices of their own logic which denies affirmation, to ultimately corrupt them and consign them to destruction. The will to act inherent to cultural transcendence meets the logically derived moral safeguard of humility, which is expressed by critical rationalism: 'we must do something', but 'we never know what we are doing.'[23] The conservatism that lies problematically at the heart of a Light and self-critical Romanticism – refusing to admit the Darkness that was warned against by Kant – creates an irresolvable tension with the emancipatory drive for cultural transcendence, which provides the animating principle of critical philosophy itself.

Like art, Light Romanticism turns against itself. It is characterized by a tendency towards inaction, which, as we are coming to understand, creates significant tensions in the operations of narrative cinema in the ways suggested by Rancière.

But before proceeding to theorize this idea of Romantic inaction in greater depth, there is one more matter I need to clarify. We need to go back and revisit that cautionary, insightful and yet problematic scholar whom I chose to help me begin this book.

Apolitical Romanticism

Carl Schmitt's *Political Romanticism* crystallizes the idea of Romantic inaction, only from a completely different perspective. The analysis is concerned only

---

[21] Adorno, *Negative Dialectics*, 153.
[22] Horkheimer, 'Traditional and Critical Theory', 209.
[23] W. W. Bartley III, 'Alienation Alienated: The Economics of Knowledge *verses* the Psychology and Sociology of Knowledge', in *Evolutionary Epistemology, Theory of Rationality, and the Sociology of Knowledge*, ed. Gerard Radnitzky and W. W. Bartley III, 423–51 (La Salle: Open Court: 1987), 425.

with a specific kind of Romanticism: a certain tendency in political rhetoric exemplified by the writings of certain authors, including Adam Müller. In essence, Schmitt presents a linguistic critique of their political aspirations, but, in doing so, provides a number of penetrating insights into the general concept of Romanticism itself. These insights will help us to understand the dualistic schema I have chosen to adopt.

For Schmitt, Romanticism represents the antithesis of political agency, and is therefore a dangerous kind of quietist and apolitical subjective attitude. Its passivity and easy appropriation of disparate elements becomes (as the quotation that opened this book proclaimed) a threat to the security of necessary moral values. We must be clear about a more specific use of the word 'politics' being used here, for it highlights an interesting and enlightening distinction. When Schmitt calls Romanticism 'apolitical', he means that it refuses to value the act of decision. As is well known, for Schmitt, there is no politics without decision and the essential choice is an absolute and structural distinction between 'friend' and 'foe'. Light Romantic indecision is based upon a principle of critique by negation, or the unrealized formal basis of freedom and choice, whereas politics (in Schmitt's terms) revolves around action, or the realization of the freedom of choice, impacting the social world by accepting risk and responsibility.[24] These competing interpretations converge, however, when Schmitt writes: 'Where political activity begins, political Romanticism ends.'[25] Here, whilst pursuing his own theoretical ends, Schmitt cuts right to the heart of the matter: '(Light) Romantic activity . . . is a contradiction in terms.'[26] It is this explanation that, I feel, tallies with Adorno's interpretation of *Hamlet* as an exemplar of the Romantic paradigm of action and the tragedy of historical necessity.

More recently, Franco Moretti has insightfully integrated ideas from Schmitt and Richard Sennett to criticize the apolitical 'Romanticism' behind Modernist and *avant-garde* aestheticism and, from a Marxist perspective, the false valorization of concepts that offer no aesthetic experiences which are qualitatively distinct from the techniques of capitalist advertising and myth.[27] However, Moretti's broadly Schmittian interpretation of Romantic indecision as

---

[24] Schmitt, *Political Romanticism*, 159.
[25] Ibid., 160.
[26] Ibid.
[27] Franco Moretti, 'The Spell of Indecision', in *Marxism and the Interpretation of Culture*, ed. Cary Nelson and Lawrence Grossberg, 339–44 (MacMillan Education Ltd., 1988), 340. In place of this problematic critical perspective, which facilitates aesthetic elitism, scholars such as Moretti and Jameson championed a reorientation of critical analysis in favour of the products of mass culture which the following decades saw enacted with considerable interdisciplinary vigour.

subjectivist quietism contains a nuance that complicates its political orientation. He also acknowledges the necessity for individual narratives to work out thematic tensions drawn between this problematic Romanticism and the various materialist pressures of historical events, which demand an ethical response according to the diegetic need for narrative expression:

> Decisions have to be made all the time; even, paradoxically, in order to ensure the existence of that realm of possibility and indecision to which romanticism and modernism have attached such a central meaning . . . irony, extraordinary cultural achievement though it is, has to recover some kind of problematic relationship with responsibility and decision, or else it will have to surrender to history altogether.[28]

This tension between aesthetic inaction and historical necessity isolates what is more broadly political about the kind of Romantic cultural representation I have chosen to analyse in this book. But before moving on to explore this idea in more detail, let's take a closer look at Schmitt's overall approach and see where his key insights lead to a number of problems.

According to Schmitt, at the root of Romanticism lies the theological 'occasionalism' of Nicolas Malebranche, a seventeenth-century French Catholic philosopher.[29] Occasionalism entails a species of causal scepticism. Events in the world are not the results of their immediate causal relationships; each action, event and object is merely an *occasio* for the actualization of the general will of God over the process of reality. God lies behind all. What Schmitt takes to be decisive for Romanticism is the replacement of God with the transcendental subject, within the framework of occasionalism. The Romantic subject sees the world as an occasion, not for the realization of God's will, but for their own productive activity; Romanticism is, therefore, 'subjectified occasionalism'.[30] Occasionalism characteristically negates the *causa* with the *occasio*; the effect of this displacement is that things cannot be calculated, normalized or validated according to economic or rational principles.[31] This is a close relative of what Manfred Frank discussed under the name of Romantic anti-foundationalism, and leads to a similar moral indecisionism. 'The Romantic attitude is that of the subject who does not commit himself', says Schmitt.[32] Flight, irony, homesickness

---

[28] Moretti, 'The Spell of Indecision', 341–4.
[29] Schmitt, *Political Romanticism*, 17.
[30] Ibid.
[31] Ibid., 16–17, 82–3.
[32] Ibid., 67.

– these ideas speak for the Romantic attitude, which refuses satisfaction with positive ascriptions regarding value or meaning. Again, these things become negative in character.

Schmitt recognized that because subjectified occasionalism meant that the Romantic has no stable ground for moral or political agency, it was therefore susceptible to any prevailing or self-appointed principle and helpless to defend itself from beliefs and maxims potentially monstrous in their results.[33] Things such as truth, meaning and value lose their quality as objects existing for themselves and become mere instruments of subjective will – just so many 'starting points' for the infinite 'novel' (*Roman*) that the Romantic makes of the world, as Novalis famously put it: 'all the chance events of our lives are (but) materials from which we can make what we like.'[34] The valorization of fragments and details turns every aspect upon which attention is focused into an *occasio* – a beginning, a footprint of a truth that lies elsewhere. Reality comes to have no independent worth, but only in its function as a palette for the self-creating subject: 'Everything real is only an occasion' for a politically indifferent moment of ahistorical self-creation.[35] Obviously, the Romantic subject did not operate under the more complete delusion that they actually 'created' the world, and so sought alternatives to God by turning to ideas such as 'the nation', 'the people' or the Hegelian 'spirit' to provide a telos for subjective activity.[36]

At this point, however, Schmitt's critique of subjectified occasionalism deviates from the schema of Romanticism as I wish to frame it. The malleability that Schmitt accuses the Romantic programme of legitimating seems – if I have understood him correctly – to overstep an important distinction.

Despite his own conclusions, Schmitt's analysis makes clear the Janus face of Romanticism, or that aforementioned tension between a Light and a Dark pole. In this passage we see Schmitt progressing from one aspect to the other: 'the romantics felt strong enough to play the role of the creator of the world themselves, and to bring forth reality out of themselves. At the same time, they were the heralds of the two new realities, community and history, to whose power they immediately succumbed.'[37] The first position is associated with the

---

[33] Ibid., 19.
[34] Novalis, *Miscellaneous Observations*, § 65, 33; Schmitt, *Political Romanticism*, 19, 84. More explicitly, Novalis also wrote: 'To the extent that a thing exists for me – I am its purpose – it refers to me – it exists for my sake. My will determines me – and thus also my property. The world is to be as I will it'; Novalis, *Logological Fragments 1*, § 76, 63.
[35] Schmitt, *Political Romanticism*, 84.
[36] Ibid., 91–2.
[37] Ibid., 64.

Light concept. Armed with the Romantic sense of boundaryless-ness, the subject perceives the world as a place without ultimate truths, which are knowable. The social world with which they are confronted is therefore incompatible with the highest truth. Cultural transcendence enacts the perpetual negation of always already insufficient standards of proper conduct and knowledge. Accordingly, 'when the traditional idea of God collapses, the other and the alien become one with the true and the higher'.[38] Romanticism attains a position of critical openness.

But then a transformation takes place. In the second half of Schmitt's statement, concepts such as 'history' and 'the people' are interpreted as surrogate first principles. Light Romanticism makes an about-face: 'Everything that is Romantic is at the disposal of other energies that are unromantic, and the sublime elevation above definition and decision is transformed into a subservient attendance upon alien power and alien domination.'[39] From a condition of Godless freedom and self-determination, it devolves into a brand of quietism that results from taking human endeavour as nothing but the realization of history, nation, spirit or any other overarching design which is beyond the comprehension of any individual or group of individuals. An 'alien power' usurps freedom through an act of affirmation on the part of the subject.

Schmitt takes elements of Romanticism and arranges them into a kind of narrative, as every explanation must. *Political Romanticism* makes some of the most illuminating statements about the ideological ambiguity of the Romantic phenomenon, and yet seems to overlook an important nuance. 'Every spoken word is already a falsehood', Schmitt writes at one point, articulating his own avatar of problematic Romanticism; 'It limits unbounded thought . . . every foundation is false.'[40] As a Light Romantic statement, this is exemplary. Freedom means to exclude no possibility through limiting determination of right or essence, for 'to avoid any definite position' means that 'the claim to the higher and the true reality is not abandoned'.[41] Even by Schmitt's own sound analysis, Light Romanticism never makes up its mind. If it does, it is because it has become something else.

Under Light Romanticism, the activity of subjectified occasionalism is stalled. According to Schmitt, the *occasio* is a 'disintegrative concept';[42] consequently,

[38] Ibid., 91.
[39] Ibid., 162.
[40] Ibid., 66.
[41] Ibid., 73.
[42] Ibid., 17.

there seems to be something inherently critical about it – no firm conviction is safe from refutation if cultural transcendence will pick upon a potentially random aspect of reality as its locus for response. Schmitt's Romanticism loses faith in the logic of cause and effect, with the result that the concept of agency suffers a decisive trauma regarding free will and action. If effects can no longer be ultimately attributed to causes, then any potential decisions or actions must be questioned according to the imagination's ability to fictionalize their unintended consequences. This, as we have already seen in the discussion of Adorno and *Hamlet*, is a familiar theme in critical philosophy. The best-laid plans often lead to the most unpredictable and unintended consequences, and the will to action is stifled by a kind of moral conviction. Schlegel and Müller's political writings made this much clear to Schmitt: 'Romantics preach complete passivity . . . resignation, humility and permanence in order.'[43] Schmitt may be right about the import of the texts in question, but it is clear now that the first half of such statements have a more ambiguous political interpretation than the second half assumes. The kind of passivity that Light Romanticism displays is related to a profound lack of confidence in the existing state of affairs as the best possible order – entailing the negating critical impulse through cultural transcendence – but, equally, an awareness that any such conditions that can be realized by taking decisive action fall short of the ideal condition a priori. As Adorno demonstrated, modern (i.e., Romantic) art declares: 'Not this, but something else' – *O Freunde, nicht diese Töne*. The dynamic of negation and freedom requires a totalizing process of critique, and the formal indifference of this process to any particular content is, perhaps, similar to what Schmitt means by the arbitrariness of the Romantic *occasio*.[44]

If negation is formalized to a condition of complete refusal finding its moral apotheosis in stasis, then there is little to separate it from formalized affirmation. Perhaps Schmitt is wrong to say, 'In the absence of the occasionalistic displacement into the higher, subjective creativity that resolves all antitheses in a harmonious unity, there is no romanticism.'[45] Such a situation is merely, as Adorno might put it, one in which Romanticism did not go far enough in its refusal of totality.

As I understand it, Schmitt's claim that subjectified occasionalism entails the justification of any position whatever, moral or epistemological, is actually

---

[43] Ibid., 125.
[44] Ibid., 145.
[45] Ibid., 148.

attacking a transition between Light and Dark Romanticism. The confusion arises because the schematic content of Romanticism in its broadest terms – passion, cultural transcendence, feeling, boundaryless-ness – carries over from Light to Dark. They are present to comparable degrees in both a Beethoven symphony and a Nuremberg rally. What Schmitt's flawed yet valuable interpretation of Romanticism gives us is a prioritization of ideas of action and decision in the theoretical understanding of this schema. Because Light Romanticism refuses final decision, Schmitt rejected it as a political concept. Yet, it is this very condition that makes it political and, according to the tradition of critical philosophy, morally valid as a philosophical perspective. However, I do agree with Schmitt's judgement that (Light) Romanticism is a doomed political concept, despite his refusal to admit that it contains any inherently critical aspect.[46] Convinced of its essentially regressive nature, Schmitt explains away the initially revolutionary aura of Romanticism on the grounds that it was operating merely according to the principle of subjectified occasionalism at a certain time and place: in Europe towards the end of the eighteenth century; it's revolutionary content resulted merely from the structural realization of Romanticism as an infinitely impressionable phenomenon, and the historical proximity of the French Revolution.[47] As we are now in a position to recognize, however, the history of Romanticism is far more complex than this explanation will allow.

Having addressed the Schmitt connection, we can now turn to the idea of inaction I want to bring into focus here. It is predicated upon the Light Romantic subject's sense of 'authenticity' – their commitment to truth and freedom, as a limit to their positive engagement with empirical reality.

Romantic inaction

The idea of inaction finds fragmented expression throughout the Romantic canon, from the image of the daydreaming poet to the films analysed in Part Two of this book.[48] Franco Moretti has explored this trope in reference to Flaubert's *L'Éducation sentimentale* (1869), for example; protagonist Frédéric

---

[46] Ibid., 161.
[47] Ibid., 99.
[48] One of the many other ways of approaching this topic might be to consider the German Romantics' conception of the passive 'feminine' spirit of philosophy itself. This theme can be discerned in aspects of Novalis, Schelling and Schlegel.

Moreau is a shade of Light Romantic indecisionism by holding back the plot rather than advancing it, and finding motivation in 'an uncontrollable aversion towards all things definite'.[49] Aversion to determinate action is a significant tendency in Romantic literature, and, as Moretti notes, forms part of the 'culture of indecision'.[50]

Light Romanticism can also be illuminated by considering *Notes from Underground* (1864). Dostoevsky's nameless protagonist makes 'irrational' choices in order to assert his free will. Passionate negation is central to their world view, along with a relentless aversion to happiness, stability, conventionality and all aspects of 'the healthy'. It is a programme that appears to validate the proximity between pain and truth advocated by critical philosophy, and, at times, it is almost as if Dostoevsky's rhetoric proceeds directly from Kantian realist anti-foundationalism. The protagonist describes a lack of faith in the absolute values (such as 'justice'), for the authority of any pronouncements made in their name will inevitably ring hollow.[51] The painful experience of the Underground Man results from what Dostoevsky calls 'heightened consciousness' – a conviction that no statements correspond to 'the true'; even the logical truism 'two times two is four' is rejected by the unhappy narrator, committed to a totalizing and self-destructive non-commitment.[52] This is a heightened consciousness that abhors 'normal' individuals – 'men of action' – who function as the narrator's discursive antagonists.

By necessity, the protagonist's own rhetorical critique has no stable foundation. It is characteristic of the Underground Man that he does not privilege his own guiding convictions any more than those he rejects. Consequently, he directs unquenchable streams of foundationless and consciously unjust spite in all directions. By retreating into his 'mouse hole', he resolves the Romantic programme of negation with an impure and self-destructive nihilism. The Underground Man advances from a state of inaction to an insular and corrosive programme of 'spite' – loathing all elements of normal life that are incompatible with his own untenable convictions. In complete contrast to the commonplace belief that the good, the healthy and the living corresponds with the active and the dynamic, Dostoevsky's protagonist reaches the opposite conclusion:

---

[49] Moretti, *The Way of the World*, 175–6.
[50] Ibid., 121.
[51] Fyodor Dostoevsky, *Notes from Underground*, 1864 (London and New York: Alfred A. Knopf – Everyman's Library, 2004), 12.
[52] Ibid., 14.

'the direct, lawful, immediate fruit of consciousness', he declares, 'is inertia.'[53] With this realization, he steps into the realm of Romantic inaction. Dostoevsky describes this conviction in some detail:

> Active figures are all active simply because they are dull and narrow-minded . . . they take the most immediate and secondary causes for the primary ones, and thus become convinced more quickly and easily than others that they have found an indisputable basis for their doings, and so they feel at ease; and that after all is the main thing. For in order to begin to act, one must first be completely at ease, so that no doubts remain.[54]

This is a typical expression of the Light Romantic attitude regarding the doctrine of action. Thinking – what the active individual does *not* do, rhetorically speaking – results in the continual retreat of so-called 'first principles' behind an ever-advancing phalanx of increasingly primary premises.[55] 'Justice' is one such falsely 'primary' basis for action, and those which support the Underground Man's own cultural transcendence – directing his 'spiteful' revenges on a world in which he cannot bring himself to participate – were only temporary, in accordance with the conviction that any such conviction regarding firm principles of action will always retreat into a seemingly illimitable obscurity, being constantly subject to 'chemical breakdown' upon analysis.[56] As with all cultural transcendence that retains its Light aspect (which does not cross that boundary neglected by Schmitt), the attempt to find a stable ground for action causes the ground itself to dissolve. The result: stasis – a paralysis finding outlet, as far as Dostoevsky's protagonist is concerned, in a relentless programme of self-loathing. The valuation of freedom over advantage is one expression of the underlying maxim: the desire to assert one's freedom to choose, above all else, even if the choice thus freely made ultimately results in personal disadvantage. 'Independence' above all – as the Underground Man puts it – 'wherever it may lead'.[57]

More acutely than Hamlet, the Underground Man is aware of the abhorrent consequences of action. His ideal is responsible for a self-consciously wretched existence. The prospect of action repulses him; he suffers physical aversion at the mere contemplation of decisive, impactful, extroverted social participation. Yet, the eternal foreswearing of all participation, certainty and happiness does not

---

[53] Ibid., 17.
[54] Ibid.
[55] Ibid.
[56] Ibid., 18.
[57] Ibid., 21–5.

provide any kind of answer to life's problems. Like many an exemplar of critical philosophy, the Underground Man also knew that positivity, or 'two times two is four', is no longer life, but, rather, 'the beginning of death'.[58] The final scene of *Hamlet* illustrates the truth of this conviction. The positivism, which is the prerequisite for activity, marks the end of freedom because it marks the end of doubt.

In order to clarify the idea of Light Romantic inaction, it is also worth considering a paradigm example of its opposite: a philosophical relative of those 'men of action' abhorred by Dostoevsky's Underground Man. Without delving into too much depth regarding another complex philosophical system, we can consider certain statements presented in *The Vocation of the Scholar* (1794) and *The Vocation of Man* (1799) by Johann Gottlieb Fichte. Although he was not a Romantic himself, there are aspects of Fichte's philosophy that are useful for clarifying the distinction between Light and Dark aspects of this schema.

Fichte saw the grand and noble 'Vocation of Man' to be an endless historical chain of rational and progressive activity. The duty, which is demanded of every rational and moral human is simply to *act* – to shape reality according to the principle of unity, to exercise free will against natural determinism and to strive for unity between the subjective and objective (Ego and non-Ego).[59] Fichte demanded that the subject '*be at one with himself – he should never contradict his own being*';[60] but since this state of perfection is dependent on a perpetually deferred harmony between subject and object, this maxim entails a continual affirmative striving of all individuals to align themselves with the current constitution of culture. It was a moral duty for the rational subject to go out into society and actively participate in culture, to make themselves useful and contribute to humanity's ongoing mastery over nature.[61] In direct opposition to the Romantic valuation of social isolation and solitude, Fichte was of the opinion that the subject 'must live in society – he is no complete man, but contradicts his own being, if he live in a state of isolation'.[62]

Dark Romanticism runs through these affirmative pronouncements: 'To stand aloof and lament over the corruption of man, without stretching forth

---

[58] Ibid., 32.
[59] See Johann Gottlieb Fichte, *The Vocation of Man*, 1799, in *The Popular Works of Johann Gottlieb Fichte*, Vol. 1, 321–478 (Bristol: Thoemmes Press, 1999), 344–8, 406; Fichte, *The Vocation of the Scholar*, 152–3.
[60] Fichte, *The Vocation of the Scholar*, 153. Italics in original.
[61] Ibid., 156, 180.
[62] Ibid., 163; *sic*.

a hand to diminish it, is weak effeminacy; to cast reproach and bitter scorn upon man, without showing him how he can become better, is unfriendly. Act! Act!'[63] Max Weber later demonstrated how this new ethos in favour of active participation (consolidated by the development of Protestant ethics during the Reformation) fed directly into 'the spirit of capitalism': the entrepreneurial duty to engage in socialized profit-making activity, as a secularization of religious doctrine.[64] This ethic of participation stood behind the rise of modern commercial industrialism, and the world of 'normal' and active people rejected by Dostoevsky's Underground Man.

In Fichte's work, we sometimes see two Romantic ideas pulling in different directions: on the Light side, the non-teleological desire for a perfect society of free and equal individuals, and, on the Dark side, a quasi-authoritarian self-permission to manipulate everything, including fellow subjects, according to a necessarily fictive standard of perfection. Light and Dark may both claim that their opposite is not really 'Romantic' at all, but, rather, the true position's deceptive and destructive *doppelgänger*. The Light and inactive Romantic is chilled by the monstrous results of such activity as Fichte calls for, and how easily the naïve Romantic programme for total unity, mutual openness, receptivity and striving for the attainment of the highest Good can degenerate into heartlessness and genocide.

Freedom beyond the will

In order to better understand what freedom means in this context, we might return to Schiller's *Aesthetic Education*:

> Man as such can be defined in respect of two states, the passive and the active. . . . The condition of the human mind before any determination given

---

[63] Ibid., 205. Revealingly similar statements are cited by Adorno in his analysis of modern myth and pro-capitalist irrationalism; see Theodor W. Adorno, 'The Stars Down to Earth', 1974, in *The Stars Down to Earth and other Essays on the Irrational in Culture*, ed. Stephen Crook, 46–171 (London and New York: Routledge, 1994), 109.

[64] Max Weber, *The Protestant Ethic and the Spirit of Capitalism*, 1904–05 (Minola: Dover Publications Inc., 2003), 75. It is important to bear in mind the complexity of the development of modern capitalism and its relation to wider social, religious and political forces. As Fernand Braudel notes, Weber's account is not to be taken as a totalizing or causal explanation of capitalist mentalities, but, rather, as a study of some revealing 'coincidence(s) and common ground'; Fernand Braudel, *Civilisation and Capitalism: 15th-18th Century, Vol. 2, The Wheels of Commerce*, 1979 (London: William Collins Sons and Co., 1983), 568.

to it through sensory impression is one of a limitless capacity to be shaped and defined ... nothing is fixed in this vast realm of the possible, so also nothing is ruled out. This condition of a lack of determinacy can be called an *empty infinity*.[65]

As Manfred Frank summarizes: 'whenever someone expresses something finite, he/she will have committed a contradiction.'[66] An idealistic desire for truth and authenticity recoils from such a compromise. By making a choice and taking action, therefore, a subject loses this primary condition of 'infinite' possibility. The very condition for 'humanity' – being free to make a choice and act upon it – is secured at the cost of negating that condition. To create a determination, to decide and to act in any matter at all is a kind of loss. It is a betrayal of everything that was not done, or a forfeiting of that sublime marker of human freedom as an unfulfilled infinite realm of possibilities: Schiller's 'empty infinity'. Hence Schiller's tragic conception of human freedom in its practical necessity to function within social reality: 'It is only through limits that we can approach reality.'[67] It is only by a negation of conceptual freedom that we can realize freedom concretely, for it is nothing but the absence of necessity, a condition that requires action. Freedom is an eternally differed category, and authentic only in the moment before its realization. In other words, freedom equates to being free to act, but not acting. It finds tortured expression in the Underground Man's obstinacy.

To demonstrate the continuity of these themes, we can identify something very similar at work in *Negative Dialectics*. Adorno writes: 'We no sooner put it (freedom) to use than we increase our unfreedom; the deputy of better things is always also an accomplice of worse ones.'[68] The correlating element that defines itself in opposition to such freedom is, of course, the attitude towards life and action which has been conceptualized as the Dark Romanticism valorized by Fichte and adopted by capitalism.

---

[65] Schiller, *Aesthetic Education*, § 19, 67. Interestingly, this was a 'soft' version of that very same position arrived at by Morse Peckham in *Explanation and Power* (1979). If the meaning of any sign is any response to that sign, it also follows that human behaviour is potentially random; Peckham, *Explanation and Power*, 164.
[66] Frank, *The Philosophical Foundations of Early German Romanticism*, 218.
[67] Schiller, *Aesthetic Education*, § 19, 67.
[68] Adorno, *Negative Dialectics*, 297. Again, the similarities with Popper's critical rationalism are striking: 'The positing of an opinion, the mere statement that something is such and such, already implies ... reification ... (yet) without a firmly held opinion, without hypostatizing something that is not fully known ... experience, indeed the very preservation of life, is hardly possible'; Theodor W. Adorno, 'Opinion Delusion Society', 1963, in *Critical Models: Interventions and Catchwords*, 105–22 (New York: Columbia University Press, 2005), 108.

Inspired by the rhetoric of Novalis' *Fichte Studies* (1795-6), we might try to understand the Romantic doctrine of action by considering two rather more abstract propositions. Novalis conjectures that '/Acting is the expression /the utterance/ of being, of reality of the I, (just as) Thought is the expression /the utterance/ of not being.'[69] This contrasting of 'acting' and 'thinking', in a way very similar to Schiller and Adorno, might invite the following conjectures:

1. Activity is the necessary failure of freedom; the moment where thought ceases to claim a moral right and makes a compromise according to the demands of history; the empirical actualization of critique in progressing beyond itself and becoming action, in an attempt to eliminate error, pain and suffering. This is the same as saying: 'Being', as Novalis' fragment has it – 'being human', and all the troubles, hopes and contradictions that accompany and make up that condition – involves *necessary action* as its expression.
2. In passive thought, which comes before such necessary action, the subject is free. It transcends the limited self and reaches out to an objectivity the value and truth of which is intuitable in aesthetic experience. Again, to rephrase this in Novalis' terms, such thought is the expression of 'not being', of being either something more than human or perhaps more fully human.

These propositions seem to be consistent with my interpretation of Schiller and extend the idea that action can be diametrically opposed to thought, just as practice is usually contrasted with theory. Again, Adorno provides a useful counterpoint:

> Thought as such, before all particular contents, is an act of negation, of resistance to that which is forced upon it. . . . Today, when ideologues tend more than ever to encourage thought to be positive, they cleverly note that positivity runs precisely counter to thought and that it takes friendly persuasion by social authority to accustom thought to positivity. The effort implied in the concept of thought itself, as the counterpart of passive contemplation, is negative already – a revolt against being importuned to bow to every immediate thing. . . . While doing violence to the object of its synthesis, our thinking heeds a potential that waits in the object, and it unconsciously obeys the idea of making amends to the pieces for what it has done.[70]

---

[69] Novalis, *Fichte Studies*, § 83, 44.
[70] Adorno, *Negative Dialectics*, 19.

The Kantian root of this position is clear. The processes of calculation – treating objects in the world as the basis for principles of action (an instrumental subjective *occasio*) – formalizes the object and disavows its status as something that exists for itself. Despite the mental processes involved in the act of calculation, it is an 'action' in the sense that its underlying principle is the elimination of this objective, purposeless, 'aesthetic' quality. The reduction of an object to an instrument entails the lack of thinking, hence Adorno can say: 'When all actions are mathematically calculated, they also take on a stupid quality.'[71] This 'stupidity' is reflected back as a value judgement onto things that do not fit the dominant ideology, as Lukács noted, for, under economic rationality, 'the human qualities and idiosyncrasies of the worker appear increasingly as *mere sources of error*'.[72] Thinking is also, as we have seen, situated in opposition to economic activity. This entire problematic between economic activity and freedom is perhaps why the poet Heinrich von Kleist declared, after reading Kant, that 'day by day it is becoming ever more obvious to me that I am quite *incapable of doing a job*'.[73]

The one who acts does not think. They do so in a moment of madness, for they lose possession of themselves as a thinking being. Action gets things done – it gets results; hence its value to capitalist rationality. Kleist also noted this: 'reflection . . . seems only to confuse, inhibit and repress the power we cannot act without.'[74] Action entails an end to thought, or a completion of thought in its grasp of truth. But this is something passionately denied by the moral prejudice of critical philosophy. Critical philosophies, in contrast, take up a discipline of knowledge that is aporetic. They prefer a perpetual stultifying dialogue with an unknowable objective reality. If it has any moral compass – if it has faith in its own project and refuses to obey its own demons – then Romanticism discovers that there is no way out.

Yet, this very acknowledgement, by which Romantic subjectivity guarantees its moral validity (Schiller's paradoxical condition for 'freedom'), is also the problematic element which may condemn it to pragmatic impotence – an ascetic intellectualism or pacifism that creates its own set of tensions when brought into conflict with history, as Schmitt well demonstrated. Since the ultimate ground

---

[71] Adorno, *Minima Moralia*, 107.
[72] Lukács, *History and Class Consciousness*, 89; italics in original.
[73] Heinrich von Kleist, Letter to Ulrike von Kleist, Berlin, 5 February 1801 (extracts), in *Selected Writings*, ed. David Constantine, 420–1 (Indianapolis and Cambridge: Hackett Publishing Company, 1997), 421; italics added.
[74] Heinrich von Kleist, 'Reflection: A Paradox', 1810, in *Selected Writings*, ed. David Constantine, 410 (Indianapolis and Cambridge: Hackett Publishing Company, 1997), 410.

for critique is the very principle of action through negation, which enables critique in the first place, then critique becomes a fictive, self-sustaining and non-teleological task. Criticism requires the adoption of a subjective claim over the grounds of truth (if not its content) in order to make statements in its name; the result is a 'magic circle' that must be subjected to a philosophical discipline – an introspective 'self-critique of reason'.[75] This eternal project 'will not come to rest in itself', Adorno states, and far from being a cause for despair, 'this is its form of hope'.[76]

It is important to stress the fact that the current interpretation of Romanticism holds the principle of striving to be non-teleological. From this perspective, then, Adorno's belief that the Romantic striving to be 'at home everywhere' leads to a subjective attitude of 'incorporation and persecution' perhaps contains an unjust criticism.[77] Schlegel's own rhetorical employment of terms that strive after totality – the 'erotic' desire to unify[78] – must be read to contain an implicit understanding that such longed-for totality is always receding. The new Golden Age will never arrive. Homesickness does not entail arrival, and, in fact, better signifies an infinite departure: a sense of being unsatisfied with any condition of being that might be experienced. If there is an irrational element to this side of Romanticism, it is in this faithful conviction on the part of the subject that, although they will never arrive home, they keep departing.

Like Schlegel's understanding of philosophy itself, knowledge never comes to rest in the limiting form of a concept, and truth is best served by a complete and yet problematic separation from pragmatic experience. As Novalis wrote: 'The key to life lies in intellectual contemplation' – in thinking.[79] Light Romantic inaction demands that there be no end to thought, or that thinking never be betrayed by any dialectic realization in action. This Romanticism, which thinks rather than acts, might be imposed upon every image of the daydreamer, isolated artist or 'hero' characterized by passivity – the social exile who can take part in the modern world only through negative capability. Yet, this quietism is an untenable position. In his short story 'Mario and the Magician' (1929),

---

[75] Adorno, *Negative Dialectics*, 406; see also Max Horkheimer, *Eclipse of Reason*, 1947 (London and New York: Bloomsbury, 2013), 123.
[76] Adorno, *Negative Dialectics*, 406.
[77] Ibid., 172.
[78] Friedrich Schlegel, 'Fragments on Literature and Poesy', 1797, in *Theory as Practice: A Critical Anthology of Early German Romantic Writings*, ed., Jochen Schulte-Sasse et al., 329–35 (Minneapolis: University of Minnesota Press, 1997), § 27, 329.
[79] Novalis, *Logological Fragments 1*, § 94, 66.

Thomas Mann illustrated the problem as effectively as Schmitt, Adorno or Dostoevsky ever did:

> If I understand what was going on, it was the negative character of the young man's fighting position which was his undoing. It is likely that *not* willing is not a practicable state of mind; *not* to want to do something may be in the long run a mental content impossible to subsist on. Between not willing a certain thing and not willing at all – in other words, yielding to another person's will – there may lie too small a space for the idea of freedom to squeeze into.[80]

The privilege of freedom as empty infinity is denied to us by history. Things need to get done, or tyrants like Claudius or Cipolla will triumph through our inactivity. As Adorno expressed, there is no Good that is not externalized in action. The category of the positive is a lie and a burden, yet it remains a tragic necessity for life itself.

As the remainder of this book will be devoted to illustrating, it is on this very point that we can seek to interpret some of the 'more Romantic' products of cinema. We will find that this reciprocal schema of Romanticism – wavering between Light and Dark – has much to say about the themes and narratives presented in certain cultural products, in addition to enriching our understanding of film's own Romantic poetics. The final pages will reflect these ideas back across images that are strikingly evocative of a cinema audience.

To briefly demonstrate what this method will involve, we might consider certain scenes from Arthur Penn's countercultural *Bildungsroman*, *Four Friends* (1981), written by Steve Tesich. In one scene, protagonist Danny (Craig Wasson) attends an uncomfortable dinner with his wealthy prospective father-in-law, Mr Carnahan (James Leo Herlihy) (Figure 10). Danny expresses faith in philosophy as a means of comprehending the world, yet the successful businessman scoffs at such idealism: only 'cowards tinker with philosophies'. Mr Carnahan's attitude mirrors that of Danny's own father (Miklos Simon), an emigrant foundry worker who, at another point in the film, implores his son to 'Fight back!' when beating and abusing him. But Danny does not fight back, and displays a faltering belief that fighting back is the wrong thing to do. These 'normal' men have no time for Danny's lyrical, unproductive and idealistic attitude to life. His values seem to insult their own, and all the more so on account of how ambiguously he seems to hold them. Forming part of an expansive background symbolizing

---

[80] Thomas Mann, 'Mario and the Magician', in *Collected Stories*, 603–50 (London: Everyman's Library, 2001), 642.

Figure 10 Danny (Craig Wasson) struggling to reconcile reason and experience in *Four Friends* (1981).

turbulent social and economic transformations, these paternal figures embody problematic and anachronistic ideologies. Metonymic representations of the economic elite and the working class are shown to draw upon the same set of proactive social values – values which need (and, in consideration of the self-destructive violence they are shown to breed, indeed demand) revision by the new generation. And yet, the response, or lack of response, on Danny's part on both occasions, and at other times throughout the film, is symptomatic of the general Romantic themes at work in the film.

Although we are shown, throughout *Four Friends*, that society needs changing, individual actions do not change anything for the better and often end up perpetuating abhorrent conditions. The resulting sense of inaction – of 'holding back', apparently guided by some ideal that escapes us in its entirety, resulting from the subject committing themselves to an empty infinity – this is characteristic of the kind of Romanticism shared by the critical philosophies, and which can be particularly potent when read within narratives that seem to offer a critique of capitalist rationality. In the following case study chapters, we will explore many cinematic variations on this philosophical theme, including paradigm instances of Light and Dark Romanticism in the moral and rational make-up of certain characters, narratives and formal practices.

Conclusion

If all action – all representation – is a kind of explanatory violence, then all action is a compromise with truth. Fidelity to truth therefore demands something that is both ideologically dangerous and, in strictly logical terms, practically impossible. Freedom equates to the complete absence of explanation, representation and action. It means to choose not to act. To shrink from violence in the name of freedom is first to reject action, and then to reject determinate thought and finally to find existence itself intolerable. To sustain the result of this conclusion is, of course, both impossible and dangerous, because the absence of response to external forces can entail an impotent acquiescence to historical conditions. Recalling, again, the favoured Adornian example of Auschwitz: to do nothing is to consent to the triumph of evil.

Here we also stand at the core of the Romantic understanding of art, for absence of response is also the paradigm of modern aesthetic experience – Kant's disinterestedness taken to its logical conclusion. In art under the aesthetic regime, the 'meaning' of the work of art extends, as Hegel and Schelling wrote, beyond the bounds of the empirical world of explanation, representation and action. It gives us something more, and leaves us unwilling, in the name of truth, to reduce its sublime excess to any empirical statement. Adorno taught us that art is a process; it refuses a determinate concept because it is essentially dynamic and historical. The aesthetic is a never-ending 'processual' event, and artworks do not have a 'being' but a 'becoming'.[81] They are always incomplete, not only in their meaning, but also in what might count as their 'being-in-itself'. In this way, all artworks are critical and conservative simultaneously; by 'emphatically separating themselves from the empirical world, their other, they bear witness that the world itself should be other than it is; they are the unconscious schemata of that world's transformation'.[82] And yet every artwork has an equal and opposite conservative function by its mere participation in the business of culture.[83] Inaction, as the nadir of aesthetic experience – standing in front of a painting, listening enraptured to a piece of music or lost in the darkness of a cinema auditorium – shows us not that we have found a pure moment of pleasure and fulfilment (the 'beautiful'), but, rather, an uncanny awareness that we are lacking something. The work of culture always draws artistic creations into a complicity with the world as it exists, becoming objects of social exchange, discussion, language, economy, and yet, 'by its aversion to praxis it (art) simultaneously denounces the narrow untruth of the practical world . . . . Praxis

---

[81] Adorno, *Aesthetic Theory*, 242. See also Friedrich Schlegel, '*Athenäum* Fragments', 1798, in *Theory as Practice: A Critical Anthology of Early German Romantic Writings*, ed. Jochen Schulte-Sasse et al., 319–26 (Minneapolis: University of Minnesota Press, 1997), § 116, 321.

[82] Adorno, *Aesthetic Theory*, 242.

[83] Ibid., 319.

tends toward that which, in terms of its own logic, it should abolish; violence is immanent to it and is maintained in its sublimations, whereas artworks, even the most aggressive, stand for nonviolence'.[84] Even those that seem to openly advocate violence do so at the inverse cost of their properly 'artistic' content. The story of art under modernism (its 'Romance') describes an oscillation between positivistic affirmation and illusionary sublimity. When equal and opposite forces meet, the result is stasis, and the displacement of energy in other and new forms.

To end Part One of this book, we will return briefly to Jacques Rancière. Beginning with an Aristotelian division between active and passive subjects, *The Lost Thread* (2014) situates the excessive detail, the non-teleological narrative and the decentring of the active protagonist as elements of a politically democratic movement inherent to the aesthetic regime.[85] The new importance of the 'useless' detail is one side of the coin. The camera which shows elements that bear no functional relation to the logical coherence of the whole is a familiar notion; Bazin, Kracauer, Deleuze and others have kept this idea central to film theory. Rancière has shown how this phenomenon – bearing with it a democratic removal of boundaries between significant and insignificant, meaningful and meaningless – demonstrates film's indebtedness to, and even formal inseparability from, the Romanticism of modern art itself.

Another side, corresponding to this reign of the insignificant, is the revolt against the active, successful and meaningful as positive categories of value. The field is impossible to delineate, and the category can accommodate diverse instances for different reasons; it welcomes Flaubert, Conrad and Balzac's anti-heroes, their failures and disappointed idealisms; the Romantic dreamer and wanderer in the pages of Keats, Rousseau and Senancour; Dostoevsky and Turgenev's 'superfluous' men; Wagner's Tristan – drugged, unmanned and annihilated; Henry James' literary 'tableaux', where nothing much happens at all; Gogol's deluded Chichikov – all such aesthetic phenomena speak for grand failures in love, morals and business.[86] Against the more Napoleonic, Byronic or Nietzschean idea of dynamic heroism amenable to capitalism – paradigm of adventurous willpower, confident decision, able reasoning, bold speculation and

---

[84] Ibid., 328.
[85] 'There is a subversive virtue in the fact of not acting'; Rancière, *The Lost Thread*, 76.
[86] Like Moretti, Rancière hints at this expansive field of literary inaction; Rancière, *The Lost Thread*, 19, 101.

successful action – what Romanticism also finds itself embracing is any Lighter image of subjectivity where this conception of the heroic is called into question.

What the aesthetic regime brought to the fore, for both the novel and cinema in its turn, was a new mode of fiction where narrative actions do not quite matter the way they used to; where what happens in the flow of events 'is no longer conceptualizable or recountable as a succession of necessary or probable actions'; and where certain values, which had been inherent to the classical conception of representational art since Aristotle, are negated.[87] Making an abstract inference from this premise, Rancière declares that equality is 'horizontal' – not simply evoking the idea of a 'flatness' that corresponds to any lack of distinction between social highs and lows, but a horizontality, rather, which finds expression in the supine Romantic daydreamer 'stretched out on a sofa or on clover'.[88] This immobility contains the spirit of social equality, even as it is insufferable to those active men like Danny's father or Mr Carnahan, who look down upon artists and their useless and impractical reveries. These active men who abhor idlers also know their place in the social totality, whether it be as a poor steelworker or as a business tycoon. They do not question the rightness of these roles and are inclined to see reflected in them a validation of mythic standards of human value, materialized in the stratifications of meritocracy and social class.

If individuals within the modern economy are driven to action, speed and decision by the mechanism of competition and economic development, then their diametric oppositions, hesitation, frustration and indecision – neurotic in structure and effect – are redefined as symbols of freedom. Light Romanticism ascribes a higher value to the failure of response. This failure results from the realization that what we truly seek cannot be attained through action. For Romantics such as Novalis, philosophy tends to arise 'through interruption... through standing still at the point where one is', without knowing exactly why[89] – like the protagonist of *Mickey One* (1965) when he encountered the old man with the broken nose. This sense of immobility is perhaps the one authentic response to the experience of life in the modern capitalist world; one in which the vast majority of supposedly free individuals, faced with a historically unprecedented level of democratic unfreedom, which it is shameful to compare

---

[87] Ibid., 30.
[88] Ibid., 83.
[89] Novalis, *Fichte Studies*, § 566, 168.

to genuine suffering, still find themselves, from time to time at least, 'struck dumb amid endless noise'.[90]

This is the relevance of Light Romantic inaction to the artistic critique of capitalism. What could be more fitting to dramatize the experience of the modern subject, given such poignant treatment in the films of Arthur Penn and Lindsay Anderson? *Mickey One, O Lucky Man!* (1973), *The Missouri Breaks* (1976) and *Britannia Hospital* (1982), and more besides, are films that perform Romantic critical theory when they reveal 'the allurements society holds out keep everyone breathless', create worlds in which it is 'no longer possible to distinguish between good and bad' and thereby condemn their protagonists to proactive failure or the tyranny of mere existence.[91] There must be no satisfying resolution, no positive programme and no 'happy ending'. The self-negating narrative conclusions addressed in the following chapters reflect the Romantic ambiguity of Rancière's assertion that, in society, in *Hamlet* and in all works of art in the modern age, 'the political wrong does not get righted'.[92]

In a previous book I suggested that Peckham's cultural transcendence and Rancière's aesthetic regime formed both Romanticism's principle of agency and part of its principle of form.[93] Cultural transcendence strives for differentiation – a breaking free from norms, rules, traditions and set ways of understanding and using things. This happens at the same time as the aesthetic regime brings all things together under the equalizing value of art and expression freed from the mimetic principle. Both imperatives – cultural transcendence and the multimedia drive supporting the aesthetic regime – find themselves confronted, in their very moment of becoming, by a dark shadow of their own highest good. A confounding and petrifying oscillation between Light and Dark, action and inaction, results: a fear of taking part, and thereby corrupting our 'empty infinity'; a fear of stagnation, death and failure; of not having given life a meaning.

Our actions, like our words, always escape us. Critical philosophies teach us what W. W. Bartley learnt, specifically from Popper and Hayek: *'we never know what we are talking about*, and . . . *we never know what we are doing.'*[94] Whatever we say or do will be wrong. There will always be a remainder. Always something that escapes us and which we may never even know existed. Since there is

---

[90] Max Horkheimer, *Critique of Instrumental Reason*, 1964 (London and New York: Verso, 2012), 133.
[91] Ibid., 31; Adorno and Horkheimer, *Towards a New Manifesto*, 30.
[92] Rancière, *On the Shores of Politics*, 103.
[93] Kitchen, *Romanticism and Film*, 27.
[94] Bartley, 'Alienation Alienated', 425; italics in original text. Sentiments that are almost echoed, incidentally, in Alan Price's soundtrack for *O Lucky Man!*

nothing to guarantee that such a remainder may not lead to unimaginable horrors, perhaps it is safest to say and do nothing. This moral conviction finds its avatar, as Rancière suggests, in the Romantic artist who strives for the Absolute, yet is condemned to create something that falls short of their ideal by the very conditions of artistic production. There is a passage written by Franz Liszt that expresses this divided Romanticism better than any I know:

> Two opposing forces are fighting within me: one thrusts me ... up to the heavens; the other pulls me down towards ... regions of calm, of death, of nothingness .... I stay nailed to my chair, equally miserable in my strength and my weakness.[95]

In comparison, here is a frank confession from Adorno:

> I always come back to the feeling I have when people ask me how I would act as the director of a radio station or as minister of education. I always have to admit to myself that I would be in the greatest possible state of perplexity. The feeling that we know a huge amount, but that for category reasons it is not possible for us to put our knowledge to genuine practical use, is one that has to enter our deliberations.[96]

Romanticism hinges on the tensions apparent within such statements. The theoretical isolation of the philosopher who agonizes over the diremption of modern subjectivity and its relation to economic exploitation finds a parallel in the Romantic artist who feels the passionate surge of inspiration, yet hesitates to put pen to paper for fear of contaminating that sublime urge with any realization that will not do it justice. The typical fate of this aporetic condition is that it transcends itself through its own failure and fuels the work of such individuals who experience it. Against its truth-content, the feeling becomes 'productive'. Symphonies, films and treatises result – works that often perpetuate the troubled conditions of their creation.

The enemy that draws the subject towards unfreedom is totality – identity thinking – yet this enemy is essential for all knowledge and action. The best lack all conviction whilst the worst are full of a passionate intensity, as Yeats wrote. The task is to maintain faith in critical reason against the pull of totality, whether the latter take the form of affirmation or nihilism. It is to maintain faith in the power of the unanswered question, and the exercise of free thought as Romantic infinity.

---

[95] Cited in Alan Walker, *Franz Liszt: The Virtuoso Years, 1811–1847* (London: Faber and Faber, 1983), 269.
[96] Adorno and Horkheimer, *Towards a New Manifesto*, 52.

Part Two

4

The artist's calling

Mickey One (1965)

One of the most significant of all Romantic narrative tropes situates the individual subject against 'the way of the world'. This is not, however, the typical paradigm of the hero versus an evil external force that threatens an authentic totality – the battle to preserve an essentially 'good' world. Romanticism often finds something uncanny in the very condition of normality that would have itself defended. A protagonist's antisocial dilemma, such as that represented in *Mickey One* (1965), can accrue mythic proportions and accommodate ambitious allegorical readings. Certainly, Mickey (Warren Beatty) is not escaping society because of any moral principle (Figure 11). He is trying to save his own skin. In debt to the mob, he goes to ground in the big city, ultimately falling back upon his skills as a comedian to make a decent living. Yet, Mickey's flight from his creditors develops a mythic dimension that activates various tropes associated with both Romanticism and capitalism. The conversation between Mickey and Jenny Drayton (Alexandra Stewart), a girl whom he encounters whilst on the run, is undoubtedly the film's 'trailer moment' of narrative and thematic exposition: 'I don't understand. Anything', Jenny says; 'hiding from you-don't-know-who, for a crime you're not even sure you've committed?' Mickey's reply: 'And the only thing I know: I'm guilty.'

The film is less concerned with generic pursuit and retribution than it is with the subjective experience of the protagonist, yet this experience is never allowed to find any solid basis against a tangible diegetic antagonism. The mob is a potent absence throughout the film. Mickey is 'on the run' in the abstract – a guilty human passionately fleeing evil forces about which he knows very little. The protagonist's actions are determined by an all-pervading absence that is felt according to suggestive traces, half-imagined shadows and, occasionally, by the violent material impact that it has upon the world around him.

Figure 11 Mickey (Warren Beatty) living under the shadow of fear in *Mickey One* (1965).

Mickey One frames its initially generic noir narrative with an expansive symbolic context of business, success and the individual's assertion of freedom against a conspiratorial social network. The film's hybridization of gangster movie, art film and satire is tempered by pointed representations of material contrast between high and low, affluent and poor, speakers and non-speakers, which flit in and out of the diegesis at regular intervals. The film prompts audiences to ask: To what extent does the protagonist's unendurable situation dramatize something characteristic about modern subjectivity in the developed world? Arthur Penn himself advocates an allegorical reading of the film in relation to McCarthyism and the need for American culture to confront and overcome a climate of fear.[1] But the dark cloud that hangs over the world of *Mickey One* can support any number of allegorical commitments, including the hypothesis that the film functions as a critique of capitalism – a critique of an expansive cultural climate in post-war America that might subsume any number of corresponding social anxieties, ranging from HUAC to Hiroshima.

Unseen forces

Whilst travelling to an audition, which might prove to be his last, Mickey's cab gets stuck behind a lorry carrying three men wearing revolutionary era costumes. Each figure holds a portable radio carelessly against their ear. According to Penn's own McCarthyist interpretation, the indifference to Mickey's story displayed

---

[1] Crowdus and Porton, 'The Importance of a Singular Guiding Vision', 7; Segaloff, *Arthur Penn*, 121.

by these three figures might symbolize the contemporary waning of American values regarding freedom and comradeship: the spirit of the founding fathers has been forgotten. Yet, this vague sense of American society 'not being all it should be' need not be limited to this idea; it is quite compatible with the broader possibility that the ideals of American freedom are now distanced from the results of one of their most significant historical consequences – the proliferation of modern capitalism. Remember that one of the most famous figures associated with this revolutionary world, Benjamin Franklin, was also a leading progenitor of Weber's capitalist ethic.[2] Indeed, the vehicle of this problematic distraction (the portable radio) is explicit concerning the significance of technological mass media. The suggestion may be that whilst Ben Franklin enjoys the latest consumer conveniences, made possible by the advance of a capitalist ethic that he advocated, Mickey One – artist and victim of the modern Western cultural and economic system – is walking into a deadly trap. His 'big break' may be the end of him.

It is in this sense that the film can be approached as an allegory of Light Romantic freedom as a negating commitment. It explores an individual's fighting passivity, directed against the dominant ideology of social participation. Like Kleist after reading Kant, the protagonist is put in a situation where they simply find it impossible to 'do a job' in accordance with their nature.[3] Throughout the film, danger seems closer to hand whenever Mickey comes near to success in his profession – to fulfilling the economic role demanded of him by diegetic forces expressive of the capitalist ideology of vocational 'calling'. Mickey's motivating passion finds expression, therefore, in a flight from the typical realizations of capitalist rationality, expressions of which are transformed into something ominous, uncanny and deathly. Destruction is the guaranteed result of 'getting out there', becoming 'successful' and holding a stake in society. Like Conrad's *Heart of Darkness* (1899) or the novels of Kafka, *Mickey One* presents us with an individual living at odds with a potent absence, but one whose meaning is defined by certain socio-economic relations.

The generic relation with the gangster film is of particular significance in this context, since, as Fredric Jameson has noted, there is a widespread cultural affinity between fictional representations of organized crime and capitalism.[4] There are few interpretive moves so widely understood in twentieth-century criticism as

---

[2] Weber, *The Protestant Ethic and the Spirit of Capitalism*, 50, 65.
[3] Kleist, Letter to Ulrike von Kleist, Berlin, 5 February 1801, 421.
[4] Fredric Jameson, *Signatures of the Visible*, 1992 (London and New York: Routledge, 2007), 42.

that which reads the mob as 'the mirror image of big business'.[5] Mickey's flight from, and tortured return to, the world of work tallies with the other 'heroic' side of the 'gangster-capitalism' experience: 'For the citizens of some multinational stage of post-monopoly capitalism, the practical side of daily life is a test of ingenuity and a game of wits waged between the consumer and the giant faceless corporation.'[6] What *Mickey One* manages to achieve, however, is to render such a game of wits irresolvable whilst revealing its violent and alien properties.

The ganger noir genre gives the film its rhetorical toolbox, but it never really opens it. *Mickey One* denies us the reassuring figuration of any powerful abstract entities within the diegesis. The threatening non-being 'behind' the official world of the fiction, which menaces the protagonist throughout the narrative, is never given a reassuring face. Mickey experiences the mob as an absence, both by fearing their appearance and in witnessing the horrific effects of their passing elsewhere. Axes in smashed jukeboxes, trashed offices, terrible scars from cut throats and half-finished sentences about broken bottles are the only traces they leave behind. Mickey's attempts to talk about the mob are met with a wall of silence. The symbolic identification between the mob and the legitimate social order – the world of business – is nowhere more plainly admitted than in the brief comic scene when Mickey successfully appeals to a local politician for an introduction to a gangster. After speaking, without result, to bartenders across the city, the door of the underworld is opened to him upon shaking hands with a prospective city committeeman: 'Only one in the whole city of Chicago can tell me a gangster to go to. Next year, damn it, I vote!' The higher up the legitimate social infrastructure, it seems, the nearer (closer to figuration) are the intangible yet violent forces that determine social life.

The film revels in its concealment of 'the real thing', as Henry James might have put it, and it is perhaps inevitable that metaphysical allegory should enter the interpretive field. Robin Wood suggests that as the film progresses, 'one cannot escape the suggestion that Mickey is Modern Man' and the real enemy seems like nothing less than 'human consciousness itself'.[7] But this consciousness has a definite historical aspect; the technological and sociocultural malaise through which Mickey stumbles makes its modernity all too obvious. Wood's critical value

---

[5] Ibid., 42. Adorno was unconvinced concerning the ability to represent the immorality of capitalism in terms of criminal allegory: 'It harmlessly interprets the seizure of power on the highest level as the machination of rackets outside of society, not as the coming-to-itself of society as such'; Adorno, *Minima Moralia*, 144.
[6] Jameson, *Signatures of the Visible*, 60.
[7] Wood, *Arthur Penn*, 34–4.

judgements prevent him from elaborating on the important fact that *Mickey One* is a 'crystallization' of Penn's 'leading concerns'.[8] Penn's own perspective on McCarthyism offers a useful interpretive key, but, as with the other case studies, I will attempt to interpret the film as a Romantic critique of capitalism, and the unconvincingness of the film's ending is an essential element. Rather than revealing – as Marxist critics often allege to be the progressive option – a positive vision of a collective utopia that stands in symbolic opposition to a coercive status quo, the film, instead, finds its organizing principle elsewhere. Not only does it offer a divided, conflicted and ultimately irresolvable experience of Light Romantic subjectivity, but also a feeling that the film has failed in its task and remains incomplete. Like Kafka's *The Castle* (1926), the allegorical tone evokes the ambiguous mythological aura of an abortive detective novel, 'in which the criminal fails to be exposed'.[9]

La dolce vita

The film begins with a group of rotund middle-aged men sitting in a sauna and laughing uproariously at a man smoking a cigar and wearing winter clothing. In this way, our protagonist is introduced through an incongruous and avowedly metaphorical situation. We get the impression that he is doing something he feels he has to do, something that is forced upon him, and not by a positive subjective valuation of the social demands which pertain to his immediate environment. If his choice of clothing is voluntary, then the decision appears to be made under an obscure necessity – he suffers discomfort for the sake of something unreadable. The opening scene immediately establishes the film's symbolic mode of address.

The following montage shows this man living the high life as a successful night club performer, and suggests that his hedonism will come at a terrible cost. Images of fast cars, beautiful young people, mirrored ceilings, beds, flowers, gambling and alcohol build a typical representation of the allurements on offer to affluent Westerners in the 1960s. The driving jazz soundtrack and mobile camerawork build a weighty dynamism, making the diegetic world seem seductive and autonomous, as if events are functioning according to an inevitable logic of their own. A host of aesthetic devices, such as underwater camera shots,

---

[8] Ibid., 31–8.
[9] Theodor W. Adorno, 'Notes on Kafka', 1953, in *Can One Live After Auschwitz? A Philosophical Reader*, ed. Rolf Tidemann, 211–39 (Stanford: Stanford University Press, 2003), 232.

overhead shots, blurred images and sound distortions, emphasize the film's participation in the European-influenced culture of the post-war generation. This dizzying vision of fulfilment evokes the contemporary vogue for the world of Audrey Hepburn, Sophia Loren, Marcello Mastroianni and the French New Wave. It creates a sense of life unleashed, and a potential to revert to something primitive and base. When Mickey witnesses a seated figure being beaten by two men down an alleyway, he turns into the embrace of his beautiful companion (Donna Michelle) and falls onto a chair himself. This doubling introduces a threatening tone to complicate the images of desire. Much like *La dolce vita* (1961), *Mickey One* constructs a paradigmatic vision of mid-twentieth-century 'high life' and yet tinges this alluring world with a poignant disquiet.

An overhead shot reveals the girl in a reverie on a deserted dance floor. She sways to the accompaniment of a jazz drumkit played by a man with a hunched back. She arches her spine like a contortionist, in a way that blurs sensuality with something uncanny, perhaps even suggestive of injury or death. At the sight, Mickey spits out a mouthful of alcohol, once again blending the erotic (spitting being conventionally associated with sexual ejaculation) with something more alarming, as if he is wilfully losing control or relinquishing something – perhaps his soul.

Mickey soon learns the price to be paid for this heady lifestyle. He owes some people a lot of money. He can work to pay off his debt, but the rest is unsettlingly obscure. When talking to his club manager, Ruby Lapp (Franchot Tone), Mickey's exasperated explanations and questions meet with no reply. Ruby's jaded expression suggests knowledge of an inevitable logic orchestrating Mickey's fate. Eventually, the attempts at rationalization dry up and the protagonist states the bottom line: 'Who owns me?' The relationships are stated in a proprietary register. Mickey talks about the girl from the opening montage as someone else's 'private stock', and, trying to guess the amount of money he owes, he expresses his estimates with growing concern: 'What, five grand? Ten . . . Twenty?' Behind each doubling number, a doubled amount of time in servitude to his job is suggested. In a later flashback scene, Ruby transforms the conditions of Mickey's debt into a transcendental experience of economic materialism; the 'wrong' unwittingly committed by Mickey, and which becomes the determining factor of his guilty identity, goes far beyond the numbers implied:

> How do you know its not all the other crap games they tore up on you? And the bookie slips. How do you know its not the car they gave you, you smashed up?

And the liquor, and the good times, and the apartment? And the clothes, and Christmas, and birthdays, and the rehearsal halls? . . . How do you know it isn't all the trips they paid for, and the 'special material', and the arrangements in music? The dentists? The lawsuits, the parties, the expenses? 'Twenty Thousand' – twenty thousand is just a fraction. How do you know it's not the – your *whole life* you're living?

The completeness of the accusation is as significant as the content. Mickey seems to be in trouble precisely because of his living *La dolce vita* of modern material prosperity – living the false totality represented by the mythologized capitalist imaginary. The things that were given to Mickey by his hidden creditors were 'favours' only so long as they wanted them to be favours. The horror of this situation is simply expressed by Mickey's quiet acknowledgement, whilst contemplating some slaughtered pigs hanging in the club kitchen: 'So they bought me. I'm tied up here the rest of my life.' Far from being the master of all the material and experiential possessions provided by his privileged vocation, Mickey has found that he is actually the losing element in a broader matrix of 'possession'. Ruby's advice, articulated in gambling terminology, is simply to 'Stick'. The experienced club manager seems to offer this as the pragmatic solution: Stick to your job. Pay the money.

But Mickey decides to run. Leaping out of the door, Ruby shouts after him: 'There's no place you can hide from them! You'll have to be an animal!' Transition shots of the moon, round and glowing white behind scrolling black clouds, are accompanied by mournful saxophone music. This circle of light is a recurring symbol in *Mickey One*, akin to a transcendental eye or spirit that oversees Mickey's trials and ultimately acts as a receptacle for his, and the film's, sublime abstractions regarding the fear which hangs over his life. At the narrative climax, a stage spotlight will carry the Word of God.

The fall of Jerusalem

Mickey burns his identity card and severs all ties with his past. He becomes a 'nobody', like the tramps he sees living by the railway tracks on his arrival in Chicago. In his hounded situation as a debtor, he's all the safer for being close to non-existence.

At a nearby scrapyard, police are recreating the disposal of a murdered body in a car crusher. Mickey is seemingly pursued by a crane and runs to escape a similar fate. Such fleeting impressions contribute to Mickey's pervading experience of being 'on the run' from something more abstract and pervasive. He continues through the scrapyard and is menaced by looming bulldozers and cranes carrying broken and twisted cars. Sparks fly, flaming tanks of fuel pour across the ground and cascades of water spew from wreckage. These images of a disoriented man stumbling through a technological nightmare, accompanied on the soundtrack by swirling and oppressive orchestral music, perhaps evoke the famous hellish vision of Moloch near the beginning of *Metropolis* (1927), when the protagonist (Gustav Fröhlich) discovers the consuming maw of exploitation that sustains his father's city. As Mickey observes the shocking explosion of a fuel tank, the scene cross-fades slowly through an image of him walking down a lonely street. The fade is drawn out long enough for viewers to get a distinct impression that Mickey is witnessing himself walking through the flames (Figure 12).

Mickey One does not offer the comfort of ascribing a class-based judgement, or even a mythological metaphor, to the disorienting experience in the scrapyard. The disquieting episode that transforms the sympathies of Freder in *Metropolis* – the sight of dozens of people being unjustly sacrificed to the technological God of status quo – is not possible for *Mickey One*. The intensified individuality of the alienated subject in post-war America gives a different significance to Mickey's own uncanny experience, focused on a *doppelgänger*-like vision, which, almost equally expressive of human spiritual destruction, is all the more ambiguous for lacking a solid basis as a represented 'wrong'. Just as Mickey never encounters the villainous presence that hounds him on account of his debts, so too does

Figure 12 The wanderer's existential and religious visions in *Mickey One* (1965).

he, instead of seeing Moloch – a clear mythic embodiment of the dread that besets him – only sees himself in flames. It is an indeterminate and uncanny apparition whose meaning lies somewhere between pity and accusation. The vision is neither demon nor soul in torment.

Sheepishly entering the door of a Christian mission, Mickey receives the hospitality of a kindly yet awkward old couple. In a conspicuously empty reading room, Mickey consumes a meagre meal as the man (Norman Gottschalk) stutters out a passage from the Book of Jeremiah:

> Jeremiah was entered into the dungeons, and into the cabins, and Jeremiah had remained there many days. Then Zedekiah the king sent, and took him out: and the king asked him secretly in his house, and said, Is there any word from the Lord? Jeremiah said . . .[10]

We do not hear what the prophet said in answer, for the scene cuts to a written repetition of the question on a board hung in the window. The significance of the selection – Jeremiah's dialogue with Zedekiah, the last king of Judah, shortly before the conquest of Jerusalem by Nebuchadnezzar II – may evoke the idea of some epoch coming to an end, or the unjust persecution of an individual burdened with the capacity to reveal unwelcome truths concerning the ruling power. But the vital and accentuated utterance – 'Is there any word from the Lord?' – carries the bulk of the scene's allegorical significance. The unanswered question reflects Mickey's situation: living in a kind of purgatory, awaiting a judgement or revelation that is continually deferred.

Far from offering any stable correlation between the expansive theme evoked by the biblical quotation and the narrative structure, the film perpetually oscillates between the two poles of hermeneutic significance. It becomes impossible to state explicitly that the film is 'about' a man on the run from the mob, or 'about' the meaning of life. As Robin Wood noted, it operates in a hazy realm somewhere between the two. What the film's chosen motto highlights, however, is the diegetic world's own particular sense of absence: a lack of something that would provide stable meaning, a comprehensible fictional world and, in Mickey's case, security. What is 'missing', exactly, is initially suggested to be Earthly Paradise itself, for, to the accompaniment of non-diegetic instrumental strains from a religious melody matching the words from Jeremiah, Mickey sees a gang of poor (presumably homeless) men rob an unconscious man who lies

---

[10] Jeremiah 37: 16-17.

in an alleyway. Mickey follows the thieves and claims a social security card as his share of the spoils. Having touched rock bottom and uncovered the essential question, Mickey uses this card to get a job under a fake name and so takes the first step on his return to the world. But the phrase 'social security' will soon become a contradiction in terms.

A manager in a large commercial kitchen says: 'Your name is Mickey One. Garbage.' This corruption of the Polish surname printed on the stolen card brings Mickey's experience at the bottom of the social hierarchy closer to that of the working-class post-war European immigrant. The word 'garbage' names both the object of his labour and the social valuation of the person whose job it is to perform. His new responsibilities include using his bare hands to scrape plates clean. Mickey falteringly adjusts to his new life. He waits unconcernedly at the back of the queue to clock out; his rhythm of life is out of sync with the bustling workers around him. Yet, the world of regular labour eats into his being. A cross-cut soundtrack edit synchronizes an image of Mickey spitting with the sound of the bell rung as workers punch out with their timecards; this gesture perhaps evokes a derisive association with routinized labour, or that every human action is moulded according to vocational experience. Mickey sleeps down an alleyway, in the very place where he spat. Yet, having established this social space – the job and the location – as one occupied by those who are only 'garbage', the film introduces a powerful element that transforms the value system represented by the act of naming: 'Mickey One. Garbage'.

The tender trap

Whilst running from the crane – symbol of that nebulous doom that haunts the protagonist – Mickey caught his first glimpse of an Asian man sitting on a cart. The pleasant-looking figure beckoned him, but Mickey continued to run. As the film continues, this enigmatical character with carthorse and dustman's clothes (Kamatari Fujiwara) is fleetingly encountered at key narrative moments, wordlessly radiating an aura of mischievous comradeship. He becomes an image of escape – an alternative to Mickey's continual flight from abstract oppression. It is eventually revealed that he is an artist, accumulating urban detritus in order to build a giant mechanical installation.

As our hero now transfers rubbish from cans to a garbage truck, he spies this mysterious artist running up some stairs with two dustbin lids. Turning, and crashing them together like cymbals, his purloined possessions become, in the hands of the artist, something like a promise; they become 'aesthetic' by transforming from refuse – being of the world which names 'garbage' and the people who work with it – into a means of creating a confounding space of uncertainty. The power of the effect is increased by the mysterious aura of value and evoked by the junk artist and his 'non-functional' role in the film's narrative: his status as an extraneous element, or a significant part of what makes *Mickey One* more than a generic crime drama. The artist figure becomes the power to challenge the socially inscribed boundaries between things and functions, and his presence in the film, through its very obscurity, marks one of the central issues of Romanticism: the tension between freedom and explanation. It is this very tension that enables us, by the film's conclusion, to orient *Mickey One*'s critique of capitalist ideology alongside a self-reflective interpretation of the film as a work of cultural production.

Soon after this encounter, Mickey wanders into a nightclub called The Tender Trap. He is seemingly attracted by the music being sung by a woman on stage: 'You're a hero. A Nero, Apollo, the Wizard of Oz. You've a kingdom, power and glory. The old, old, oldest of stories is new, true . . .' The lyrics of the song, which draws Mickey back towards his old profession, and towards danger once more, are dense with mythologised images of individual fulfilment.

The compere (Benny Dunn) begins a series of hackneyed jokes. Acts come and go throughout the night, and, when the audience has thinned considerably, the host eventually comments on Mickey's iron constitution for club life. Our hero begins mouthing the comic's punchlines, finishing his jokes, and eventually overtakes the man on stage by delivering his own lines and evoking rimshots from the house band. The compere eventually recognizes Mickey to be a member of his own profession – 'Brother Rat!' – and invites him onto the stage. Yet, Mickey immediately turns and waves away the invitation, reminded, it seems, of the danger that public exposure means to him. In another more generically conventional film, this may be 'the big break', or the moment when the hero gets his chance to have a foot on the ladder of success. For *Mickey One*, it is the shadow of death.

Fearing for his life, Mickey visits an indoor arcade and finds time to think. Camera shots isolate details of a brightly lit public hall crowded with games and attractions, creating a montage of poignancy, violence and disorientation. The scene is somewhat reminiscent of Lindsay Anderson's early documentary *O Dreamland* (1953), which also constructs a mood of bleakness and tragedy in a similar arcade environment, recording the forlorn pleasures on offer to the postwar working-classes. An artificial woman shuts her mechanical eyelids; this image is juxtaposed with a toy machine gun firing at figures in the windows of a model house. A woman marches up and down upon a raised platform, rhythmically clapping her hands as if rallying customers, whilst behind her hangs a banner advertising grotesque nose remodelling procedures. These images and sounds iterate the ideas of death and pain, identity and obscurity, which are weighing on Mickey's mind. Yet, the dialectic of shots contains punctum-like elements that are not subsumed by reference to Mickey's narrative situation. He observes a shirtless man turning slowly on the raised platform beside the clapping lady; his torso, covered in tattoos, is incongruous with his meek and bespectacled appearance, as is the careless yawn, which elicits its own medium close-up shot. Certainly, a life on the stage, such as Mickey experienced, to his cost, is not so glamourous for everyone. In the introduction to this book we saw how Mickey's next encounter – the old man with the broken nose – exemplifies the political significance of such intrusive and vital contrasts in social existence.

Mickey investigates a mutoscope (a 'what-the-butler-saw' machine) and sees the girl he romanced in the film's opening montage pouting for the camera. This embodiment of the life that intoxicated and then destroyed Mickey is now set before him as an object of purely illusory desire. As in *O Dreamland*, mocking high-pitched diegetic laughter accompanies Mickey's confused fumbling with the machine and the tantalizing object of desire that lies within. The final image of the arcade scene is the girl's seductive expression, but this time only filling a

Figure 13 A vision of mocking temptation (Donna Michelle) in *Mickey One* (1965).

fraction of the screen, as if at a distance, leaving her image floating in a darkness to the muted accompaniment of frantic taunting laughter from a nearby arcade machine (Figure 13). It is as if the film's metalanguage is accentuating the mocking lie behind the temptation, the evil force that is slowly but surely drawing Mickey back into the maw of capitalist desire by social participation, and the sensual and sublime allurements it employs. The beautiful yet unreal thing in the machine is perhaps as close as the film ever comes to giving an actual face to the thing that stimulates Mickey's fear.

Xanadu

The allure is apparently too much. We will come to understand that Mickey genuinely loves his job. The stage is the one place he at least feels 'free'. He contacts an agent, George Berson (Teddy Hart), and eventually resumes, at a degree of personal risk, his work as a stage entertainer. The transition is accomplished with narrative pace and ellipsis. Knowing he has a success on his hands, the film has no need to explain the unquestioned economic and social logic that makes Georgie tout his new client at the Xanadu, a big downtown nightclub. He is a typical – indeed, clichéd – theatrical agent; it is only 'natural' that he should promote his assets. *Mickey One* manages to create a situation where that mythic quality also becomes deeply portentous.

The Xanadu itself becomes emblematic of capitalist principles. The first thing we see inside the club is a man in a waistcoat aggressively shouting at a cowed man in overalls: 'You want to get paid, huh? How much? How much, huh? I'll pay you in poison . . . Get outta' here!' The dominant figure is Larry Fryer (Jeff Corey), one of the managers of the Xanadu and a conventional 'boss' type: aggressive, demanding, self-confident, unsympathetic to populist audience sensibilities. Georgie pushes his new client and Larry seems quietly interested. He pokes his head through an office door and asks his co-manager to give Georgie an interview. The use of off-screen space and the deferential aspects of the other actors' performances serve to introduce Ed Castle (Hurd Hatfield) as a powerful and aloof figure (Figure 14).

The word 'castle' connotes strength, continuity and hierarchical social authority. A castle will protect the correct social distribution of means and relations. It is something proud and venerable, hard-won by besting innumerable attackers; conservative, and yet ready and capable of meeting and mastering the

Figure 14 Ed Castle (Hurd Hatfield) in *Mickey One* (1965).

future. As co-manager of the Xanadu, Larry says he works under Ed Castle, the partner who is in 'complete charge', and, moreover, 'a gentleman and a king'. It is he who will make the ultimate decision whether to patronize Georgie's new client.

Ed's office is palatial. The room is like a shrine to the triumphs of modern commercial society. There are large metallic sculptures evocative of vehicles, machinery and other technological contraptions. At our first glimpse of Ed, he is using an electric juice processor to make a smoothie – a rare possession for the mid-1960s, and a contemporary marker of affluence and technological consumerism (the old-fashioned Georgie cringes when Ed takes a sip of his healthy concoction). We will later see Ed using an electric toothbrush. When Georgie enters, Ed says: 'I'll be with you in a moment' – a phrase typical of the busy modern professional. The objects on Ed's desk are evenly arranged and precise, mirroring his speech and bodily motions; a single disapproving look is enough for Georgie to realize the propriety of snatching back his hat, after it had been inappropriately placed upon the table.

In this way *Mickey One* establishes Ed Castle as an emblematic figure of modern business success. His surroundings, performance tropes, dialogue and wider narrative placement provide a host of conventional signs of managerial authority whose realization borders upon the regal. Ed is such a 'good' businessman, it seems, that his initial characterization can concern itself with things removed from the practicalities of what his job may hypothetically involve: smoothies and organic food. This distancing is a representational trope sometimes associated with rich and powerful characters whose wealth and success has resulted in a displacement of their supposed responsibilities and tasks into a privileged experience of alienated luxury. This aristocratic register often operates in reference to populist interpretive sympathies. In many a narrative, lower-class characters encounter a rich and powerful figure who is represented as isolated, untouchable, sedentary and concerning themselves with activities, behaviours and pastimes whose very distance from the hierarchy of the social, political or violent relationships that support them, gives their character a quality of disassociation and irrationality. The name of the club, 'Xanadu', evokes a paradigmatic example of this trope in *Citizen Kane* (1941). It symbolizes how wealthy and powerful figures are 'out of touch' with the world and behave according to a differentiated system of moral values. Ed belongs to a certain representative tradition in which affluence and social untouchability brings about a kind of mental, physical or moral degradation, which works in at least two ideological directions at once.[11]

Ed is interested in health and purity, ideas that are intimately connected to the modernity of his economic and social situation. His ideal is a 'toned' body that is able to absorb all 'nutrients'. He praises organic foods, with their connotations of 'goodness' towards ourselves and our 'fellow man'. This monologue about bodily purity might recall the unstable General Ripper (Sterling Hayden) from *Dr Strangelove* (1964), strengthening the association between social abstraction and madness. Does Ed's obsession with health and purity imply some corrupting opposite – an unwholesome sickness – within the managerial type he represents? As noted in the previous chapter, if neuroses and fixations have an ability to allegorize the conflicted and unfree condition of the modern subject, does Ed's obsession with goodness compensate for some evil that lurks behind the immaculate surface of his world?[12] As the film progresses, and Ed's complicity in the danger pursuing Mickey increases, this potential becomes more distinct.

A significant layering of meaning takes place here resulting from the wider historic context of the text's reception. Part of what makes Ed such a fascinating figure in *Mickey One* results from the lasting relevance of the signifiers of

---

[11] First, an audience's populist attitudes can hold a satisfying sense of superiority over these figures, whose possession of social and material capital has been shown to bring about various conditions of unhappiness. This superiority might equate to a process of emancipation from the relational system of social judgements, which treat wealth and power as desirable goals for individual social action. Secondly, the very satisfaction brought about by this potential reaction creates an ideologically weighted judgement in favour of maintaining the 'lower' social and material conditions of those who experience it; the attitude maintained by this judgement might be expressed as: 'Leave the madness, debilitation and moral bankruptcy to the rich, then. We, without such corrupting wealth, are better off as we are.'

[12] On the truth-content of neuroses, see Adorno, *History and Freedom*, 218; Adorno, 'The Stars Down to Earth', 114.

professional economic and cultural identity that surround him. Perhaps serving as markers of denial regarding some hidden corruption, the phrases and tropes used by Ed may also seem disquietingly familiar to modern twenty-first-century spectators, accustomed as we have become to health-conscious consumerism and technological lifestyles, facilitated by disposable incomes and ever more refined attitudes towards the importance of public image. The smoothies, organic foods and electric toothbrushes that mark Ed as a figure of difference, pretension and possibly unstable Otherness in *Mickey One* also become the most 'normal' and contemporary things about the film itself. If we are able now to look at this film and see, in these 'normal' things, something 'not quite right', it will be a telling fragment of the text's overall potential to critique the capitalist world view.

Ed may be a 'castle' – something that stays the same and reveals new meanings as we spectators change with time – but his power is not so secure as it first appeared. When Ed is introduced, the film shows him in possession of authority and power. Co-manager Larry's attitude does much of the initial work: 'Ed Castle is in complete charge here – all this kind of stuff . . . I'm only the business end.' Larry displays a self-deprecating placement of himself as 'just' a businessman who works under Ed as someone in 'complete charge' – 'a gentleman and a king!' The sliding door to Ed's office opens automatically from bottom to top, making Larry momentarily bend down like a supplicant in order to enter the room. However, over the course of the film, this initial hierarchical ordering becomes gradually destabilized. After Ed declares his lack of interest in finding out more about Mickey, Larry intervenes: 'What the hell, we could at least go look at this guy? . . . . Of course, I'm only the business end. It's your say-so . . .' A series of reverse shots show Ed's face registering disapproval, Larry's twitchy expression of casual persuasion and a knowing smile creeping onto Ed's lips; the scene cuts to the three men sitting in an audience and laughing at Mickey's act. The man supposedly in 'complete charge' is shown to have acquiesced to the wishes of his junior partner. In another of the film's characteristic cross-edited sound transitions, Larry's raucous laughter appears to initially accompany Ed's thoughtful smile in the office. As the managers of the Xanadu appreciate Mickey's act, the shot frames Larry's swaying body loom back and forth across the foreground, with Ed situated behind (Figure 15). One obvious reading of this moment might hold that Larry is figuratively eclipsing Ed's managerial authority, but there is also something grotesque in the image. Larry's raucous laughter adds something mocking, Punch-like and diabolic to the scene, and this somewhat alarming quality increasingly colours the power

Figure 15 Co-manager Larry (Jeff Corey) eclipses Ed (Hurd Hatfield) in *Mickey One* (1965).

balance between the two characters. Ed's interest in maintaining order and health in his own domain perhaps functions as compensation for some deeper experience of submission, which it is at first difficult to recognize. The world of business is a highly unsettling space in *Mickey One*, and the instability of the professional relationship between Ed and Larry is a major factor contributing to this effect.

Ed is ultimately entrusted with the responsibility of securing Mickey's tenure at the Xanadu, and frequently reassures Larry with a manager's certainty: 'I'll get him.' Given what we know about Mickey, however, this certainty may be misplaced. The hierarchy at the Xanadu is now decidedly problematized. When Larry and Ed meet on the street, the transformation of their relationship is plainer still. Larry is adamant: 'I need that kid to be here today. He's your responsibility.' This last line is repeated, and the shot duration and facial expressions in the brief back-and-forth dialogue sequence make that recognition seem more like a threat. The doubt that Ed expresses concerning the identity and motivations of Larry's associates – considering their professed interest in auditioning Mickey – leads us to suspect that Larry is, in fact, the Xanadu's connection to the underworld. Just like Mickey, Ed is living 'the high life' on dubious favours bestowed by an arbitrarily powerful entity he doesn't really understand. But, again, Larry rapidly changes the tone and object of his statement, as if to allow a threat to pass unquestioned; he tells Ed that any expenses incurred on business trips can be reimbursed by 'the company', on whose behalf Larry speaks. Perhaps we see here a cyclical process? It was this very kind of institutional privilege that led Mickey into debt in the first place. Company expenses really are 'favours so long as they want them to be favours', just as Ruby Lapp intuited about the mob.

By the end of the film, it is almost as if Larry has been keeping Ed as some kind of dupe, managerial puppet or employed hostage. The one who initially seemed the most secure and rewarded for his position in the economic system is revealed to be just as menaced and trapped as Mickey. In their last scene together, Ed and Larry have a serious argument and the power balance reaches an extreme opposite of the initial presentation. Mickey disappears after his audition for Larry's contacts and the 'businessman' demands that Ed find him again. The two men argue hotly with raised voices and gestures. But by the end of the short scene, Ed has been stunned into immobility by Larry's waving arms, trumpeting voice and gesticulating body, bending and bobbing with a level of vitriol seemingly out of proportion with the needs of the exchange. He bellows with authoritarian pauses and emphasis: 'I want him here tomorrow! . . . . He's your responsibility!' The scene is framed with the camera outside the door of Ed's office, as if afraid to be any nearer to the conflict. Within a few short seconds Larry's tirade won't even allow Ed room to reply; Larry smashes a vase placed on a nearby table and marches out, leaving Ed in puzzled shock. Although this scene reiterates the power of the criminal forces that threaten Mickey's safety through the aura of fear and violence determined by the supposed wishes of Larry's unseen associates, there is also more going on. Ed's shocked expression, the wildness of Larry's gestures and the shift in the power balance creates an excess which is not explained away by the idea that the management of the Xanadu are living under the shadow of the mob. The dialogue's emphasis on individual responsibility – certain duties expected of certain people – maintains the fundamentally commercial register of the argument, whilst also reiterating the relationship between the culture of business and that intangible atmosphere of violence which casts a dark shadow over the entire film. Indeed, when separated from the alarming physicality of Larry's actions and its formal presentation, the rationality of the argument is convincingly valid from a business perspective: Mickey has gone missing and it is, indeed, Ed's responsibility. This is a sound and reasonable point of business, only one whose cinematic presentation boils over with a physical terror, making this underlying rationality seem alarming and motivated by covert and sinister forces.

Mickey's calling

The more exposure Mickey enjoys as a performer, the greater are his chances of being discovered by the mob. The scene in which Ed first approaches Mickey in his dressing room is one familiar from a host of genre stories about a protagonist 'making it big', only here the values are turned inside out. Our hero is given a prestigious booking that will advance their career. Slowly wagging a finger with significant pause and emphasis, Ed gives a parting word: 'Splendid!' – this boy will surely 'go far'. But Mickey is not interested.

Ed next visits Mickey's apartment and makes a generous offer to coax him to the Xanadu: an increased salary, with tantalising 'favours' and 'extras'. Yet, Mickey is adamant to remain in comparative obscurity, away from success and away from danger. In the attempt to change Mickey's mind, Ed employs the affirmative rhetoric of the managerial muse: 'There is no jump. Not for people like you. Your talent is a bridge. You'll walk across.' Even the sensualized materialism of a 'milk-white Cadillac . . . portable bar and air conditioning' doesn't tempt Mickey. Ed's sales pitch becomes more desperate and ludicrous – 'Money, clothes, success! . . . . Al Jolson had a hundred and fifty waistcoats in his closet when he died!' – and Mickey finally kicks him out of the room.

With an employer hammering on Mickey's apartment door and demanding that he be reasonable, *Mickey One* comes face to face with what Max Weber called 'one of the fundamental elements of the spirit of modern capitalism': 'rational' economic conduct on the basis of a vocational 'calling'.[13] Ed makes it plain to Mickey that he is more than a desirable commodity. It is not even in Mickey's own interests alone that he is encouraged to exploit his gift, but, rather, a matter of higher significance. He is a born talent; a 'natural'. To be a stand-up comic is Mickey's 'calling': a supposedly preordained function among worldly affairs that God has been gracious enough to reveal ("O, Lucky Man!"), and certain men privileged to communicate, only parenthetically furthering their own interests as a result.[14]

The persuasive aura that often surrounds the notion of a 'calling' is intimately linked with the idea of success and its familiar quantitative standard: money. Certain representations of this aura connect its object with a kind of disorientation. The sublimity of a successful condition determined by wealth is well exemplified by a passage from *The Wings of the Dove* (1902):

> this was what it was to be a success; it always happened before one could know it. One's ignorance was in fact often the greatest part of it. 'You haven't had time

---

[13] Weber, *The Protestant Ethic and the Spirit of Capitalism*, 180.
[14] Ibid., 79.

yet,' he said; 'this is nothing. But you'll see. You'll see everything. You *can*, you know – everything you dream of'.[15]

Lord Mark's words to the wealthy yet doomed Milly Theale display the same kind of abstract awe and seductiveness used in Ed's rhetoric. The manager of the Xanadu is a diegetic mouthpiece for a sublime yet Mephistophelian promise based on mythic fate, which is shown to be, in this particular narrative context, as intimately entangled with ideas of death and false plenitude as Henry James' novel.

The tragedy is that Mickey remains a 'natural' comic. To run from success in this way goes against his fictional nature. During his first conversation with Jenny, Mickey expresses these fragmentary yet poetic thoughts whilst playing melancholy chromatic chords on a piano. He feels 'free' when he is on stage – 'the best person in the world, you always wanted to be. Yourself. The one exactly they (the audience) want you to be. They clap for. The same. One. Where else? In your dreams? In bed?' There is a genuine artist in Mickey; the film has made it so. When relaxed, he often talks in jokes. But when Jenny asks if Mickey is in 'the theatrical business', he suddenly seems threatened and asks her why she wants to know. By evoking the economic and mythic aspects of a vocational calling, *Mickey One* problematizes the very conditions under which the protagonist can act according to his 'natural' state. The idea of associating Mickey's natural being – his being 'very quick', as Jenny puts it – with a professional commitment becomes, through the logic of the gangster narrative, something intolerable for our hero. This division between the protagonist's sense of authentic being and the social necessity to make this only a prerequisite for an economic role is an essential part of *Mickey One*'s critical Romanticism.

The powers of art

The junk artist is not the only figure in the film who creates moments of escape. With Ed still hammering at the door, Mickey searches for a way out of his apartment building and is violently startled by the appearance of a burly man at the window. With the use of slow-motion film, the man appears to move up and down in a ghostly and airy manner, mouthing and gesturing in a way that

---

[15] Henry James, *The Wings of the Dove*, 1902 (London and New York: Alfred A. Knopf – Everyman's Library, 1997), 110.

suggests an alarming interest in Mickey's situation. We know that Mickey is on an upper floor, adding an extra quality of strangeness to the apparition. Weary as he is of murderous assault, Mickey drops down to the floor in sudden panic. Orchestral music, somewhat reminiscent of Ravel's *La valse* (1920), appears on the non-diegetic soundtrack and creates a poignant yet playful mood at odds with the initially alarming visuals. As Mickey cautiously approaches the window, the music continues, transforming the ambiguous appearance into something that possesses an attractive sense of aesthetic potency; it is something like a transient moment of filmic 'magic', which, as will soon be confirmed, works towards Mickey's salvation. Inexplicably, a man is jumping on a trampoline outside his window. The music appears to underline this very inexplicability and frame it as a wonderous thing. The stranger vacates the equipment and Mickey is able to jump out of the window, cushion his landing and escape.

Like the junk artist, the trampoline man is there because it contributes to the character of the fictional world as one containing inexplicable forces for both good and evil. If the antagonistic elements in the film can be conceptualized as the seductive yet violent forces of capitalism, then the 'saving power' which places the trampoline under Mickey's window, and accompanies it with awe-inspiring music, is the 'art' of the film itself: the 'Romanticization' of the world – the valorization of that which does not fit, which seems out of place or which has a perplexing autonomy at odds with the expected course of narrative events.

On several occasions *Mickey One* stages the collapse of this aesthetic freedom into its opposite, such as the sequence in which Mickey tidies his room after Jenny's arrival. The activity is shown with speeded-up film, to the accompaniment of an effervescent *allegro* arrangement of the Ravel-esque theme that is now associated with a sublime experience of dynamic indeterminacy. During this sequence, Mickey is 'putting on a show' for Jenny – engaging in a playful and possibly sarcastic display of productive activity by making his room supposedly more fit to live in. But Mickey is also touched by the spirit of the junk artist who banged the dustbin lids together. Against the representative regime, it offers an 'unconsciously' determined aesthetic occurrence that stands apart from narrative function. The domesticity of the task is explicitly contrasted with the playful mode of its presentation. But this is not a 'playful tidying scene' in the same register as *Mary Poppins* (1964); this is film's playfulness rebounding upon itself, for it comes across as something like a celebration of pointlessness. There is no conceivable reason for the change in formal techniques, or to show Mickey tidying the room at all. It just occurs – an arbitrary moment of Romantic self-creation. An aesthetic excess. It may strike audiences as a paradigm example of the Schlegelian desire to make the world Romantic – a *Gesamtkunstwerk* without politics – yet the result is deeper still, for the representative regime reasserts itself to put the lie to the sublimity of aesthetic celebration. No work is without politics, and a claim to totality makes it all the more allied with suffering.

The performative aspect of the event is accentuated by the way it ends: with Mickey sitting down at his piano and creating a discordant noise with the self-conscious and mock-causal placement of his elbow. However, the sublime mood is soon undermined by a sudden and discomforting contrast. Turning to his sole audience member, Mickey sees that, far from sharing in the film's elation at the playful mockery of domestic activity, Jenny has turned away from this performance, head in hand, and is apparently in tears. Mickey suddenly adopts a sympathetic attitude. The anti-climactic impact on the keyboard now becomes only a knowingly conventionalized vulgarization of the aesthetic 'spirit' of freedom.[16] Going far beyond the rhetorical level manifest in the text itself, we might read this moment as a perplexing and troubling instance of the central Romantic schema of art: a moment when the intoxicating and invigorating spirit of aesthetic freedom – finding expression in a Romantic satire of purposive activity – runs up against an eruptive and unpredictable experience of human pain. Mickey's reply is a spontaneous respect for the suffering before him. 'Cry', he says; not as a command, but more as an acknowledgement that things are so.

More than this, however, Mickey's next response is rooted in his 'natural' abilities as a comic. To make Jenny feel better, he starts telling jokes. This mobilization takes place in a different field to that which is being forced upon him by Ed and the wider social world. He uses his power to combat the pain of a fellow human in distress. Mickey can be authentic not only by and of himself, but also in the presence of another in need. It is this sense of authenticity – framed, initially, in opposition to the economic principle embodied by Ed – that provides the vehicle for a sense of aesthetic freedom as the negation, not of what is 'natural' to the subject, but only of its false and mythologized 'fulfilment' within the economic totality.

Shortly after this revelation, Mickey and Jenny are shown to begin a romantic relationship. A montage sequence follows, accompanied by the same Ravel-esque music, which underscores the possibility of escape from the oppressive world of vocational commitment. The oppositional powers of art mobilized in

---

[16] It is for this very reason – strangely enough – that it reminds me of the final note of Liszt's Piano Sonata in B minor (1854), one of the most significant texts in nineteenth-century Romantic culture.

Mickey One are also consolidated in the activities of the Japanese junk artist, whom Mickey and Jenny next encounter at the end of the romantic interlude. He wordlessly invites them to attend the unveiling of his masterpiece.

Surrounded by an applauding crowd on the Chicago riverfront, the junk artist unveils an immense installation: a moving sculpture in white metal constructed from urban detritus (Figure 16). The result is reminiscent of the chaotic edifices of Jean Tinguely and the clattering good-natured contraptions of Rube Goldberg and William Heath Robinson. Cycling, wagging and spinning semi-autonomous excrescences in painted scrap conjure a symphonic clattering, and the machine creates an audiovisual cacophony of eccentric activity. Parts recall familiar aspects of urban life: snapping dustbin lids, blocks thumping on piano keys, swaying conveyor belts and jumping shapes representing all kinds of industrial and purposive activities. The whole becomes something very much like an artistic vision of the modern world, with all its music, transport, commercial routines, public conveniences and industrial installations. We hear that this strange creation is called *Yes!* – a vision of oppressive complexity, absurd redundancy and cosmetic whiteness. *Yes!* performs its automated movements with the jerkiness and speed of a calculated mechanism, like a playful satire of capitalistic efficiency. All this feverish activity is going nowhere, achieving nothing and shaking itself apart. '*Yes!* will come alive even while destroying itself', narrates a member of the crowd, quoting from a pamphlet; 'Its greatest freedom will come out of its greatest threat. For *Yes!*, courage is freedom.'

Figure 16 Yes! – the art installation made from collected scrap. *Mickey One* (1965).

A Marxist interpretation might gravitate towards the internal contradictions imputed to exist within the functioning of the capitalist economy. The greatest 'freedom' capable of being produced by a bizarre and imposingly senseless system of movements and relationships is that which is realized in the moment of its undoing. The Hegelian teleology behind capitalism's internal unsustainability translates into the self-destructing aesthetic object. In this sense, *Yes!* 'comes alive' by fulfilling the self-destructiveness of what it hypothetically represents. The vision of an artwork representing a 'mad' world that destroys itself upon its unveiling seems to invite many theoretical comparisons, not least Adorno's comment about aesthetic experience as an 'apparition' or 'firework'.[17] *Yes!* is a 'perfect' artwork, in the sense that it is tied so intimately to its historical present that it burns itself out in its very presentation. The comparison is particularly apposite, for the artist ignites a host of fireworks imbedded within the sculpture. It begins to crumble and shake, emitting a fountain of sparks and smoke. This is no accident, but, rather, the necessary 'becoming' of the work's aesthetic moment, for the artist dances in triumph as his work is transformed into a raging inferno.

Fire engines arrive and *Yes!* is engulfed in extinguishing foam. To the accompaniment of mournful non-diegetic music, axes are used to smash and dismantle the unruly artwork, and the crowd turn away coughing and gesticulating. The rational face of social reality returns as the firemen work to extinguish this blazing public spectacle. The alienating artwork has been ideologically designated something 'bad' – a judgement displaced into the rational need to resolve a dangerous conflagration. For a fleeting but pregnant moment, the sequence presents strange images of the foamy surge around the abandoned sculpture, accompanied by low and ominous non-diegetic piano and a rhythmic clanking reminiscent of shipping tackle in the wind. This sea of foam might be read to embody typical anxieties pertaining to a 'postmodern' world in which all difference is reduced to a sterile plateaux of mass-produced churning surface. As a filmic symbol, this sublime and hellish vision is the narrative product of society's most normal functioning: the fire brigade extinguishing a fire. The foamy ocean can function as a symbol of the dominant social ideology: powerful yet impossible to fight, all pervading and yet impossible to grasp, numbing to the thinking faculties and yet sublimely intoxicating to the senses.

As a result, when the audience disperses, it is not clear if they are lamenting the interrupted performance of the truth-revealing artwork, or showing their

---

[17] Adorno, *Aesthetic Theory*, 111–18.

revulsion for something which has been revealed, in turn, as a meaningless wreck, both useless and dangerous. The metaphorical presentation of diegetic events throughout *Mickey One* means that this event remains open to both interpretive possibilities, and more besides.

However, it is important to recognize something. The unveiling is attended by several hundred spectators at the Marina City complex – a contemporary symbol of American metropolitanism, technological innovation and the integration of business and culture. Indeed, the attendees seem like exemplars of post-war American affluence: wealthy, cultured and able to appreciate *avant-garde* art. At first, the crowd applaud enthusiastically whilst Mickey and Jenny adopt body language suggesting uncertainty or distrust. Yet, Mickey and Jenny are alone in remaining after the sea of foam has engulfed the charred skeleton of *Yes!* After the crowd has dispersed and as the artist laments the wreckage of his masterpiece, the two are the sole witnesses to the fact that *Yes!* is not entirely defeated. Mickey and Jenny share the artist's joy at discovering that one fragment of his eccentric work remains alive. According to a logic quite impossible to rationalize, a clock on the end of a long metal arm, rather like a fairground target, begins to wave up and down whilst chiming quietly. The little group wordlessly celebrate this lingering aimless vitality, which, for all its strangeness, is endowed with an anthropomorphic charm. A dissolve to the following scene featuring the smiling faces of the artist and Jenny makes it seem like the third personality on-screen, that of *Yes!* itself, is also smiling (Figure 17).

Mickey and Jenny have become a second audience – those who 'see again' and see anew. They now see *Yes!* through new eyes and partake in the artist's joy

Figure 17 Art's fleeting emancipatory potential. *Yes!* smiles along with the junk artist (Kamatari Fujiwara) and Jenny (Alexandra Stewart). *Mickey One* (1965).

at the work's ability to function, whatever ironic meaning that pseudo-activity might entail. Yet, there is no absolute meaning to *Yes!* We can only conjecture as to what, symbolically, was being smothered by the foam. Was it the chance of an affirmative culture in defiance of McCarthyism, as Penn believes, or was it the artistic revelation of the active madness that unconsciously motivates the dominant social system? Does the affirmation in the work's title mark the desire for political optimism, or does it perform the ironical defamiliarization of the positivist ideology supporting an elusively hostile world? Whatever its meaning, *Yes!* creates an invigorating sense of outsider community. Immediately after their emancipating encounter, Mickey, now sat in a restaurant with Jenny, crams a handful of breadsticks into his mouth and bites them in a playfully uncivilized manner. Perhaps this mood of liberating childlike unpredictability is facilitated by their encounter with critical – self-negating – art.

The audition

Mickey is finally convinced to go to the Xanadu, where Larry's contacts are waiting to 'audition' him. Ed tells Mickey that this 'marvellous opportunity' could ensure his career. But this privilege is soured by an ominous mood created by multiple filmic elements: sinister microphone feedback emanates from the dark club auditorium; the fact that there are no supporting musicians, only flickering lights on the stage; the bizarre revelation that the unknown visitors have ensconced themselves in the light booth at the back of the hall; and Ed's counterproductive reassurance: 'I promise you there's nothing to fear.'

There is genuine ambiguity surrounding the nature and intentions of the presence in the light booth. The gruff male voice that rasps over the club speakers engages at least two sets of schematic cultural associations – two representational types – which are common to Hollywood productions: 1) the gangster type, and 2) a species of lower-class managerial figure, perhaps typified by theatrical impresarios, casino officials or newspaper editors. The strangeness of their chosen vantage point seems to immediately confirm Mickey's suspicions that the visitors are here to kill him. If there was to be a sniper-style assassination of someone on the club stage, the light booth is an obvious place from which to shoot. Yet, many of the suspicious conditions laid down by the unseen figure can also be explained as a form of 'eccentricity' that draws legitimacy from capitalist (ir)rationality. His wanting a deserted and darkened auditorium, without music, nor any audience except himself – '*I'm* the audience!' – none of this is conclusive in regard to Mickey's fears. Perhaps the strange terms under which Mickey must audition are really some kind of 'test'. By putting the talent in a vulnerable situation, the boss can see how well they perform under pressure. The unseen figure certainly is 'the boss'; when Ed begins to argue over terms, he is interrupted with a resounding and authoritarian 'Out!', and Mickey is left alone to brave what may be his final performance.

The tense audition scene functions according to a continually deferred explanation regarding the nature and motivations of the presence in the light booth. We share Mickey's uncertainty as to whether they are really here to kill him, and the question of identity soon dissolves into the vague fact that he is at the mercy of an unknowable agency. Mickey's dialogue consists of improvised jokes and comic lines; he never shatters the pretence that he is auditioning, yet there is a running possibility that he will be shot at any moment: 'What, are you laughing or aiming? . . . . Boy, if I'm lucky, I've got the greatest finish in show business' (Figure 18). For all the life-threatening tension, which causes his body to stiffen and sweat to appear on his brow, Mickey continues to do that which comes naturally to him. Timing and performance make it seem as if Mickey is thinking in jokes – that under the most extreme pressure, his 'true self', his natural talent, remains his support. The audition scene shows how intimately Mickey's character is possessed of comic talent. In this scene, *Mickey One* frames what is ostensibly a job interview as a symbolic fusion of spiritual revelation, persecution and ritual execution. By making the moment of Mickey's impending destruction also the moment of

Figure 18 Mickey (Warren Beatty) in the spotlight. *Mickey One* (1965).

his greatest professional triumph, the film dramatizes a defamiliarization of the rarefied and privileged experience of discovering one's economic calling.

As noted, a 'calling' evokes irrational ideas of preordination and the positive value ascription holding that devoting oneself to a particular line of activity becomes a way of manifesting God's will. To discover and adopt one's calling means that the will of the individual and the will of some higher absolute power supposedly come into alignment. That is perhaps why a spirit of agnosticism permeates *Mickey One*. The stage spotlight becomes the symbol of Mickey's physical and psychological presence in the very place towards which the diegetic world has been dragging him as the fulfilment of the narrative. Standing petrified in the glare of that spotlight – immobile, uncertain, 'free', as he himself avowed, yet also within the shadow of death – this moment is when Mickey is closest to meeting his maker, in more ways than one. We will see this scene dynamic repeated, with more explicit diegetic connections to authorial control, at the climax of *O Lucky Man!* (1973). As the previous chapters have prepared us to acknowledge, such moments of intolerable inactivity can inspire deeply ambiguous Romantic interpretations.

Stand-up comedian is a vocation that can be characterized by the subject being situated alone, exposed and vulnerable on a public altar. Like a prayer or lecture, a comedy set is a ritual display and re-inscription of the individual's assertion of identity and their right to exist, speak and fulfil a certain functional role in society. Their presence on stage is justified only on the grounds that they *do* something – ideally, something interesting. Their being-on-stage, as a social placement, creates an ideological demand for action. The common experience of 'stage fright' exposes the social value of the performer who can act under pressure, and against the threat that there will appear some creeping feeling of danger in being 'exposed', alone against society, held up as something between a victim and an exemplar. In this way, Mickey's ability to tell jokes under these stressful conditions suggests something heroic. The film audience may feel a sense of awe in the presence of this man who can stare down the barrel of a gun and tell jokes, but this is a rifle that is sublimely allegorized as both the eye of the public world, as experienced by a professional performer, and the eye of a judgemental God. Weber summarizes this association quite distinctly: 'the idea of a duty in one's calling prowls about in our lives like the ghost of dead religious beliefs.'[18] This is the tragic and universalized condition of an individual who is

---

[18] Weber, *The Protestant Ethic and the Spirit of Capitalism*, 182.

forced, in Mickey's own words, to 'make jokes on my own grave', through the very act of being in the world.

Eventually, Mickey manages to escape, and, still uncertain about the validity of his fears, continues his flight from the spotlight and all it connotes. The religious symbolism of the encounter is accentuated as the escaping Mickey runs past a Salvation Army band singing that recurring thematic question: 'Is there any word from the Lord?'

'Stick'

After a crisis of conscience, Ed eventually advises Mickey to get 'out of the business'. When he had wanted to secure Mickey's employment, Ed sang his praises and told him he could go all the way to the top. But now that things have changed, Ed uses the opposite approach: 'You're wasting your time. You're not good enough. You're too weak for a big room . . . . You'll spend your life in deadfalls . . . . You're a talented amateur.' Calculated to deter Mickey's zeal for confronting his mysterious persecutors, Ed's words come across as an attempt to save his life. It is from Ed that Mickey now learns of Ruby Lapp's death: 'First with a broken bottle in the face, before they . . .' – the sentence is interrupted, building that sense of unspeakability, which characterizes the film's antagonistic forces. Ruby, the man who told Mickey to 'stick', is now contrasted with the reformed figure of Ed himself. Ed's advice is not to 'stick', but to 'run!' We see here the damage done to Ed, and his attitude towards himself, by his placement in the world – a damage that reveals itself in the rambling urgency of his unconvincing self-acquittal:

> I swear I'm not touched by them. I happen to work in a field they control. I have the right to my work. They don't control me. In the real world you have to be realistic. You have to make certain compromises.

Ed exonerates himself from the machinations of an avowedly oppressive society, and yet admits plainly, in a common-sensical business register, that being 'realistic' equates to making compromises and betraying your own self-respect.

Mickey suddenly stumbles into some glass shelves, which smash to pieces on the floor. Sprawling unharmed on the carpet, Mickey is just about to roll his face onto a shard of broken bottle when Ed scrabbles down and removes the dangerous object. Ed looms over the prostrate Mickey with the broken fragment in his hand, seemingly the more shocked of the two to find himself in the act of mimicking the murder he had falteringly described only moments before. Coming so soon after his frantic and contradictory attempt at self-justification, Ed's troubled appearance now suggests a strong sense of guilty complicity in the all-determining climate of fear.

And so the film moves towards its ambiguous conclusion. Mickey tells Jenny: 'No more running away. I haven't got any more the guts to live that scared'. These lines encapsulate the double valuation characteristic of the film's central Romantic problematic between freedom and explanation – art and society. They suggest that the ending of the film, which presents Mickey going back to work on stage at the Xanadu, is an admission of weakness, a personal failure: one that is raised by the film to the level of a poignant victory by means of a sublime filmic rhetoric.

The mob is still out there, and possibly maintaining their plans to assassinate the unfortunate comic. When Mickey emerges from the wings at the Xanadu, the audience are disconcerted to see that the comic's attention is awkwardly divided between looking at the allegorical spotlight and searching the audience for the missing Georgie, who has disappeared under mysterious circumstances, possibly having been killed by the mob. Larry and Ed position themselves at the side of the room and observe warily as the comic begins his new job.

Larry has got his way, after all. Mickey has followed his calling and gone back to work. The world is as it should be. Looking significantly into the glare of the spotlight, as if searching for an answer during a prayer, he says: '. . . so this is the Word, huh?' The film audience does not know what exactly has been revealed. It is the intuitive fulfilment of the potent lack which has haunted the diegesis from the very beginning. As the closing music rises, the camera pulls back to reveal Mickey standing alone in darkness, bathed in the glow of the spotlight. He then sits at a piano framed against the Chicago riverfront and skyline (Figure 19). The Xanadu has dissolved, and this sublime revelation has enabled Mickey to transcend the material conditions of his narrative situation and profession. He is now making music in tune with the world in which he lives. The separateness implied by his isolation in the spotlight, alone in a sea of darkness below the lights of the metropolis, is complicated by his participation in the larger 'city symphony', which brings the film to an end.

For Penn himself, Mickey's decision to go back to work was akin to a show of defiance towards HUAC.[19] The protagonist's choice certainly seems to

---

[19] Segaloff, *Arthur Penn*, 121. The specific reference is to Lillian Hellman and the much-publicized industry criticism of HUAC's investigations into communist influence in post-war Hollywood.

Figure 19 The final transcendent affirmation of both individual and society. *Mickey One* (1965).

acknowledge that the dominant social order is not what it should be, but what else does it impart? Mickey's most explicit reason for returning – the words 'Ruby Lapp', implying a sense of responsibility for his old manager's death – is an ideologically significant moral concession. It suggests respect for the martyrs of his own efforts to live authentically. Perhaps he believes Ruby died in a tragically pointless effort to protect his incognito, and he therefore owes Ruby, and possibly Georgie, his own life as a kind of purifying 'payment' for a cosmic debt. Either that, or Mickey has come to realize that living under the shadow of fear is, as Ruby once told him, the best and only way to live. Mickey's efforts to break away and achieve greater freedom have created only violent and unforeseen consequences.

In this way, Mickey's abdication from his position as a social outsider is reconciled with the conventional ideological means of mythologizing the hero's return to the status quo: his own willingness for self-martyrdom – the special 'strength' he now displays, for the audience of the film to recognize, despite his own previous confession that he no longer has any 'guts' – becomes a means of purifying his troublesome desire for cultural transcendence. This is not the only conventional valuation device used to mythologize Mickey's choice to return to the economic and social role that has been forced upon him by sinister powers. He also tells Jenny: 'I gotta live the only way I'm at least free: with you.' The desire to remain authentic in reference to his own sense of freedom – rhetorically validated by the film (typically for classical Hollywood) through the establishment of a well-matched heterosexual couple – is tragically consistent with the pathway to destruction and unfreedom that he has been heroically avoiding all through the narrative. Ultimately, there is not so much of a difference between the way Mickey chooses to live 'at least free' and the 'certain compromises' that were admitted by Ed.

In this sense, Mickey's choice to return to work is a failure – a concession to the terror of social totality. It is as if the Ancient Mariner had gone inside to join the wedding feast with the shadow of the albatross still upon his shoulders. Suggestively, the dialogic summation of the film's thematic resolution occurs just before the film cuts to an image of two dancers spinning erratically before an audience of smiling old white men in suits:

> Are you frightened, Mickey?
> As long as I live.

The false ending

Although the film ends with a superficially progressive vision of an artist remaining faithful to their craft and finding freedom in its insular yet transcendent domain, this faith is also shown to be a collaboration with forces of terror. Mickey's return to work is a compromise, which is promoted by an aesthetic of filmic sublimity into an allegorical condition of modern experience.

This is how the ending becomes two things simultaneously. First, a positive affirmation of moral conviction in the face of a terrifying uncertainty: as the strength to say, as Mickey does, when dazzled by the light: 'I'm staying around to see my finish. Now who's up there?' The film articulates the need to include what is excluded – the hidden violence that shapes human life, little old men with broken noses and the irrationality of the 'natural born worker' who refuses to work. Art is endowed with this power even as it is problematized, for this tendency towards freedom – epitomized by the Ravel-esque fantasy scenes – is also allied with a return to the very economic and social role with which such events had previously seemed most at variance. No longer is the film positing freedom as a direct alternative to the vocationalism that figures such as Ed and Larry have been pushing Mickey to assume; now, with the semi-tragic acceptance of 'the Word', the film seems to agree with what it has, all along, been most at pains to represent as an evil. The film's failure to resolve this tension is what allows it to narrativize the aporia of modern freedom under capitalism described by Adorno: 'Spellbound, the living have a choice between involuntary ataraxy – an esthetic life due to weakness – and the bestiality of the involved. Both are wrong ways of living.'[20]

Critical consensus has defined the ending of *Mickey One* as a 'qualified affirmation', and this is correct to the extent that such affirmation results in an ambivalent political conservatism.[21] If the endings of texts remain the most crucial points for determining the ideological commitments constructed on a text's behalf through interpretation, then the progressive element of critical Romantic aestheticism in *Mickey One* is circumvented by something distinctly problematic. The cathartic effect of the final camera shot, moving out over the lights of the city – a 'sigh' of operatic closure – celebrates the social totality and its mastery over the individual just as much as it does the individual artist's isolation, their ability to comprehend, however abstractly, the meaning of that totality and, more abstractly still, the power of cinema to represent and explore philosophical, political or artistic problems.

Mickey's unanswered question 'Who owns me?' plays its part in the evocation of a world where the idea of ownership is all sufficing and ineludable. Ruby and Ed know that there exists some 'higher' force that organizes the necessary and normal arrangements of life. Its authority is both absolute and regrettable. Someone who possesses the personal qualities, talents, charisma, wit, intellectual agility and the simple luck required to make a success of themselves in their calling, finds the enticements and promises laid out before them transform into just so many dark and shadowy alleyways down which they could lose themselves in unimaginable ways. The film creates a space in which the desirable privilege of being favoured for success becomes an experience of anxiety and fear. The idea of purgatory maintained throughout the narrative – never to hear the 'Word from the Lord' – maintains a structural relation to the Romantic condition in which subjects never find the homeland for which they pine. Mickey falls from grace as a Light Romantic figure of uncertainty as soon as he hears the Word of God – as soon as he goes back to the job that society has desired for him.

As in Jacques Rancière's reading of *Heart of Darkness* (1899), the false affirmation that ends the story encapsulates the aporia of the aesthetic regime.[22]

---

[20] Adorno, *Negative Dialectics*, 364.
[21] Crowdus and Porton, 'The Importance of a Singular Guiding Vision', 4.
[22] Rancière, *The Lost Thread*, 47. At the end of *Heart of Darkness*, the protagonist lies about a man's dying words in order to protect the feelings of their bereaved fiancé. This is despite the fact that those supressed words have come to stand for the central 'truth' which is revealed by the fiction: the brutality of the colonialist project and its supporting capitalist economy.

The spectator of *Mickey One* has known the terror of being called the Golden Child of success, and, like Conrad's Marlow, has seen the horror that lies at the heart of the capitalist enterprise – the severed heads on sticks behind the closed doors of business. Marlow's lie to Kurtz's bereaved fiancé – which overrides, through an expediency of narrative, the revelation gleaned throughout his journey regarding the myth of civilization's industrial progressiveness – is related to the same falsity that ends *Mickey One*. The grand final camera shot that celebrates the film's aesthetic ostentatiousness becomes, again, the lie which is told 'in order to end the story . . . to subtract the truth of sensible moments from the false tyranny of stories'.[23]

Yet, the false ending brings its own message. Throughout the aesthetic regime, stories find strength in moments of failure – in that which is uncertain and unconvincing, that which 'doesn't work'. But moments free from functionality are always drawn back in. As in Conrad's novella, 'there is no good ending', and what remains to speak the truth against the myth of totality is 'the *deus ex machina* that arrives from outside to put an end to a chimeral story that has no reason to stop'.[24] In the case of *Mickey One*, we could say that this appearance is not entirely from outside; the sublimity of the junk artist character reflects back upon the closure of the narrative as a fulfilment of something woven into its very structure – a transcendental moment of aesthetic freedom that masks an acquiescence to the status quo. It is this very moment that is radicalized, and refuted all the more forcefully, by the other endings we will explore in the following chapters. The lie that ends the fiction honestly imparts a negating truth over the discontinuities of the whole.

---

[23] Rancière, *The Lost Thread*, 47.
[24] Ibid., 45.

5

Enemies of promise

O Lucky Man! (1973)

A moment of silent inaction – a transcendental flash of truth revealed in stillness – has been hard won by the final scene of *O Lucky Man!* (1973). Mick Travis (Malcolm McDowell), protagonist of *If....* (1968), has perhaps finally reached maturity. He has certainly come a long way since his days as a 'Crusader'. War upon the sterile and absurd conventions of the English public-school system, as well as the mythic class culture that this system perpetuates, has seemingly come to an end. Perhaps the final scene of *If....* was a daydream, a vision of a revolution that never took place, where defiant optimism turned to anxiety and chaos. But if the efforts needed to overthrow a despised system are shown to lead to hopeless and bloody destruction, then perhaps Travis would do better to join the party. Acquiesce instead of protest. Embrace rather than destroy. By the opening scenes of *O Lucky Man!*, then – *If....*'s spiritual sequel – it was time for Mick Travis to 'play the game' and enter the race of life.

For Lindsay Anderson himself, the transition from *If....* to *O Lucky Man!* was certainly an artistic maturation. The 'sweet' idealism of the heroic Crusaders had transformed into a bitter and satirical 'realism'.[1] He considered *If....*'s sequel to be a post-Romantic film, as far as his own artistic productions were concerned. Yet, this transition can also be read as the failure and rebirth of Romantic idealism across different social imperatives, through the tragedy of compromise and association, and dramatizing the inevitability of the Romantic individual's perpetual flight from a homeland. Travis' grand experiment in 'playing along' with the system he once sought to destroy leads to a transcendental moment of inaction, which is very similar to those found under the glare of the spotlight in *Mickey One* (1965). It happens during another audition scene, following that climactic moment when Anderson himself breaks the boundaries of the diegetic

[1] Anderson, 'Stripping the Veils Away', 131.

Figure 20 The 'Zen' smile. Mick Travis (Malcolm McDowell) at the climax of *O Lucky Man!* (1973).

world and slaps Travis with a script. The camera holds on the protagonist's face for a few significant seconds as he very faintly smiles (Figure 20). There is a complex blend of emotions at play in this expression: anger, peace, irony, pain and understanding. Travis appears energized and yet tired. It is a smile (just), but he also seems on the verge of tears.

Previous interpretations have suggested that this smile is a moment of 'Zen' awakening, marking Travis' quiet acquiescence to a treacherous and permanently unmasterable world.[2] The smile that is achieved here is certainly of a completely different character to the one elicited during the opening sequence. It is not the ingratiating, warm and falsely sincere smile of the salesman who affirms – affirms themselves, the product, the interlocutor and the capitalistic world view, which underscores the relationship between them. It is, instead, closer to the smile of the tragical ironist. The sublime gaze that Travis directs back into the camera at the end of the film is more than a Brechtian shattering of the fourth wall. It is also suggestive that our protagonist now possesses some 'truth' which extends beyond the diegesis. Perhaps this is a Blakean moment of altered consciousness: a positive Hegelian dialectical synthesis.

The 'Zen' interpretations of Travis' smile may be accurate, but, ultimately, they tell us very little about the film.[3] Appearing at the culmination of a long

---

[2] Izod et al., *Lindsay Anderson*, 139. Anderson himself advocated the significance of the Zen idea; see Lindsay Anderson, '*O Lucky Man!*', 1994, in *Never Apologize: The Collected Writings*, ed. Paul Ryan, 126–8 (London: Plexus, 2004), 127–8; Anderson, 'Stripping the Veils Away', 135–6. It is true that the trajectory of *O Lucky Man!* consists, in part, of Travis making the transition from one kind of smile to another; see Izod, et al., *Lindsay Anderson*, 139. See also Hedling, *Lindsay Anderson*, 123–5.

[3] Erik Hedling provides detailed analysis of the Zen reading, whilst admitting that this theme does not provide an exhaustive interpretation; Hedling, *Lindsay Anderson*, 125.

and episodic narrative that articulates themes associated with capitalism, individualism, subjectivity, intention, freedom and politics, the smile on Travis' face at the end of *O Lucky Man!* can also be illuminated in reference to the idea of anti-capitalist Light Romantic inaction I have described in previous chapters. To a certain extent, this present case study will attempt to accomplish the superfluous: it will offer an interpretation of *O Lucky Man!* as a satirical allegory of capitalism. Yet, the hypothesis that *O Lucky Man!* is a Romantic film rests, not on the reasons given by Frank Cunningham (see Chapter 1), but, rather, on the basic understanding that the text critiques the spirit of capitalism whilst negating its own efforts.

Thwarted fables

O Lucky Man! draws from a rich literary heritage. From classical tropes to modern devices, including ideas from ancient myth, satire and the *Bildungsroman*, the film invites association with a host of narrative forms.[4] The structure is certainly picaresque. The genre of the itinerant trickster or scoundrel, conflating ideas of adventure, parable, allegory, crime, philosophy, drama and comedy, the picaresque mode legitimates the ironic, the formally disconnected and the episodic. The distance between the object-language of the diegesis and metalanguage of the narration creates a space of critical distance amenable to the Brechtian *Verfremdungseffekt* favoured by Anderson. As commentators have noted, the film's narrative structure brings out the distanced, alienating or journeying associations within the protagonist's very name: Travis as 'traverse', or travel.[5] Ideas of quest and adventure pervade the film: the feeling that Travis the adventurer is an epic hero striding out to fight dragons and discover treasure. He encounters Herculean tasks, monstrous foes, deceptive tricksters and mighty conflicts, which are met bravely, in a world that, for all the modernity of its themes, seems strangely out of its own time. Like *Mickey One*, some intangible and malevolent force seems to hang over everything. Our hero is often spared grizzly and untimely deaths by only the narrowest of margins.

The title 'O Lucky Man!' combines this fortuitousness befitting the classical adventure – Travis surviving encounters with powerful dangers by having a

---

[4] The film was also inspired by *Candide* (1759) and *Sullivan's Travels* (1941); see Hedling, *Lindsay Anderson*, 113–14, 136–42.
[5] Hedling, *Lindsay Anderson*, 119; Izod, et al., *Lindsay Anderson*, 138.

metanarrational 'fate' on his side – and a distinctly modern demand that the structural framework of such encounters be the pursuit of material and social success in its capitalistic form. Perhaps Travis' journey of trial and fortune recalls the fairy-tale aura of capitalist mythology associated with the works of Daniel Defoe. As in *Colonel Jack* (1722), the protagonist exists in a fictional realm where riches and prosperity promise to fall onto his shoulders (sometimes literally, as in the case of his 'golden' suit) by the grace of authorial omnipotence.[6] Yet, the film's title has a double aura of myth. As a result of its mythic overdetermination, this affirmation of freedom and fulfilment rings with a poignant sense of deception and disappointment. By the end of the narrative, this affirmative sentiment will seem like a false promise, and become enmeshed with a quasi-apocalyptic authorial tyranny.

Other features contribute to this sense of anachronistic bricolage. Notwithstanding the steady reporting of distant news events over Travis' radio, the world of *O Lucky Man!* is one where a lot of news, in fact, never seems to travel at all. Travis witnesses nuclear explosions, grotesque scientific experiments, monstrous war crimes, almost all of which are shown to have no serious consequences. This segregation of autonomous episodes and encounters recalls the dreamlike effect of children's stories such as *Alice in Wonderland* (1865). It makes contemporary Britain seem like a kingdom in a fable, where great battles and disasters take place just over the horizon, but about which no one out of direct earshot knows anything at all. Like Alice, Travis wanders through a disconnected kingdom, each corner of which is absorbed in its own uncanny affairs.

Extending the literary heritage, Travis' story might also be compared with that other anti-capitalist epic *Dead Souls* (1842). Gogol's scheming Chichikov, so adept at moulding himself to various social scenarios in order to emerge with his sought-after material profits (the legal ownership of dead serfs), is driven, so the narrator tells us, by a passion born of his historical age, and which will eventually 'throw man down in the dust and make him kneel before the wisdom of the heavens.'[7] This, as we will see, might also characterize the later scenes of *O Lucky Man!* Like Chichikov, Travis is a singularly ineffectual protagonist who moves among broadly drawn characters representative of a new commercial era, an inconspicuous and unheroic guiding thread, leading the meandering narrative

---

[6] On Defoe's championing of capitalism, see McVeagh, *Tradefull Merchants*, 60.
[7] Nikolai Gogol, *Dead Souls*, 1842–52 (New York: Alfred A. Knopf – Everyman's Library, 2004), 279.

through a satirical cross-section of contemporary society, 'a living picture of the age, a chart of its uses and abuses'.[8]

The film's resultant mixture of classical and modern elements seems, at times, to dramatize the reversion of progressive and enlightened sensibilities to the aura of mythology, as described by Adorno and Horkheimer in *Dialectic of Enlightenment* (1947).[9] Questing and journeying mark a point of symbolic overlap between modernity's capitalistic imperatives of entrepreneurial endeavour and speculation alongside older and more irrational forms of storytelling based on faith, risk and violent ethical retribution against the transgression of natural order. The more Travis the adventurer seeks to master his environment, therefore, the more inevitably and alarmingly does control comically slip from his grasp.

In this sense, too, *O Lucky Man!* evokes the *Bildungsroman*, which Franco Moretti names '*the* "symbolic form" of modernity' – one intimately tied to the social and economic transformations of the eighteenth and nineteenth centuries.[10] The development of this literary form dramatizes a crisis of narrative, subjectivity and socialization via the delegitimation of maturity. By validating the act of social integration, the initial 'classical' *Bildungsroman* is decidedly anti-Romantic.[11] The happy marriage and the communal unity equates inaction with acceptance of the status quo. For Moretti, the classical *Bildungsroman* was able to validate this kind of affirmative narrative conclusion only in reference to a 'pre-capitalist' social reality.[12] Later post-classical developments would not only accentuate the capitalistic aspects of the diegetic world, but also the Light Romantic impulses of their protagonists, who find a happy ending always just out of reach. Like the protagonist of Goethe's *Wilhelm Meister's Apprenticeship* (1796), Travis attempts to become the master of his own life. He goes out into the world, hoping to realize his potential by playing the roles that life requires him to adopt. Yet, by structuring the narrative according to this ideology of *Bildung*, *O Lucky Man!* also performs the same critique as Balzac's *Comédie humaine* (1829–48): not that the narrative judgement uphold 'a society's professed values', but, rather, present a 'violent rejection and open derision of anyone who tries

---

[8] Richard Pevear, 'Introduction', in *Dead Souls*, 1842–52, Nikolai Gogol, ix–xxii (New York: Alfred A. Knopf – Everyman's Library, 2004), xvi.
[9] Theodor W. Adorno and Max Horkheimer, *Dialectic of Enlightenment*, 1947 (London and New York: Verso, 1997), 6–13.
[10] Moretti, *The Way of the World*, 5, passim.
[11] Ibid., 15–73.
[12] Ibid., 27.

to realise them.'[13] As in *Dead Souls*, the protagonist experiences this 'violent rejection' in their attempt to master the world according to its own terms:

> The narrative of youth is no longer the symbolic form able to 'humanise' the social structure . . . (nor simply) to question its cultural legitimacy. It only acts to magnify the indifferent and inhuman vigour of the modern world, which it reconstructs – as if it were an autopsy – from the wounds inflicted upon the individual.[14]

Rather than rebelling against the cultural dominant (*If. . . .* shows the ambivalent aporia of destruction to which this leads), *O Lucky Man!* explores the tragic consequences that follow when someone stops saying 'No!' It does this by dramatizing the critical dialectic described by Adorno: 'The infallible eye for anything trumped-up, for unsubstantiated but commercially-angled intellectual pretentions, unmasks those who failed to measure up to their own higher standard. This higher standard is power and success, and manifests itself, in their bungled attempt to reach it, as itself a lie.'[15] The film reveals the state of unfreedom into which the subject falls when they accept the false totality of capitalist ideology. In this sense, *O Lucky Man!* is the autopsy of *If. . . .*'s Romanticism.

The myth

> I did my duty. I only wanted to be successful. I did my best.
>
> Travis

Mick Travis embarks upon a quest for fortune and fulfilment. Along the way he adopts multiple vocational roles, becoming, for much of the narrative, an embodiment of the proactive capitalist entrepreneurial spirit. Under advanced capitalism, says Adorno: 'the idea of freedom from labour is replaced by the possibility of choosing one's own work. Self-determination means that within the division of labour already laid down I can slip into the sector that promises me the greatest rewards.'[16] Travis' goal is fulfilment within the current social system,

---

[13] According to Moretti's interpretation of Balzac; Ibid., 120.
[14] Ibid., 164.
[15] Adorno, *Minima Moralia*, 211.
[16] Adorno and Horkheimer, *Towards a New Manifesto*, 16. In reality, however, this possibility is not so easy to act upon, as anyone familiar with the modern job market will attest.

and so the exact nature of the vocational role he pursues to fulfil this ambition becomes immaterial. Accordingly, *O Lucky Man!* conflates affirmative action (a subjective attitude that accepts the social totality as given) with the formal paradigms of literary adventure. The quest for 'fortune', in which our hero can slip between social roles and functions with a freedom permitted by the conventions of the literary form, returns as a modern image of entrepreneurialism.

Success is a normative concept. Whether realized in the form of profit or power, success is colloquially understood to be capital acquired though labour – the end beyond the means. For one whose end is 'success', pure and simple, there is no determining value in means themselves. In a sense, Travis becomes the internalization of that same principle, like the secularization of the Protestant work ethic described by Weber. The dramatization of this impulse, in the narrative form of the legend or adventure, complements the Homeric allegory in *Dialectic of Enlightenment*[17] – both Odysseus and Travis become exemplars of the capitalist doctrine of action. But whereas the modern 'successful' individual becomes 'the *imago* of unleashed freedom and unbounded productivity, as if those (ideals) might be realised always and everywhere' by any free individual, *O Lucky Man!* represents this aura of success only to dramatize its essential untruth as ideology.[18] Travis can choose any job he wishes and feel confident of succeeding because it is the continuity of the attitude behind the interchangeable role that really matters. The players change, but the game remains the same, as the lyrics in Alan Price's soundtrack attest. Accordingly, an illusory self-determination motivates Travis' wanderings. He sees the same pot of gold at the end of every rainbow.

Not only is the choice of work dependent upon a great deal of economic and social freedom, which is denied to a large section of the working population in even the most advanced societies, but freedom of self-determination regarding work also obscures the overarching principles of rationality upon which the frameworks of such choices are based. The freedom to choose your vocation from among innumerable jobs directed at the same quantitative standard of 'success' replaces the idea of work as something fulfilling in itself. In doing so, it undermines that Romantic conception of human freedom that Marx inherited from Schiller's *Aesthetic Education* (1795), and which fed into the concept of alienation. Aided by the literary hybridity of the text, Travis then moves through

---

[17] Adorno and Horkheimer, *Dialectic of Enlightenment*, 43–80.
[18] Adorno, *Negative Dialectics*, 342.

a vision of the modern world beset with an aura of alienation reverted to myth. Choose what vocation or opportunity for self-realization he might – coffee salesman, scientific guinea pig, private secretary, arms dealer, altruistic social worker – he finds the same kind of archaic madness and violence everywhere. As an allegorical space for the development of modern economic subjectivity, the diegetic world of *O Lucky Man!* becomes a place of deception and danger, and the protagonist is free only to choose his poison.

The mythic rhetoric satirized by the film, and particularly in the musical interludes, requires only that Travis have the will to play the game of capitalist totality – confidence is all; Fichte's will to action against all odds, or 'stamina', as Travis himself puts it. The ability to shake off failure and 'get back on your feet' counts among the highest virtues of this ideology. Social Darwinism is raised to a truism by the need for the subject to attune themselves to the current of the world: 'You will see terrible things. But "grow hard", even as Nietzsche said. Rest only in order to build strength to go on, and know from the start that you are going to win. If you survive, enjoy the comforts afforded by your success. They are, 'it is proclaimed', 'fair compensation for all you have lost.' All this is something like the object-language ironically professed by Alan Price's songs and operant in the world through which our hero moves, deluded.

The new crusade

First, the film establishes a rhetorical method. The opening scene is reminiscent of a silent documentary film about life on a colonial plantation. A guard (Brian Glover) catches a worker (Malcolm McDowell) stealing coffee beans. A title card appears – 'Unlucky!' – and the worker is tried before a dribbling Rabelaisian official. The brutal and alarmingly anachronistic punishment involves the removal of the thief's hands with a machete. The unfortunate worker submits with awed terror.

Such is the vision of the past which opens *O Lucky Man!* The word 'Now!' grows on the screen and bursts the cropped aspect ratio of the *mise-en-abyme*; it marks the end of this thematic overture, but produces a double effect, which characterizes the film's satirical method. The opening sequence may operate either on a distinction or on a continuity between past and present. The object-language and the metalanguage seem to make both of these propositions at once, by giving the word 'Now!' different things to do. The film-within-a-film distinguishes between the injustice and cruelty of the old world and the comparatively enlightened times of the film's present. The metalanguage, on the other hand, obliterates this distinction by stressing the continuity of historical conditions and the social violence they are suggested to contain. As the film progresses, we are encouraged to understand that the opening sequence at the coffee plantation is not a transiently barbaric period in the development of the capitalist economy, but a distillation of the essential violence upon which the whole is dependent. Violence continues in advanced capitalist social life, only in different forms.

We are then transported to a modern coffee factory, where Travis and a number of other young men dressed in white overalls are attending a workplace induction. Compared to the plantation, this is a pleasant environment. There are no guns, the workers smile and chat and the modern representation even flirts with a conventional mythic validation when Travis ducks under a conveyor belt to talk to a girl (Christine Noonan). It is as if some workplace romance is about to begin. But he only has enough time to make a brief but significant comment about the irrationality of taking Nigerian coffee beans, packing them up in the UK and then shipping them back to Nigeria for distribution. 'Frightening, isn't it?' says the girl. This dialogue suggests that, yes, modern globalized business is irrational, but 'never mind'. In contrast to the nightmarish world of the plantation, it seems as though capitalism has come a long way.

We understand, then, that Travis' desire for difference has taken a new path. He wants to stand apart and be distinguished, but not, as in *If . . . .*, against society as a whole, but, rather, as an outstanding individual within the system itself. He will now take part in society, but only to the extent that he can still rise above the majority. He once mounted the roof of a public school with a Bren gun, but now capitalism provides him with pre-established behavioural principals for conduct and rationality, and he is determined to rise in the world by adhering to them better than everyone else. In short, he will distinguish himself by becoming a 'success'.

The lyrics of Alan Price's song 'Poor People' accentuate the discrepancy between a willingness to go do whatever is necessary to attain success, and the doomed condition of 'poor people' who fail to understand this willingness. As we have seen in Part One, according to the ideology of modern capitalist 'freedom', it is your own fault if you are poor. If all humans are equally free to make successes of themselves, as this regime will assert, then success is hard won and well earned. Poverty results from a fundamental lack of some essential personal quality, such as intelligence, imagination or, as Travis puts it, 'stamina'. The metalanguage of Price's song seemingly offers no distinction between the falsity of the condition experienced by 'poor people' and the second order character who believes in what is being sung ironically. They are both – poor people and those who sing whilst on the road to success – in conditions of ideological mystification. Such is the rhetorical method of *O Lucky Man!* The film articulates such an ideology in order to render it monstrous and obscene.

The factory guide asks why split coffee beans are returned to the production process. Mr Biles (Brian Pettifer) is tasked with providing an answer to this question, but his reply is stereotypically unsatisfying: 'I've been off sick, sir.' Economic rationality has no criteria for human sickness, save as a guarantee of lower quantifiable results. Alone among the group, Travis answers appropriately: 'Eliminates waste, sir.' He drops the pronoun, for an impression of maximum verbal efficiency, whilst maintaining 'sir' as a necessary social honorific. Economic irrationality has taken hold of his values.

The salesman stands between production and consumption, and the whole success of the operation symbolically devolves upon them. They are the lynchpin of the operation, and sales executive Mr Duff (Arthur Lowe) employs the terminology of battles, adventures and struggles to add a mythic quality to the salesman's task. Another manager, Ms Rowe (Rachel Roberts), asks the trainees to demonstrate good sales 'psychology', and a nervous and ungainly man (Glenn Williams) makes his way to the front of the training room. 'Smile, Mr Spalding', she says, but his slouched and twitchy appearance does not satisfy. 'People don't buy things just because they're good', says Ms Rowe, 'they have to believe.' And, as salesmen, '*you* have to believe' as well. More explicitly, she uses the words 'sincerity' and 'honesty' whilst directly reversing their meanings. The executive advises her trainees to create an arbitrary sincerity, which will help them succeed in business: 'Smile . . . . Give with all your heart! Don't think of yourself.' This falsely altruistic injunction is exposed by the capitalist maxim that stands behind it (personal interest), and when this injunction is internalized as an effect of socialization, it marks a loss of freedom.

The salesman must unite the human and the mechanical by using the aura of human conviction to convince others to buy their product, whilst adopting the values that are demanded of them by the company and what it needs to sell. The conviction that 'the product is good' becomes their own – their faith – whether or not it is 'really' believed. Romantic and philosophical notions of the human remaining true unto themselves do not matter to capitalism; like the excuse of sickness given by Biles, they are extraneous to the need for the quantifiable measurement of profit and efficient calculation, and enter the purview only as a deficit. It is this reduction of the human to the mechanical and the valuation of ends over means – as necessary for capitalism as it is abhorrent to critical philosophy – that Travis will cultivate and exploit throughout the film, in the certain knowledge that it is his ticket to success.

When Travis is asked to introduce himself, therefore, he knows just what to do. He steps forward to meet Ms Rowe; she does not have to come to him. He extends his hand in greeting first; others had not done this. With unwavering eye contact, he wears on his face, like a mask, a big 'sincere' smile. Glowing with artificial affirmation, Travis has perfectly demonstrated his recognition and adoption of the correct ideology. Ms Rowe is pleased. He has internalized all the right falsehoods, made all the necessary concessions to thought and conduct and will undoubtedly make an excellent salesman.

Enemies of promise

The chairman of the company (Peter Jeffrey) informs his executives that an immediate sales appointment is required. Surveying the trainees, he asks Ms Rowe to select the top candidate. This scene suggests that important business decisions often come down to subjective instincts, which are, in this instance, borderline irrational in their animalistic connotations: 'What's your instinct say?' the chairman asks, 'Can you sniff him?' Travis is lucky. A vacancy has appeared, and he is in the right place at the right time. His smile – the personal factor, the part over which he appears to have control, even though determined by the needs of his immediate socio-economic context – was just the golden ticket (Figure 21). Opportunity for success is here merely a combination of chance, the personal dispositions of others and a willingness to fit into a gap in the system that it is necessary to fill in order to ensure the system's perpetuation.

'The future is in your hands Mr Travis. Take it', says Ms Rowe. The intoxication of this sublime promise of freedom and opportunity is augmented by a romantic embrace, as the two characters fall into each other's arms. With a new job and a promising future before him, Travis sets out to fight the dragon of failure. The chairman gives him the equipment he will need: a map, compass, car keys and, with significant presentation, an apple – a piece of quasi-Christian symbolism perhaps suggesting loss of innocence, as well as banishment from Paradise.

Figure 21 An affirmative and adaptable Travis (Malcolm McDowell) smiles at fate. *O Lucky Man!* (1973).

Whilst driving on the road to success, Travis' car is passed by a noisy red convertible. After sounding his horn, the impatient driver (Jeremy Bulloch) overtakes the protagonist, and the two men share a moment of meaningful eye contact. The speed at which they both appear to be careening down the narrow country road is somewhat alarming, especially when combined with the almost competitive suggestion of their prolonged stares. With arrogant demeanour, chequered flat cap, driving gloves and scarf, the man presents signifiers of affluence and may function as an embodiment of the idea of success against which our hero now measures himself. The 'successful' young man accelerates away, leaving Travis in his dust.

Plunging through a bank of fog that suddenly appears on the road, Travis hears squealing tyres and a crash. Emerging from this unexplained haze (arising, it seems, due to a fairy-tale logic of omnipotent malevolence), he comes upon a tragic accident. The convertible has crashed into a truck, and, as Travis attends the scene, he finds the man dying among the debris. In innocent tones, which contradict first impressions, the injured man falters out the pathetic words: 'Tell my mother I'm all right. It's her birthday.' This young and 'successful' man, who at first aroused the potential for a range of feelings between antipathy or admiration, is now reduced to a pitiable condition. The overall structure of the scene invites the interpretive possibility that Travis and the dying man are taking part in 'the race of life'. The mythic 'luck' of the film's metalanguage was at work here; the treacherous mist appeared solely in order to crash the car. Having implicitly transcended the condition of 'poor people', the man in the red convertible could not outrun his ultimate fate: the 'curse' of a rotten world engineered by the fiction. If we feel these things – framed as they are by an allegorical framework, in a world that seems unpredictable, plastic and hostile, operating according to a logic which is independent of diegetic agency, and banking on a radicalization of the principle of chance against all hopes of self-determination, no matter how tirelessly they are affirmed by a fictional world that, in the same breath, overturns that promise – then we feel the affective cruelty of that paradox which the film satirizes: 'Take it, O Lucky Man! Control the uncontrollable.'

The rationalization that the crash happened because of 'bad luck' is, then, disavowed by the film's narrative conventionality, which contextualizes the event as an ominous foreshadowing of our hero's future: 'And when you, too, run out of luck, and crash your car and die on your mother's birthday, the presentation of your humanity will make you seem alien to yourself.' If the man in the convertible symbolizes a pure will that ends up broken and twisted into an incoherent identity, then his meaning can be illuminated by Adorno's words: 'The pure will . . . is falsified by anyone who believes it to be in his possession. Negatively, it breaks through in the subject's painful perception that in their reality, in what become of them, all men are mutilated'.[19] The Romanticism of this painful perception – and what distinguishes it from the sense of affirmation which helps the capitalist entrepreneur forget their chance upsets, get back on their feet and get back into the race – emerges in the moment of suffering or *weltschmerz*, an awareness that the world is wrong, and that to get back in the race would only perpetuate this wrong. If Travis feels it here – with the dying man in his arms, with the radio blaring a jolly pop song about tenderness and companionship, and with the police who arrive on the scene outrageously more interested in claiming spilled goods from the lorry and threatening to frame Travis for manslaughter than in helping the injured – then he will not accept it just yet. As he says in the following scene at the hotel: 'Stamina! . . . you've got have it.' The policemen offer him a share of the spoils, and Travis accepts the principle of exchange – even as he took the apple – still with a willingness to believe that the world is a 'fair' place, when all is said and done.

For the present, luck is on Travis' side. After a faltering run of coffee sales, he secures a successful meeting with a hotel manager, Charlie Johnson (Arthur Lowe). The scene is significant because it suggests certain propositions: (1)

---

[19] Ibid., 297.

Successful sales performance requires no skill. Travis simply walks into the hotel, meets the manager and the sale falls into his lap. Mr Johnson does most of the talking and effectively brings Travis up to the condition of his predecessor automatically. There is no need for Travis to re-secure the sale. (2) Success is dependent upon the establishment and maintenance of social relationships, which, in themselves, are nothing to do with the product or the process of selling it. When Johnson says that he will put in a good word for Travis among his friends, the strong implication is that this will improve Travis' sales. If the current meeting sets a precedent, Travis may soon get excellent commissions without actually 'selling' a bean. (3) Again, luck and uncontrollable subjective considerations are the ultimate determinants of success. Johnson has no obvious motivation for promoting Travis' interests. He seems to be willing to do this out of a somewhat unfathomable favouritism; but the two men have only just met. Like Travis' initial appointment, a supposedly meritocratic system is shown here to be dependent upon arbitrary and unpredictable conditions.

Mr Johnson escorts Travis to a live sex club, where several local officials quickly get on friendly terms with the lucky salesman. Ever the social Darwinist, Travis is rewarded for adapting to his environment by meeting several powerful new business contacts. He joins the crowd's raucous chorus of 'Chocolate sandwich!' directed at the stripping stage performers, without, perhaps, knowing what it means. With a cigar in his hand and a girl on his knee pouring alcohol into his mouth, Travis seems to be enjoying himself. He will arrive back at the hotel with a crate of scotch (presumably a gift from one of his new business associates) to find the landlady waiting for him in his bed. Devotion to his work is beginning to 'pay off', then. What could be more 'natural', according to the ideology of capitalism, than this spectacle of a salesman relaxing after a successful business deal? It demonstrates the variety of the ways in which Travis follows the unwritten programme of capitalism. He uses his initiative, attempts to fill gaps in the market and enjoys the results. This element of enjoyment is important, for it is the justification for the personal costs that are paid in following the dogma of economic rationality. The promise of sensual and social gratification becomes the reward for the relinquishment of autonomy.

Some higher power is driving Travis onward. A mysterious old man (Ralph Richardson) gives him a golden suit as a gift, like a blessing from the Gods in a Greek legend. The old benefactor is a mixture of classical character types from innumerable fables, myths and novels; he combines aspects of the friend figure who advises and equips the hero, the trickster who dooms the unwitting adventurer with an ironical smile, and the wise old sage who already knows how the story will end. As Travis leaves the hotel, the old man gives him a parting word of advice; but the advice wisdom gave to posterity in *Wilhelm Meister* – 'Remember to live!'[20] – becomes here something altogether more sinister: 'Try not to die like a dog.' By evoking an idea of animalistic annihilation, this warning transforms the enlightened world of promise through which Travis journeys seem not so much a land of golden opportunity, but a perilous and fantastical realm on the borderland of reason.

The capitalist's progress

Travis' next adventure takes place at a mysterious nuclear facility. He is captured by soldiers who put a hood over his head and escort him into an office with a picture of Queen Elizabeth II on the wall. His mask is removed and the door is locked. As Travis wanders about the room, however, he discovers that there is another door, and this one is unsecured. Travis sneaks through the deserted corridors to the accompaniment of ambient diegetic sound suggestive of industrialized scientific activity. He finds an observation window and sees figures dressed in bulky protective clothing occupied with a large technical installation. Travis is then swiftly recaptured, and his interrogation begins.

There is something absurd about the way Travis' blindfold is removed this second time. Despite his armed escort, having a bag over his head and being locked in a room in a concrete bunker, Travis has managed to wander around and see precisely that which (presumably) all this effort was directed at preventing him from seeing. Menacing officials demand to know the identity of Travis' employer. They don't appear to believe his story about being a coffee salesman. A guard (Brian Glover) begins strapping Travis to his chair. In one of the film's few moments of generic comedy, a tea lady (Dandy Nichols) wheels a trolley into the interrogation room and serves refreshments to the officials, whilst the man whose job it is to provide the coffee in the first place is being unjustly coerced as an alleged spy. One of the officials (Philip Stone) assures Travis that he will ultimately sign the confession, despite any resistance. Again, he adapts to his environment and capitulates. When the questions start coming, Travis gives the

---

[20] Johann Wolfgang von Goethe, *Wilhelm Meister's Apprenticeship*, 1796 (London: J. M. Dent and Sons, 1944), Vol. 2 Book VIII, Chap. V., 98. The quote given is an alternative translation.

officials the answers they want to hear. He admits to being a member of 'the Party' and to being paid 300 roubles a month.

An ominous siren rings throughout the building. The interrogators hastily exit the room and the sound of rushing feet subsides into the distance off-screen. The seriousness of the interrogation has been alarmingly usurped by some matter of apparently greater concern. Again, with comic timing, the tea lady comes back into the room and frees Travis, complaining all the whilst about the mess. Outside some serious conflagration is underway. Smoke pours from one of the great doors in the side of a scientific installation, men in lab coats join scores of panicked civilians and soldiers and fire engines race onto the scene. Travis makes his way through the confusion and escapes into the hills. For an indeterminate time, he scrambles up a steady incline without looking back, and shortly his desperate ascent is exacerbated by a series of tremendous off-screen explosions somewhere behind him. He is soon surrounded by smoke, debris and flames, with the strong implication being that he has narrowly avoided being caught in a nuclear explosion. A hellish scene now before him, Travis uses the bag containing his golden suit to protect himself from a sudden rainstorm seemingly brought about by the quasi-apocalyptic event he has just survived.

It is an alarming episode. Aside from the implication that hundreds of people have died off-screen, and that our hero's survival was dependent not only upon this catastrophe, but also the absurd eventuality that he was released by a tea lady, what is perhaps most disturbing about the scene comes from a more insidious and structural relation between the diegetic elements at play and the political ideas they evoke. The explosion, it is suggested, was caused by the people whom it killed. It was a self-destructive event, resulting from the implied making of plans and their actual and unforeseen consequences. In purely formal terms, this sequence in *O Lucky Man!* dramatizes, in affective guise, the kind of 'madness' that lurks behind positivistic principles of subjective rationality – the absurdity of all positivist pretensions to absolute control.

To begin, it is significant that Travis is left to wander freely around the building after his first capture. His situation has gone from one in which he is totally controlled – literally surrounded by a group of armed men in an alarmingly overdetermined manner – to being completely uncontrolled at the heart of a top-secret facility. This is a representation of an official world populated by the kind of people who 'control things' and 'know what they are doing'; but many things are being left unattended, overlooked and inadequately supervised. The overdetermination of control expressed by the squad of soldiers and the interrogation officers is undermined by the ultimate fragility of the entire facility to an offhand event of total annihilation. Travis and the explosion are related; their respective presences at the secret base are both 'mistakes', which a desire for totality has been unable to control. Recalling the earlier discussion of critical philosophy and its negation of positivism, the forceful manipulation of Travis according to the will of his interrogators seems to dramatize the idea that truth is not reducible to empirical observation: so long as Travis gives the right answers, truth can be reduced to a false equation between the given and the real. Government officials with pictures of the Queen on the wall can force all the obedience from individuals they desire, yet real truth – the objective condition that nuclear material does not 'sign' if you force it, and that Travis really is innocent of the charges brought against him – this objectivity will always be beyond manipulation. Maybe the nuclear explosion appears, in this sense, as a return of the repressed: actual and uncontrollable truth emerging as a kind of crisis in order to refute, as Popper might have put it, the authoritarian identity of reason and reality.

Perhaps in this image of Travis squatting on a muddy bank, huddled under a plastic bag, we sense an echo of many indefinite images of destruction wrought on the fringes of the capitalist system by military conflicts, political disturbances, industrial accidents and social displacements (Figure 22). The hellish explosion becomes a metonymic representation of the uncontrollable chaos that is positivism's collateral. The following vision of the salesman wandering the wasteland in his glittering suit – a small personal compensation for the desolation with which his world has been cursed – is also ripe for allegorical interpretation. Social Darwinism holds that survival is granted to the strongest;

Figure 22 Travis (Malcolm McDowell) wandering in the wasteland. *O Lucky Man!* (1973).

thanks to the diegetic events that brought him to safety, however, we can only wonder how acutely Travis really believes that. He did survive, but taking that survival as a sign of strength or 'stamina' seems beyond rational comprehension. As the following scenes suggest, if Travis' faith in the capitalist ideology was at all shaken by his apocalyptic experience, it will take more than an earth-scarring mass slaughter to shake his conviction that he is on the right path.

On the outskirts of the wasteland, the exhausted Travis stumbles upon a scene of pastoral beauty. Having survived a hellish experience, the fiction succours him with a vision of paradise. Following the sound of choral singing, he enters a church and collapses next to a mound of harvest offerings. A woman kneels by his side and, with eyes lifted upward in holy grace, allows Travis to suckle from her breast. Cinematic realism is now openly tempered by metaphor: Religion and Woman become regenerative comforts for men who need to find the strength to go back into the world. Having passed his trial, Travis leaves this rural idyll in high spirits, swinging a stick as he marches the through fields, accompanied by happy children and triumphant piano music, which mixes religious, Romantic and popular registers.

The pilgrim eventually comes to a highway and hitches a lift. For the capitalist, eager to get back in the game, it does not take long for another opportunity to present itself. For when Travis learns that the occupants of the car are on their way to take part in a paid medical experiment and need extra volunteers, he immediately negotiates a larger fee. On his journey south, Travis opportunistically resolves to make some money from the Millar Research Clinic.

The ant and the pig

A noisy group of people march into a reception room. Several anxious doctors are gathered around a tall and confident middle-aged man in a stylish grey suit. Prof Millar (Graham Crowden) has made his first appearance in the 'Mick Travis trilogy'.[21] Like others whom the protagonist encounters throughout the film, Millar sees potential in our adventurer. Convinced that the new arrival can advance his research, the Professor commences a long monologue about human

---

[21] Now is not the time to turn our attention to the significance of Prof Millar – his apparent beliefs, actions, symbolic potential, schemas of cultural representation or their relevance to the dynamic of Romantic critical philosophy, explanation, freedom and power explored in this book. This will be a task for the final chapter on *Britannia Hospital* (1982), when the Professor will return in a more central role.

survival in the modern world by asking Travis a simple question: What is the most 'successful' animal that has ever lived? Without much deliberation, Travis arrives at a tentative and rather comic answer: 'The ant?'

It is a curious choice. It invites some speculation concerning Travis' criteria for 'success' as a concept. We are given no reason to doubt that Travis gives the answer sincerely, and the questioning tone in which it was stated situates this as another instance of Travis willingly adapting to his environment. If so, he is attempting to give Millar an answer that will best suit his own interests in the current network of power relations. In short, Travis, as on other occasions throughout the film, apparently does his utmost to give his interlocutor the answer he believes they want to hear. In this way, the answer invites certain hypothetical propositions concerning the relationship that Travis authenticates between the two individuals.

From a human perspective, ants work hard within a hierarchical team structure, which results from natural evolution. Individuals are units that make up a naturally determined whole (a 'colony'). What is, for Travis, the determining marker of their 'success' may involve a combination of an anthropomorphised validation of a simple and rigidly maintained social system and a holistic programme of industrialism dedicated to survival and proliferation regardless of time, space or other contextual factors. In other words, Travis may take the typical ant colony to be some kind of capitalist utopia. The fact that this system admits no room for individualism presents no serious contradiction; if Travis is really giving Millar the answer he thinks will please him best, then his choice merely operates according to Travis' own desire to fit in with the dominant power, to mould his priorities accordingly and excel on existing terms. In Price's words, Travis is willing to sell everything he stands for. When faced with another figure of authority, did Travis give the answer he had hoped would please them best? Did he try to adapt to his environment? Did he adapt in a way that reduced his own condition to that of a mindless worker drone? The malleability of Travis' principles does have its price – literally. The volunteer is willing to go along with everything Miller asks of him, so long as one question is answered to his satisfaction, the only question a capitalist entrepreneur might be expected to ask: 'What are you paying?'

Later in the evening, Travis investigates one of his fellow volunteers. He finds an agitated young man (Jeremy Bulloch) lying in bed and asks: 'How much are they paying you?' Pulling away the sheet, Travis discovers the disturbing and absurd nature of Millar's grand attempt to improve humanity. The young man's

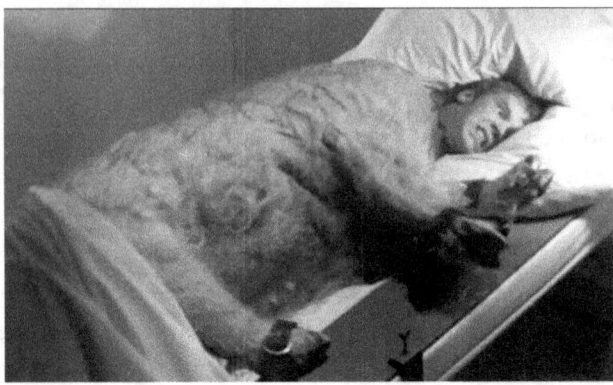

Figure 23 The unlucky victim of human 'progress' (Jeremy Bulloch). *O Lucky Man!* (1973).

head has been transplanted onto the body of an animal (Figure 23). Considering it a glimpse of his own future, Travis screams, runs down the corridor, jumps out of a window and makes his escape on a bicycle.

Travis has saved his own bacon, but the political connotations of this horrific discovery are thematically consistent. An encounter with the potential to foster feelings of sympathy, empathy and a moral outrage that may create the potential for real social intervention – all this is rendered unthinkable through the affective horror created by this nightmarish creature in a state of helpless distress. The film articulates the subjective experience of encountering a suffering Other as a thing to abhor and escape – to distance from the act of thinking. The poor victim is 'obviously' beyond help, and is not even entirely human. Travis' wild scream is the moment where the social abjection is consecrated, for it brings him, too, momentarily into the animal kingdom. The object-language of the experience that Travis undergoes says: 'People in trouble are abject' – untouchable. It says this just as strongly as it does: 'Look after number one', or 'Success is the highest virtue'. It says: 'Leave him to his fate,' because what could Travis do, even if he wanted to? There is no adequate rationalization provided for Millar's implied actions. For both Travis and the film viewer, the idea of thought itself flees the hospital room in a state of panic.

In these terms, the discontinuous transition to the following scene is not, as it first seems, a radical break with these themes, but a direct articulation of Travis' 'stamina' – his ability to forget, or his ability not to think. Escaping by bicycle, the panicking Travis is run off the road by a van. He crashes into some bushes, and the occupants of the vehicle, who turn out to be Alan Price and his band, pull up to see if he is all right, and the musical narrator of *O Lucky Man!* offers the protagonist a lift. Despite having made a horrific discovery concerning the intimate and literally monstrous effects of institutionalized practice only moments before, Travis is now clambering out of roadside foliage, suddenly more concerned with the disarrangement of his prized golden suit. Having survived another 'traumatic' episode, Travis' speedy reversion to a state of normality is suggestive of the narrative mode and its relation to character development. The literary 'trial', familiar from the fairy tale or *Bildungsroman*, is not something from which Travis learns anything at all. He does not emerge from the nuclear facility, or from Millar's clinic, a wiser, enlightened or more thoughtful person. This distortion of realist character consistency not only results from the film's exploration of capitalist 'stamina', but also contributes to that anachronistic sense of formal construction. A part of the dreamlike quality of *O Lucky Man!* can be attributed to the protagonist's periodic reversion to a seemingly untroubled state of innocence. For a considerable portion of the narrative, the idea of character development is seemingly supplanted by a Homeric willingness to 'shake off' troubles and brave the next adventure.

Grow hard

Some hours later, after waking in the arms of Patricia (Helen Mirren), Travis witnesses the van's arrival in London – a global financial hub with the 'biggest money market in the world', as Travis himself puts it. If the capitalist opportunist can 'make it' anywhere, it will be here. The inconsistent character Patricia evokes multiple schemas of feminine representation, ranging from the Maiden to the Vamp. She is associated with the metanarrational perspective of Alan Price and the band, and yet is seemingly closer in spirit to her tycoon father, Sir James (Ralph Richardson), stories of whose unscrupulous business achievements she whispers into Travis' ear with relish.

Sir James puts Travis' capitalistic boasting in the shade. His returns on multimillion-pound investments are staggering; his personal time is worth £500 per minute; and he reputedly drove half a million peasants off their land in Bolivia, causing mass starvation. Sheer size of numbers develops a pornographic allure; mathematical sublimity facilitates a tabooed pleasure in the admiration of social distinctions in wealth and power. Whilst Travis hears about such things, with an adoring woman in his arms and his eyes fixed on a monolithic tower block framed against the London skyline, Patricia's words become the stuff of an earlier and more barbarous age. As Weber suggested: 'When the imagination . . . has once been turned toward purely quantitative bigness . . . this romanticism of numbers exercises an irresistible appeal to the poets among businessmen.'[22] Whether Travis can really be called a 'poet among businessmen' is debatable, but his reaction to Patricia's testimony certainly evokes something close to the numbing rhetoric of a Kantian mathematical sublime. It is as if Patricia's father were some great pharaoh or king, whose glory is measured by the number of dead beneath their temples.

Travis's brief experience working for Sir James might be compared to Chichikov's encounter with the wealthy landowner Kostanzhoglo in *Dead Souls*.[23] In both stories, the ambitious yet satirized protagonists, eager to stride down the road to a fancifully conceived economic paradise, encounter a man who becomes, for them, an embodiment of success. In the subjective views of both protagonists, these men represent the end-goal of their ambitions. In order to replicate their all-too-obvious material successes, our heroes instantly decide to mould their own actions and mentalities to complement those of their idols, despite the fact that both Travis and Chichikov make this choice before they have even laid eyes upon them. The adventurers initially survey, from a distance, the land and possessions of wealthy and powerful businessmen, and hear impressive stories about their economic finesse and amoral pragmatism. Everything extraneous to the material display of wealth and influence (the idea of displaced villagers when seen as anything except evidence of the power that made them move) falls by the wayside.

During Travis' interview with Sir James, the distraught Prof Stewart (Graham Crowden) charges into the executive's office. Recently fired by the ruthless tycoon, he throws himself out of a window, taking with him an innocent assistant, William (Michael Bangerter). Again, breaking with conventions of realism, Sir James immediately calls together some senior staff members and reads an impromptu eulogy on behalf of the late academic. Sir James thrusts a portfolio under Travis' arm and wordlessly gives him the job that was so recently entrusted to his unmourned assistant.

The world of big business is characterized here, above all, by an institutional callousness, trivial ritualization and an almost dreamlike strangeness in the bearing of its wooden figures with stern faces (Figure 24). Much like *Mickey One*,

---

[22] Weber, *The Protestant Ethic and the Spirit of Capitalism*, 71.
[23] Gogol, *Dead Souls*, 350–7.

Figure 24 The sinister and conspiratorial world of big business. *O Lucky Man!* (1973).

the most telling aspects of the film's critical mode of address are perhaps to be found in the creation of a vague sense of unease within commercial environments. Moments such as Travis' sales interviews and his experiences with Sir James evoke that elusive mood of disquiet canonically described by Marlow in *Heart of Darkness*.[24] Negating the traditional idea of a capitalistic 'space of opportunity', the atmosphere is thick with an aura of conspiracy and unspoken violence.

As Dr Munda (Arthur Lowe), leader of the fictional African country Zingara, insinuates at the start of his meeting with Sir James, the world of business likes to be recognized as one of facts and figures.[25] All things should be direct, practical, unambiguous and serve to facilitate clear decision, without elements that are unnecessary to the demands of economic rationality. 'A man of business' equates, without much of an interpretive leap, to someone whose life is organized according to a non-human quantitative conditional. For the brain attuned to 'business', in an abstract and ideal sense, instrumental reason reigns triumphant. Cut out the superfluous elements from a meeting – in other worlds, make it somewhat 'inhuman' – and you have the ideal condition for conducting

---

[24] In Conrad's novella, the protagonist arrives at his company building for the first time and, despite all things seemingly being 'normal', nevertheless feels as though he is entering a world where something is 'not quite right'; Joseph Conrad, *Heart of Darkness*, 1899 (London and New York: Alfred A. Knopf – Everyman's Library, 1993), 13. See previous chapter.

[25] The infamous case of Arthur Lowe blacking up in order to portray Dr Munda facilitates a thematic reading. The multiple performances given by actors such as Lowe, Crowden and Richardson create a decided sense of 'falseness', which spreads its effect concerning both the film as a Brechtian text and within the diegesis as a critical representation of a false and deceitful capitalist society. The film is both false as a fiction, and a fiction about something false – something, like Anderson's actors, hiding behind a deceptive surface.

business. *O Lucky Man!* presents a pointed realization of these assumptions, as business is bluntly allied with inhumanity.

Like Travis, we witness events in this problematic world with somewhat of an outsider's eye, yet any sense of outrage at the injustices taking place is frustrated by Travis' apparent willingness to be complicit in their immorality. Travis' quiet complicity with 'the way of the world', embodied by the actions of Sir James and his associates, exemplifies the connection between the capitalistic imperative to pursue one's own interests without regard for the condition of others (such as Prof Stewart or the Zingaran people) and a species of violence to the self. Adorno describes a figure very similar to Travis: 'one pursues one's own advantage before all else, and simply not to endanger oneself, does not talk too much. That is a general law of the status quo . . . The social monad, the isolated competitor, was the precondition, as indifference to the fate of others'.[26] The idea of quietly going along with whatever sets itself up as inevitable is shown to be a concession to inhumanity – a passive apologia, taking the falsely affirmative and economized form of Nietzsche's 'grow hard'.[27]

This meeting between Sir James and the Zingarans starts innocently enough. They watch a film designed to promote corporate investment. Hotels, resorts and native African dancing are all advertised for their ability to provide enjoyment and recuperation for Western workers with disposable incomes. As the sales pitch continues, however, we see the drastic lengths to which the government will go to secure its economic interests. Native workers are forced to live in segregated housing and are paid mere pennies each day. But if the government does squeeze their domestic workforce and go out of their way to provide luxuries for Western expats, it is merely a matter of accommodation. In the same way that Travis adapts to the needs of his environment, so too does the economic policy of Zingara adapt itself to the competitive demands of global capitalism. The government stresses to Sir James that European workers who relocate to their country can expect the same standard of living as is to be found in the developed world. It is this willingness to adapt to the dominant expectations that secures Zingara's hypothetical status as a 'developing' nation, or as one ready to take its place on the world stage, with an affluent ruling elite and a massive, exploited underclass.

---

[26] Theodor W. Adorno, 'Education after Auschwitz', 1967, in *Critical Models: Interventions and Catchwords*, 191–204 (New York: Columbia University Press, 2005), 201.
[27] See Ibid., 197.

As the conference continues, the investment meeting transforms into something else. Colonel Steiger (Wallas Eaton) next reports on the military efforts of the Zingaran administration to supress a group of anti-government rebels. This topic is introduced as an elucidation concerning the protection of returns on foreign investment – a development which, although somewhat 'unrealistic' in its representation, remains within the normally understood purview of the military-industrial complex. Footage of wartime atrocities comes too close on the heels of promotional tourist media to maintain the separation between globalized business and armed conflict. The rebels pestering Dr Munda's government introduce an element of uncertainty into the business venture – an uncertainty that is unacceptable to economic rationality. In the true spirit of positivism, this element must be eliminated with violence. Therefore, to guarantee the security of Sir James' investment, Steiger needs to defeat the rebels with chemical weapons. The military virtues of substance codenamed 'Honey' (similar in effect to napalm) are couched in quantitative terms: planes carrying so much can cover so much ground in so much time, and so forth. What such language excludes is the gruesomeness and inhumanity of the images on the screen; but burnt corpses in various states of dissolution are reduced from evidence of suffering to an economic message: the product is efficient. Relying upon this tension, the filmic metalanguage emphasizes a scandalous disproportion between the normality of the business affairs being represented and the moral bankruptcy by which they are sustained.

Baffled to fight better

Our affirmative hero goes along with this illegal arms deal, of course, and eventually becomes the scapegoat when the police intervene. Like the unlucky plantation worker in the opening sequence, Travis is tried and convicted as a criminal. Five years later he emerges from prison with a supposedly new attitude: no longer that of the entrepreneur, but one which is no less exculpated from the affirmative falsity of the world around him. Although Travis has put the ideal of capitalistic success behind him, his redemption remains illusory.

Clichés come thick and fast during the farewell speech given by the paternal prison governor (Peter Jeffrey): 'daily bread', 'the world is your oyster', 'the brotherhood of man', 'sweat of their brow', 'move mountains', 'it belonged to my grandmother'. Despite its variance from the individualist and amoral ideology to

Figure 25 The prison governor (Peter Jeffrey) baffles Travis to 'fight better'. *O Lucky Man!* (1973).

which Travis has previously been adhering, the governor's speech also encourages our hero to participate in the world uncritically. These hackneyed words reveal the hollowness of Travis' transformation and the affirmative world view he still embodies. As with the protagonist's previous experiences, the privilege to begin anew – to pick yourself up and make a fresh start – is articulated as proof of the goodness of what does not change. It is almost as if Peter Jeffrey were again playing the headmaster from *If....* Despite everything, the world still 'goes on the same', as Alan Price elegiacally confirms.

Embracing his student with paternal affection, the governor says: 'You have eyes like Steve McQueen' (Figure 25). Like Ed Castle in his attempt to bring Mickey to Xanadu, the mythology of social participation has adopted the rhetoric of the latest adverts and fashions, exaggerating, to a point of absurdity, the benediction – the 'You, and only you' – which every mythic utterance imparts.[28]

The governor reads a slightly misquoted passage from Robert Browning's 'Epilogue' from *Asolando* (1889):

> One that never turned his back, but marched breast forward
> Never doubted clouds would break,
> Never dreamed that wrong would triumph,
> Held we fall to rise . . .
> Sleep to wake.

The recitation advocates the viewpoint pronounced by Browning's stanza, and positions the final line so as to suggest the value of seeing past obvious conditions

---

[28] See Roland Barthes, *Mythologies*, 1957 (London: Vintage Books, 2009), 149.

('fall' and 'sleep') to an ideal, cyclical and organic condition in which these things are balanced with their immediate opposites ('rise' and 'wake'). What is most significant about this passage is its effect of ideological mystification; meanings are found in opposites, and no doubts are to be found. Although the meanings of such texts are always particularly elusive, it is perhaps significant that (in addition to other changes) five words are omitted from the Browning quotation that alter its potential meaning. The original runs as follows:

> Held we fall to rise, are baffled to fight better,
> Sleep to wake.[29]

Who is being 'baffled to fight better'? Perhaps this describes what the governor is doing by reading the poem to Travis in the first place? His sentiments 'baffle' in order to make Travis go and 'fight better' in the name of the doctrine of action that maintains the lie of a good world. The governor sees 'the spark of idealism' in this young man. He can see Travis building motorways – forging new paths. Romantic idealism is, again, transformed into something Dark and insidious: new paths and new roads to be traversed by lorries bringing products, money, jobs, exploitation and 'inhumanity', all in the name of a mythic ideology of positive activity.

Armed with the governor's philosophical phrase book, Travis next attempts to save the life of a woman contemplating suicide. But the reformed humanitarian's potted quotations make no impression upon Mrs Richards (Rachel Roberts) – a poor working-class mother with no money, a family to feed and an unemployed husband. The governor's humanistic philosophy turns Travis into a mouthpiece for a phantasmagorical ideology that displaces the experience of tangible material inequalities and privations into a stoic and enlightened sense of satisfaction with 'the gift of life', 'fresh air' and 'sunshine' – those 'natural' human rights available to every free citizen – a displacement which, when contrasted with the plight of Mrs Richards, appears to be engineered to distract the needy and exploited from their privations. Turning to his book of philosophical aphorisms for guidance, Travis reads:

> Life is mostly froth and bubble,
> Two things stand like stone.
> Kindness in another's trouble,
> Courage in your own.

---

[29] Robert Browning, 'Epilogue', 1889, in *Robert Browning's Poetry*, ed. James F. Loucks and Andrew M. Stauffer (New York: W. W. Norton and Co., 1979), 485.

Having asked the writer's name, and upon being informed that Adam Lindsay Gordon was the poet, Mrs Richards takes this sentiment as evidence that the writer was a 'fool'. Artists, the implication seems to be, do not have any real answers. Being categorically divorced from the materiality of human life, yet lamenting the absence of a Golden Age that would see that materiality transcended, the products of artists – such as *O Lucky Man!* itself – are mired in that aporetic condition of guilt we saw described by Adorno in Part 1. This is the realization that the film's self-negating ending will soon confront: that art, too, is an opiate of the intellectuals.

'Revolution is the opium of the intellectuals'

As Travis observes a group of homeless people gathered around a mobile soup kitchen, some very curious graffiti is visible in the background (Figure 26). The main implication seems to be that 'revolution' (talk of revolution, or action that attempts to make a tangible and positive change in social conditions) does not 'do any good'. As such, the statement – perhaps part of the film's metalanguage – is profoundly pessimistic regarding positive agendas for political praxis. The statement also implies a distinction between 'intellectuals' and the masses, suggesting that education, and professions that foster the development of revolutionary ideologies, form a special class distinct from the people whom such ideologies profess to emancipate. In short, the slogan seems to concern,

Figure 26 'Revolution is the opium of the intellectuals'. *O Lucky Man!* (1973).

not actual revolution as a historical system of categorical events, but, rather, revolution as an 'idea' – as a rhetorical figure that prefigures and survives such actual events.

As we have seen, Romantic critical philosophy broadly agrees with this graffiti. Revolutionary praxis cannot be trusted to bring about a better world, or at least cannot safely be made a fetish object for progressive thinking. Certainly, in the bleak and threatening world of *O Lucky Man!* we can easily imagine that revolution would not make any substantial alteration to the 'goodness' of its moral and political distributions. Travis had his own 'revolution' in prison, and emerged a 'new man', but outside he finds a world just as eager to deceive, rob, confound and fling him into deadly and uncontrollable scenarios.

Seeing a woman dispensing soup to the homeless (Vivian Pickles), Travis asks if he can be of any assistance. She gives him the task of feeding another group gathered around a bonfire not far away. He is a little nervous, but she has some advice: 'It's simple: Just be yourself! Don't put on an act. They don't like that!' But this, of course, is easier said than done. Travis has never been 'himself' throughout the whole of *O Lucky Man!* Perhaps he, like many other Romantic literary figures, is a 'man without qualities' – unknown to himself, and grasping through life in search of something never to be found. As the hero now moves among the prostrate figures, a large flickering fire casts over the scene an archaic impression of social devastation. The dark and grimy underbelly of industrial capitalist Britain has now reverted to something more like a scene from Goya. The homeless do not appreciate Travis' naïve efforts to bring them comfort. One irate figure (Graham Crowden) demands that the do-gooder leave them alone. Striving to awaken some common bond of humanitarian kinship, Travis attempts a faltering but impassioned speech; but his words – 'comrades', 'charity', 'dignity', 'love', 'brothers!' – fall upon deaf ears. The homeless chase him through a desolate urban wasteland, appearing to embody a justified rage against a symbol of a world that brings about and perpetuates such a life. Yet, the impression remains that the energies of an almost revolutionary anger are misdirected against an undeserving object. The scene ends with a slow-motion shot of a trash can rolling down a slope into the camera; a cynical and animalistic underclass has snuffed the flames of humanitarian idealism.[30]

---

[30] The ambiguous valuation of 'the proletariat' is a highly significant theme in Romantic culture. Travis' failed attempt to validate his humanism by appealing to the poor echoes the experience of Romantics such as John Thelwall, friend of Wordsworth and Coleridge, whose troubling encounters with the working class exemplify a typically Romantic tension between the claims of 'education and experience', as E. P. Thompson suggests; see E. P. Thompson, *The Romantics: Wordsworth,*

In contrast to the prison governor's rhetoric, we see now that things are not so different after all. Travis' eyes have been opened to the pain and confusion proliferating in a world he so recently attempted to master. Yet, still clinging to the feeble ideology of affirmative action that permeates and supports this world, he is overwhelmed yet again by a 'reality' unfit to be understood through inherited schemas and second-hand philosophies. Travis is all too eager to adapt in order to fulfil his 'true' nature, to learn from his 'betters' and 'make use' of himself. But in a world that is beset with falsity, this desire for self-determination entails an endless wandering which makes activity itself into a kind of degradation – a perpetual deferral of authentic experience. Travis' embodiment of social affirmation only ever exacerbates inauthenticity and corrodes his desire for a utopian condition. 'Act, and therefore be', said Fichte in *The Vocation of Man* (1799). But what errors and misfortunes will Travis not suffer as a result of this incessant activity?

Despite his best efforts, Travis has had startlingly little impact on anything. Whether he aimed to come out on top of the economic and social hierarchy, or sought to transform it from the very bottom, he has met with failure. Saving his own neck has often been about as much as his agency really amounted to. Travis, like the film viewer, has been given no opportunity to find a functional orientation in the diegetic world; the protagonist's exaggerated reversal of primary drives in the final act of the film, following his release from prison, has removed even the one certainty that had given him a sense of cohesive identity: that capitalist principles of economic rationality are to be his guiding star. Without this, what is left of him? Emptied of all sense of value and purpose, he seems closer to us all – a Romantic wanderer.

A different smile

There is something curiously divided about the idea expressed in this quotation from Horkheimer: 'Freedom is not the freedom to accumulate, but the fact that

Coleridge, Thelwall (Woodbridge: The Merlin Press, 1997), 4–31, 167–8. In both cases – Thelwall and Travis – the desire for political emancipation is problematized by a thwarted myth of proletarian authenticity. After the French Revolution, Thompson explains, radicals are no longer able to justify their political programmes with a myth of the 'Holy Peasantry'; English Jacobinism gravitates towards disillusionment upon feeling the acute cultural divide that separates the emergent artist-intellectual type from the working class on whose behalf they preach the virtues of equality; see Thompson, *The Romantics*, passim. Soon after his own dispiriting failure to communicate with the subjugated classes, Thelwall retired from political life to live on a farm in Wales – a type of quietist retreat that Travis is ultimately spared due to the diegetic intervention of Lindsay Anderson himself, who resolves the film's political dilemma in a very different way.

I have no need to accumulate.'[31] His words seem to cross a rhetorical borderland between modern Western critical theory and Eastern spirituality – Marx and Zen – in a way not unfamiliar to the history of German philosophy. If Travis has been accumulating something over the course of *O Lucky Man!*, it is not material possessions, but, rather, a great deal of experience – a *Bildungsromanesk* experience of life itself, which seems now to weigh upon him. This meeting between the critique of capitalism and a certain loosely defined transcendental spirituality may account for the similarities between Romanticism and the film's oft-cited Zen motif. We are now close to that sublime smile which, as we saw, evidences an elusive moment of freedom distinct from all previous diegetic events, within which ideas of spiritual transcendence, capitalism and Romantic critique are enmeshed, and which brings Travis' journey to such an ambiguous conclusion.

With nowhere to go and with no ideal to guide him, our wanderer takes a leaflet from a man with a billboard advertising an open casting event. Travis and the man share meaningful eye contact. If the viewer has been alert to the Brechtian recycling of cast members throughout the film, they may recognize Jeremy Bulloch, the actor who played the ill-fated young man with the sports car and the man with porcine appendages in Prof Millar's clinic. In that moment of eye contact, Travis and the tout seem to recognize something – a shared destiny, or an intersecting of paths. A similar effect was created when Travis left the prison in the company of his comrades from *If. . . .* and the coffee sales training programme. Travis, it seems, is merely the film's chosen representative of some common condition. Like the tragic and bewildering news events being reported on the billboards and radios scattered throughout his adventures, other stories of absurd injustice, delusion and misery are playing out unseen all around, epitomizing modern subjective experience in the developed world.

At the audition, Travis, hero of *O Lucky Man!*, meets the artist responsible for the world in which he has his fictional existence. Now an on-screen presence, Lindsay Anderson orders subordinates to hand Travis a pile of books and a prop gun. It is as if Travis, or Malcolm McDowell himself, is being auditioned for his role in *If. . . .* Both Travis and McDowell collapse into one and the same figure, and it is impossible to decisively separate actor and character. Anderson tells Travis to 'Smile', and the public hall, which until this point had been filled with the sound of bustle and talking, falls silent. Despite the director's cool instance,

---

[31] Adorno and Horkheimer, *Towards a New Manifesto*, 16.

Travis refuses to comply. Eventually, Anderson takes a copy of the script and slaps Travis over the head. At this point the camera cuts in close to the young man's face, and that strange ghost of a smile slowly appears on his lips. The shot holds for a duration conventionally sufficient to signal the imminent ending of a film.

As suggested at the beginning of this chapter, the smile's enigmatical-ness is indicative of its critical nature. The smile is non-functional – it says nothing, it does not invite any positive effect, but, rather, creates a space of meaning, which, by its very indeterminacy, allows the film to pause long enough to end: a sublime moment of closure in openness. But this is precisely what is so parodically undermined by the joyous dance, which thereafter provides a coda, somewhat like the 'jigs' that end Elizabethan comedies.

We must look at this moment very carefully.

To begin, we might consider another of Horkheimer's aphorisms: 'To achieve the condition of an animal at the level of reflection – that is freedom. Freedom means not having to work.'[32] After being hit by Anderson, perhaps Travis, too, has achieved the condition of an animal at the level of reflection. When Travis refuses to smile, he is finally free from work. He no longer possesses an internalized desire to act – to be successful at something or, indeed, anything, according to a need imposed upon him from outside. Initially, he is still pliable. Anderson gives orders that Travis, at first, carries out without protest; but in the end, he refuses. The simplification of Travis' condition down to the direct giving of monosyllabic orders and his mute and unresisting performance has made plain the authoritarian nature of the power dynamic. Holding a gun or books by command – acts that expand the film's self-reflective intertextuality – do not force him to be at odds with himself, and he complies without apparent comprehension or pleasure, awkwardly, as if something new is stirring in him. The smile is qualitatively different, however.

The radio report that Travis heard upon his arrival at the nuclear facility stated that Zen was all about 'living in the moment' and forgetting the past and the future. 'Illumination comes suddenly', like a great flash of light. Now, mirroring the nuclear explosion, which chased Travis out of Hell, something else has happened off-screen; this time, inside Travis himself. It is a moment of stillness which is not 'rest' – not a moment justified by the prospect of gaining strength to go on, as when he visited the church, but, rather, something else: a

---

[32] Ibid., 11.

moment when the idea of going on becomes something unthinkable. Zen was not an inappropriate concept to evoke here, for it is, as Heinrich von Kleist knew better than anyone, a matter of life and death – being and nothingness. Goethe's 'Remember to Live!' contains an idea that places Romanticism in problematic proximity to capitalism. 'Remember to Live!' functions not only as a call to turn away from the prosaic everyday world in expectation of something more, but, rather, as a validation of a dialectic and pragmatic compromise – a compartmentalization of lived experience, where work and play have their proper place. Hearing these words, the Romantic sees their own grand programme of schematic values and behaviours laid out before them: 'feel, think, be free, travel, experience the new, value every moment – do not let sterile and corrupting socialisation get a single foothold.' The capitalist, however, may recognize these same values and yet arrive at a different conclusion, seeing them as a validation of that paradoxical collaborative process whereby one lives to work and works in order to live: 'feel, think, be free, travel, experience the new, value every moment – enjoy the pleasures that your vocation has allowed you to purchase as compensation for your depleted personal time and effort.' To save Romanticism from itself, then, we need something opposed to the words offered by Goethe. The Light Romantic finds freedom – a Schillerian empty infinity – in their precise antithesis, but which is, as we have seen, no less vulnerable to corruption: 'Nothing! – as if you are dead already'.

Travis' true awakening comes at the moment that is perhaps nearer to self-destruction than any of the 'close calls' he has experienced from nuclear bombs and medical experiments: the moment of defying the author himself, even if this defiance is still an authorized part of the fiction. If all art is complicit in the social totality by virtue of the very rule of its form, then the truth-content of Travis' moment of inaction is to be found, like *Mickey One*, in its potential to undo the fiction itself. His stillness transcends the order of aesthetic explanation by refusing all that is certain in a rotten world and retaining the potential to become anything at all that is different. This, as Schiller implies, is a real but defiantly 'useless' freedom.

The false ending

After Travis' climactic moment of understanding, the actors in Anderson's Brechtian satire – McDowell, Roberts, Lowe, Crowden and so on – divest themselves of their disguises and dance to Alan Price's musical reprise of the film's title theme. The film ends with a celebration, but whether it is affirming Travis' moment of enlightenment or the power of cinematic art itself to foster an enriched understanding of the world around us, neither of these interpretations seems entirely plausible.

In Chapter 1, I disagreed with Frank Cunningham's conclusion that Travis finally accepts an organic and changing universe. Cunningham seems much closer to the mark when he identifies, on the way to this conclusion, 'Anderson's disgust with arbitrary systems of thought'[33] – when people unthinkingly adopt externally imposed maxims, whatever they may be. What is left when such systems are stripped away is not (as Cunningham interprets) a sublime acceptance of a contradictory and uncontrollable world, but, rather, a moment of profoundly critical negation, a moment in which all participation comes to a halt, leaving a truly 'free' individual standing mute in a condition of inactive indecision. This rereading seems to bring *O Lucky Man!* closer to Adorno than Brecht, Coleridge or Blake, and a different kind of Romanticism. Cunningham reads the final dance as a utopian promise – a vision of humanity when 'ideologies have been abandoned'.[34] How, we may ask, does such a triumphant ending tally with the cynicism and satirical vitriol to be found throughout the trilogy? What place do party balloons have in this supposedly 'ideology-free' reverie?[35]

The dance that ends the film really makes sense only if it is interpreted ironically. The moment when Travis and Anderson embrace can be understood, not as a sincere homecoming, but as a knowing disavowal of the narrative authority that constructs and authenticates such moments. Like F. W. Murnau's *Der letzte mann* (1924), the film ends with a generic gesture the tragical force of which comes from its very overdetermination as a 'happy ending'. What *O Lucky Man!* provides, to those inclined to read it this way, is an affirmative catharsis that resounds with an aura of absurdity and untruth – a playful acknowledgement (to return to Rancière's reading of Conrad) of the lie which ends all stories, no matter their politics.

Perhaps the most significant element of this ending is the diegetic presence of Anderson himself as the film's avowed 'author'. For John Izod, et al., this apparition is the Jungian 'archetypical figure of the wise old man', like the 'priest,

---

[33] Cunningham, 'Lindsay Anderson's *O Lucky Man!* and the Romantic Tradition', 260.
[34] Ibid., 261.
[35] Although some commentators read the party balloons to be symbolic of the easily punctured 'illusions' from which Travis has finally been liberated; Hedling, *Lindsay Anderson*, 125.

doctor, magician or holy fool' who confronts and transforms the hero with their aura or 'mana'.[36] But Anderson here seems more like God the creator. He steps onto the screen in an act of self-creation possible only for an artist or a God. The slap he gives Travis is, in this sense, more akin to the climax of Elgar's *The Dream of Gerontius* (1901), in which a similar moment of acoustic 'impact' condemns the Everyman protagonist to Purgatory – a deferred judgement over an ambiguously misspent life. Like God in Elgar's musical interpretation, Anderson does not appear in order to aid the hero on his journey, but, rather, to impart a sublime and painful judgement, difficult to understand, and which brings everything material to a close. As Gogol foretold, our misguided hero has finally been thrown down in the dust and made to 'kneel before the wisdom of the heavens'.

In the tradition of the *Bildungsroman*, 'the more unaware and bewildered the hero, the wiser and more far-sighted the narrator.'[37] In this moment, Travis is perhaps the most bewildered and yet the wisest we have ever seen him. What does this say about Anderson? There is something sinister about the director in this scene (Figure 27). He seems commanding, as perhaps an artist (and more so, a film director) should be, but this quality steps over into the brutal. As the sinister and treacherous workings of 'fate' throughout Travis' adventures have prepared us to understand, it is not only our protagonist who has a dark side, but also our auteur – the self-confessed condition of the text itself and its powers of critique.

Figure 27 Lindsay Anderson as the authoritarian artist. *O Lucky Man!* (1973).

---

[36] Izod, et al., *Lindsay Anderson*, 162; see also Hedling, *Lindsay Anderson*, 122.
[37] Moretti, *The Way of the World*, 135.

The spirit of destiny that has motivated Travis' adventures has subjected him time and again to the evil effects of its influence. By the final scene, his desire for growth and success has become an aimless and non-teleological wandering. The mythic pronouncement made by the film's title has become a mocking lie. It is almost as if Travis is cursed, reflecting the condition of a cursed capitalist world: 'On the one hand, the world contains opportunities enough for success. On the other hand, everything is bewitched, as if under a spell. If the spell could be broken, success would be a possibility.'[38] But what is the nature of the 'spell' bewitching Travis in this film? Why is he so unlucky? This evil influence results, in fact, from the text's authored and allegorical nature – from its very 'meaningfulness' as a work of art – which is dependent upon the presence of its authorial voice. It is a voice that makes itself appear through Brechtian fragments and excesses, until the final scene, when the wizard steps out from behind the curtain in the recognizable and awe-inspiring form of that honest liar, Lindsay Anderson.

Art, the conclusion seems to be, is far from innocent regarding the deceptions, promises and cruelties of the modern world. Goethe's vision of *Bildungsroman* offers an ideological reconciliation between humanity and nature, an acceptance of the necessary conditions of life as part of self-creation: an 'art of life'. Anderson denies his protagonist a similar experience of mythic affirmation. But when art flirts with its own failure in this way, it remains able to conduct a revealing kind of self-critique. It determines Anderson's appearance in the film, not only as the most seductive monster of them all – one whose mysterious calls for 'Books' and 'Gun' contain a desirable sense of mystery, exciting viewers familiar with the iconography of *If....* – but his appearance also lays bare the mechanism of terror which runs through the whole system. The violence of Lindsay Anderson's director does not disguise itself. It is an honest terror, inviting uncertain reflection rather than acceptance. In this sense, then, he does 'free' his puppet protagonist.

Back at the nuclear plant, Travis' interrogator foretold his ultimate fate: 'There are three things you can be sure of: the pain is not going to stop; you will remain conscious; and in the end you will sign.' What he did not explain is what that 'signing' – the smile – would mean: a transcendence, within the category, of what that act of complicity means. Adorno wrote about this often. It is a transcendence made possible by the aesthetic mode and the self-negating presence of Anderson himself. The artist must appear as a tyrant in order to reveal the tyrannical in general, and so reveal the space to be filled by something new and uncertain.

[38] Adorno and Horkheimer, *Towards a New Manifesto*, 14.

6

Dialectic of enlightenment

The Missouri Breaks (1976)

The Missouri Breaks (1976) promised to be Arthur Penn's most commercially viable production. Jack Nicholson and Marlon Brando star as the leader of a band of horse rustlers and the ruthless 'regulator' hired to hunt them down, respectively. This pairing of two of Hollywood's biggest celebrities in a revisionist genre production was a shrewd filmmaking decision. Brando and Nicholson were at the height of their careers, having recently delivered lauded performances in films such as *The Godfather* (1972), *Last Tango in Paris* (1972), *Chinatown* (1974) and *One Flew Over the Cuckoo's Nest* (1975). Even the atmospheric and nostalgic soundtrack was written by John Williams, fresh from the success of *Jaws* (1975). Yet, as the result of a remarkable discontinuity at its heart, *The Missouri Breaks* failed to realize its potential both financially and culturally. Returning to the inverted hero/villain dynamic of *Bonnie and Clyde* (1967), the film follows Nicholson's sympathetic outlaw Tom Logan, whilst the representative of the law is an eccentric, cruel and irrational murderer. In one of Marlon Brando's most unusual performances, the villain Robert E. Lee Clayton presents a Mephistophelian combination of absurdism, terror and allure, which complicates the film's broadly genre-realist aesthetic. As contemporary reviews suggested, Brando's bizarre characterization is one major reason why the film was not a success.[1] The entire dynamic of hero and villain becomes fatally imbalanced.

Like other films considered in this book, the judgement of aesthetic failure not only creates space for alternative critical interpretations of the text's meaning, but also plays into the rhetorical significance of failure as a Romantic theme. Beyond

---

[1] See Vincent Canby, '"Missouri Breaks," Offbeat Western' [sic], in *The New York Times*, 20 May 1976. https://www.nytimes.com/1976/05/20/archives/missouri-breaks-offbeat-western.html; accessed 1 March 2021. Fredric Jameson judged that the film remains trapped in the 'pathos of a self-pitying and individualistic vision of history'; Jameson, *Signatures of the Visible*, 67.

key thematic elements in the narrative, the tensions between the film's hero and villain – their characterization and represented actions – make it possible to read *The Missouri Breaks* as a Romantic critique of capitalism. Where Clayton can become an embodiment of the irrational and Darkly Romantic 'spirit' of capitalism, as a form of Enlightenment returning to mythology, Logan's own plight as an ineffectual hero – deferring all action against evil until a moment when action is revealed as an evil itself – can be illuminated in reference to the schema of Light Romanticism.

Disproportionate punishments

The Missouri Breaks begins by establishing an unjust social system. David Braxton (John McLiam) is a landowner and community leader in Montana who has begun hanging criminals without trial. This is powerfully demonstrated by the death of Sandy (Hunter von Leer), a member of a horse-rustling gang, whose execution will soon be reported to his fellows by Little Todd (Randy Quaid). The landowner's daughter, Jane (Kathleen Lloyd), clarifies the 'message' to be taken from all this: a cavalier attitude towards the taking of human life in the name of law and order is a necessary condition for material success. Jane, who confronts her father about his cruelty and unfairness, suggests that affluence and social distinction are bought at the cost of losing something essential to an implied conception of humanity itself. Jane's opinions overlap with those of the film's metalanguage, and, in one sense, develop the themes of capital and ethics woven throughout *The Missouri Breaks*: labour, profit and the morality of the methods used to orchestrate these things. The film explores means and ends, and the variety of autonomies, tensions and imbalances between the two.

Compared to *Mickey One* (1965) and *O Lucky Man!* (1973), the narrative is conventional in structure. It follows the criminal enterprises of the gang, led by Logan and Calvin (Harry Dean Stanton), as they recover from the loss of their former comrade. They have ambitions to expand their rustling operation across the Canadian border and establish a new base on land owned by the reviled Braxton. At the same time, the latter hires the infamous freelancer Robert E. Lee Clayton to protect his property and hound out the criminals (Figure 28). Whilst most of the gang are away in Canada, and Clayton's suspicions fall on Braxton's

Figure 28 The eccentric 'regulator' Robert E. Lee Clayton (Marlon Brando). *The Missouri Breaks* (1976).

new tenants, Logan begins a romantic relationship with Jane. Clayton eventually hunts down and kills the gang members with ruthless efficiency, leading to a final confrontation with Logan.

At the beginning of the film, the rustlers are represented as a contained, autonomous and interactive social unit functioning according to broad principles of equality in privilege and labour. They prosper under the need to work according to common goals, but also find room for flexibility and an emotional, critical and quite literally 'playful' articulation of individual desires and impulses. The gang joke with each other, play tricks and pranks, laugh whilst working outside in the sun; these naïve and nostalgic scenes are accompanied by equally playful non-diegetic music, which validates the represented behaviour. The group displays a loose and informal hierarchical structure, with Logan and Calvin directing most of the gang's endeavours. Yet, at several points in the film, we are shown that each member of the group has the opportunity, and the self-actualized inclination, to voice his opinion to the whole. Logan and Calvin are willing to act upon suggestions made by the others. The decision to rob the train, which eventually bankrolls their purchasing a share of Braxton's land, results from an angry outburst by Little Todd. A practical, profitable and successful action that benefits the group as a whole is shown here to result from an emotional and democratic source and be raised as a part of an open communal discussion.

Although Calvin is a kind of authority figure, refraining from partaking in the jokes and play-fights of his fellows, his dialogue, clothes, behaviours and social status are not markedly differentiated from those of the gang as a whole. Typically, he does not give orders, but makes requests based upon motives for 'safe' results. For example, he asks with a 'please' for a fellow member of the gang to carry tools down from the roof of the cabin, instead of throwing them. Calvin does not act as an authority figure who stands apart from the gang, precisely, but, rather, as an embodiment of a kind of 'rational' individual whose thoughtful engagement with the concerns and priorities of the social order is alert to the contradictions and lack of control over outcomes, which stands as its eternal Other, and, as a criminal, becomes a social 'outsider' as a means of escaping that contradiction. This separation of the outsider individual from the legitimate social order is expressed as a kind of trauma through the inclusion of Calvin's story about the fate of his dog. He tells Logan that his faith in so-called 'honest' work died the day his uncle killed his dog for putting its tongue on a pat of butter. The dog story encapsulates Calvin's loss of faith in the dominant order – both its professed rational method of granting a standard of living equal to the quality and quantity of labour practised by each individual, and its valuation of the hierarchical paternal authority on which that system of professed equality is based. The implicit claim that the organization of life under the contemporary capitalist system derives from a just and coherent value system is cruelly undercut by the emotionally affecting disproportionality of the dog's punishment. It reflects the injustice done to Sandy by Braxton and the system he represents.

But the utopian, 'outsider' space created by the outlaw gang is complicated by a sense of fragility, as well as a certain ironic tone in the representation achieved through the use of generic tropes, which, in an almost Brechtian sense, accentuate its fictiveness and historical abstraction. This effect is particularly notable in the musical score. Much like Penn's Bonnie Parker and Clyde Barrow, then, Logan and his gang are flawed and 'lovable rogues' – romanticized outlaws perched precariously on the edge of a violent and oppressive legal system that will ultimately seek to destroy them. The allure of the outsider existence is shown, in Penn's films, to be inseparable from the threat of assimilation or complete punitive annihilation. As in *Bonnie and Clyde*, that punishment will be carried out by agents acting on behalf of the social order, and their methods will be shown to be as alien, shocking and cruel as the heroes' own actions are, in turn, sympathetic and – as Robin Wood puts it – 'human'.[2]

---

[2] Wood, *Arthur Penn*, 71.

Atrophied society and its discontents

In order to raise the money needed to commence their enterprise, the gang decide to rob a train. The light-hearted and comic tone of this episode creates an atmosphere of 'fun' around the gang that contrasts with the comparatively bleak opening scenes.

Logan forces a train guard (Danny Goldman) to open a safe and hand him the money. The fact that Logan accomplishes this daring feat alone, takes the trouble to learn the guard's name and escapes without violence contributes to the construction of audience sympathies towards Logan and the values and attitudes that he embodies. Logan tells the guard, named Nelson, to uncouple the mail car from the rest of the train, in order to make escape easier; but the panicking official says: 'I'm not sure I'm able to do it.' Nelson insists that, because he is a clerk, he is not mechanically minded. The shock of being robbed is defensively and humorously displaced by anxiety over being asked to do something beyond the skills and responsibilities associated with his vocation. Opening the safe to get the money, too, Nelson says: 'I'm not permitted to touch this.' Nelson's reaction is suggestive of a social tendency to reduce the capabilities of any individual to the patterns assigned to them as part of the wider economic system. The intrusion of a rogue element – Logan with his gun – encourages Nelson to hold all the more firmly onto the security and displacement of responsibility that such patterns provide. Later in the film we will see how Braxton's elderly manservant (Vern Chandler) would rather die than see his master killed. Under pressure, Nelson is transformed into a mere operant of coded responses. Perhaps this train guard, for all his generic and comedic elements, is an ancillary symptom of something fundamentally 'wrong' with the established social order of economic rationality, which has been rejected by Logan, Calvin and the rest the gang. The 'good' and 'responsible' worker is reduced to a clownish figure.

Other filmic elements contribute to this vision of an inflexible and atrophied society. For the gang's next daring endeavour, they steal horses from the Canadian Mounties. The choice of target is significant, for the Mounties – 'the best police in the world' – function as an embodiment of social ordering. More than this, however, Calvin's plan is predicated upon recognizing and exploiting the fictive nature of ideology itself. 'Them Mounties scare me, Cal', says Logan, and Calvin replies, 'They scare everybody. That's why it's going to be so easy.' The widespread recognition of the Mounties' authority means that no one considers them viable targets for rustling. Having seen the myth for what it is, Calvin is convinced that 'the powers that be' are vulnerable to exploitation. As Pierre Bourdieu famously theorized, the magic wall of social distinction doesn't protect the powerful if it is not recognized by the subjugated.[3] Calvin's raiders eventually steal the horses whilst the Mounties are singing in a chapel. The inflexibility of social institutions is what enables the inevitable cracks in the system to be exploited, as Calvin explicitly states when the rustlers finally make their move: 'Now they're locked in with Jesus.'

In a sense, then, the gang are entrepreneurs.[4] They identify and exploit opportunities for profit, considering each one beforehand in reference to potential risks and gains. Although their criminal activities are structured according to capitalist principles of action, the egalitarian and pacifistic values of their community are contrasted with the hierarchical and violent world of Braxton's legitimate society. The adoption of certain mercenary tactics is acceptable provided that no one is hurt; Nelson and the Mounties are left unharmed, and the postal service and the police are powerful enough to take the loss. But if Adorno and Horkheimer read Odysseus as a paradigm for the capitalistic entrepreneur – one who calculates and takes risks in order to succeed; who adapts and goes without in order to win through; whose gains are morally justified by the risks and strenuous efforts involved in the process of acquiring them[5] – then *The Missouri Breaks* presents, conversely, the cruel undoing of that empowering myth. Logan and the gang's own 'Odyssey', to deal in stolen horses right under the nose of the Cyclops Braxton, is soon ended by Marlon Brando's ruthless and diabolic regulator, who comes to resemble all the monstrous creatures of the islands in Homer.

As mentioned in Chapter 1, some 'more Romantic' films can refuse to designate any positive ideal of political organization. Braxton's farmstead is represented very differently from the criminal gang, but neither is suggested to be a practicable social system. Both groups are flawed, but in different ways: where the former is anachronistic, harmful and self-destructive, the latter is conflicted, besieged and challenged to survive in the face of antagonistic forces.

First, Braxton's home contains features suggestive of anachronism and decadence: a chandelier that is too large for the low ceiling, a decrepit servant

---

[3] See Pierre Bourdieu, *Language and Symbolic Power*, 1991 (Cambridge: Polity Press, 2018), 50–1.
[4] In these terms, *The Missouri Breaks* functions as a satirical and revisionist example of 'the professional western' sub-genre, in which 'expert' protagonists band together for financially motivated endeavours – a trope discussed by Will Wright in *Sixguns and Society: A Structural Study of the Western* (Berkeley: University of California Press, 1975), 97.
[5] Adorno and Horkheimer, *Dialectic of Enlightenment*, 57–62.

who would rather die than see his master murdered and a library where quality is measured by size (Braxton equates the number of books on his shelves, rather than their content, with the degree of civility they represent). These features attest to a condition of lived existence out of proportion to frontier life – conditions that Braxton himself simultaneously valorizes, mourns and seeks to defend. With its opulent décor and loyal domestic servants, Braxton's home evokes a European past. This domain is also self-destructive due to the ultimate effects of the actions Braxton takes to defend it. The employment of Clayton leads, through a loose and suggestive logic of cause and effect, to the landowner's own eventual enfeeblement and ruin. Adorno and Horkheimer suggested that the standard of living enjoyed by any individual under capitalism essentially corresponds to how rigidly they are 'bound up with the system'.[6] Conversely, if the system becomes crippled, then also crippled are those who have used it to climb higher than others, for they have further to fall. By the end of *The Missouri Breaks*, Braxton's pact with the devil is shown to come at a terrible price, as Clayton's actions rebound upon his employer.

But, again, there is no positive alternative. Logan's community of outsiders is also a flawed environment. It displays several characteristics that render it partial, riven and unstable. The comic interludes of jocular camaraderie and playful teasing among the gang are, by their generic conventionality, liable to be read as somewhat hollow and inauthentic. The nostalgic mood of the gang's joyful moments is mixed with a critique of that very utopianism itself, proclaiming its insufficiency to cope with a changing and hostile present. The gang is exclusively male, and its precariousness results partly from the total subtraction of women from their community. In a later section we will see how the introduction of a female causes a period of profound reflection at odds with the aims and identity of the overall group. Jane's arrival precipitates a crisis in Logan's ability to act – to be the 'hero' the film needs him to be, and make a decisive contribution towards the resolution of the narrative and its dramatic tensions. The problematic encounter between the gang environment and an autonomous female presence happens when the sense of unity provided by that exclusively male unit is momentarily postponed. Jane, as an Other, opens the door for something genuinely New and disruptive for Logan.

But the reigning totality will have its say, too. The symbolic significance of the farmstead as an enclave for the interaction, development and strengthening

[6] Ibid., 150.

of alternative value systems and social relations is recognized as a threat by the legitimate social order. The liminal community formed by the gang is, therefore, besieged by forces seeking its destruction.

Evoking the spirit of capitalism

Early in the film, Logan laments that a criminal such as Sandy would, only a few years ago, not have been hanged for his offence. Lenient punishments are a thing of the past, and it seems as though there is 'something new in the air'. Throughout *The Missouri Breaks*, that 'something new' is embodied by one particular character. The professed difficulty of making a living on the frontier appears to demand a willingness, from both legitimate businessmen and those who exploit them, to take expedient measures. This 'hardening of life' under extreme economic conditions, linked to the historical development of the American myth, is condensed and parodied within the Mephistophelian character Robert E. Lee Clayton (Figure 29).

According to a mourner at the funeral of Pete Marker – Braxton's former 'ramrod' – the late employee 'personified the American West in the days of its rowdy youth'. This encourages an interpretation of the estate's newest arrival, Clayton, as a personification of the West in its 'new spirit'. Unleashed by the system, Clayton becomes the white blood cell of the capitalist establishment, purging all threats to the economic and ideological standards upon which the

Figure 29 Clayton (Marlon Brando) as a Mephistophelian spirit of capitalism. *The Missouri Breaks* (1976).

system depends for its survival. Yet, the process also entails a fatal autoimmune condition, as the civilizing process makes itself felt as the performance of a barbaric mythology. Adorno and Horkheimer's assertion that enlightenment must return to myth is supported by Joseph Schumpeter when he writes: 'Capitalist rationality does not do away with sub- or super-rational impulses. It merely makes them get out of hand by removing the restraint of sacred or semi-sacred tradition.'[7] It is only fitting, therefore, that Clayton's introduction contain something of the spiritual, not long before things really do get 'out of hand'.

During the funeral, Jane goes outside and surveys the rolling Montana scenery. In a moment of narrative pause, audiences are prompted to share Jane's thoughtful experience at the border of civilization, between society and nature, suffused with all the mythic significance and symbolic power of the Western idea. Accompanied by the faint sound of a chapel organ, two packhorses come rattling down a slope towards the house. When they descend from on high, there is a sense of spiritual evocation as the unaccompanied animals draw up outside Braxton's door. Suddenly, a human head with grey hair standing on end appears sticking out sideways from behind the front of the horse. Jane is shocked at this unexpected apparition, which immediately introduces itself as 'Lee Clayton'. The new arrival explains that riding suspended sideways on his horse is a precaution against being spotted, but the overall effect is one of comical strangeness. It is as if Clayton uncannily emerges from the horse itself – protruding like a second head.

The animal symbolism used to represent Clayton (he is frequently associated with birds, horses and other creatures throughout the film) serves multiple functions, some of which are too obvious to be worth dwelling upon at length. One that is particularly pertinent, however, concerns the link between Clayton as a reputedly successful freelance worker and the social Darwinism that directs his behaviour. His underhand violence whilst working in Braxton's interests takes the 'survival of the fittest' mentality to immoral extremes. Despite his strangeness, therefore, Clayton is, at heart, primarily an economic agent who finds his significance in a functional relationship with Braxton's world of business and economic rationality. This is suggested as soon as Jane asks: 'Who shall I say is calling?' and the visitor replies, curtly: 'Lee Clayton. I just said that.' Speaking in short, functional statements that suggest no time for social pleasantries, the visitor says he is 'From Wyoming' and 'Here on business'. Clayton's mild

---

[7] Schumpeter, *Capitalism, Socialism and Democracy*, 129.

impatience is suggestive; for unnecessary repetition is not appreciated by this agent who will, throughout the film, pride himself on his efficiency and professionalism.

Clayton praises Braxton's library, stating that readers should devote themselves only to those books that will help them understand the difference between 'right' and 'wrong', 'otherwise how are we to find our paradise amongst the stars?' Several things are happening here: (1) Clayton is adopting, in twisted and imitative form, the discourse and registers of Braxton himself. Absorbing the evidence of the bookshelves, Clayton has, rather like Travis in *O Lucky Man!*, adapted to master his environment. It is almost as if Clayton had seen, as the audience had seen earlier in the film, Braxton's pride in his library. (2) Clayton is proclaiming (perhaps ironically) the positivist doctrine that truth can be discovered by appealing to what has been handed down by tradition. This is a primary dictum of capitalist ideology, since the justification for the legitimate dominance of that economic system is predicated upon the fact that it currently exists – the positivist Darwinian fallacy that whatever simply survives is the best of all unrealized alternatives. (3) Finally, Clayton is suggesting, in his evocation of a 'paradise among the stars', that his own being might be a Miltonesque 'fallen angel' cultural type. He seems very Mephistophelian, having been summoned by Braxton's Faust, who doesn't fully understand his own desires and actions, as well as their implications. These interpretive possibilities create a supernatural atmosphere around the new arrival, which is not refuted by Brando's idiosyncratic performance. Is Clayton the devil in human form? When he contemplates a burning cabin later in the film, he says: 'I'd like about anything but getting burned up.' Perhaps the fires of Hell are all too familiar?

With the wake still in progress, Clayton apologizes for his inopportune arrival. Yet, within seconds he chastises his new employer for neglecting to terrorize useful information from Sandy before his execution: 'You pampered the man.' Clayton's devotion to his job is shown to exist alongside a sociopathic disregard for morality and convention. To everyone's horror, he reaches into the coffin and rhetorically gesticulates with the corpse as a means of emphasizing his argument.

After Clayton leaves, there is a moment of shocked silence. The assembled company are amused and disconcerted, but Braxton is quick to assure them that his new employee comes with the highest recommendations. Anecdotes and jokes then pour forth from the erstwhile mourners concerning this infamous regulator, and a rowdy discussion ensues concerning Clayton's attributes and eccentricities. Jane leaves the room, followed shortly by her father. The strong implication created by the timing of their exits during the dialogue is that whilst Jane is affronted by the jocular discussion of Clayton's marksmanship, and, therefore, his association with violence and death, Braxton himself is ashamed of having to rely upon the assistance of a man whose eccentric conduct – including liberal use of lavender perfume – has attained the status of common knowledge and become a subject worthy of derision. Despite Clayton's reputation as an effective worker, there is also something here from which Braxton shrinks. Although a decidedly alien figure in the world of 'civilized' society, Clayton nevertheless plays a vital role in the economic system; he is a 'regulator', literally a guarantor of order and stability. Perhaps his eccentricity, and Braxton's negative response, allegorizes the disavowed immorality of what must be 'regulated' in the first place. Braxton's lack of tolerance for his new employee's conduct becomes – like Ed Castle's obsession with purity in *Mickey One* – evidence of some deeper underlying corruption. Clayton is something unleashed by Braxton, but something he is ultimately unable to countenance or control. It is in this sense, then, that he can be understood as an 'evil' embodiment of the irrational positivist and instrumentalist spirit of capitalism and its violent and authoritarian relation to objective reality.

The tension between reason and irrationalism in capitalism is most clearly recognized in the contradictory attempt to reconcile the two most basic imperatives of economic rationality: maximum efficiency of means and the maximum attainment of ends.[8] To act according to both requires a fundamental cognitive dissonance. Critics of capitalism often speak of the modern worker as one whose lived experience – extending this split condition of rationality – becomes divided into a work life and a private life. As André Gorz summarizes, 'professional success becomes the means of achieving private comfort and pleasures that have no relation with the qualities demanded by professional life.'[9] The result is a schizophrenic lived experience, organized in accordance with contradictory value judgements: 1) equating rational conduct with economic imperatives; and 2) seeing work to be a mere necessary sacrifice, tolerated on account of the need to earn money and secure the pleasure and free time it affords. The irrational figure who accepts these mutually contradictory positions is, according to Adorno and Horkheimer, 'already virtually a Nazi' by virtue of

---

[8] See Ernest Mandel, *Late Capitalism*, 1972 (London: NLB, 1975), 510.
[9] Gorz, *Critique of Economic Reason*, 36.

their willingness to hold two different ideas of 'right' at the same time.[10] The good worker is completely committed to their job, as every good manager expects; yet, they avowedly work in order to afford to enjoy time spent away from work. These contradictory maxims must be upheld by a subject who embodies the ideal of economic rationality. Clayton can be read as a grotesque actualization of this schizophrenic adherence to opposing modes of life. He is obsessed with his task and yet treats his employer with derision. We see him relax after a hard day's stalking and killing by birdwatching, eating a hearty meal at Braxton's table and taking a foamy bubble bath.

Alongside this divided personality, Clayton displays qualities of instrumentalism – the disavowal of objective autonomy according to the pragmatic needs of the subject.[11] Clayton didn't think twice about grabbing a corpse from a coffin to make a point about crime and punishment, for example. But a more obvious sign of this instrumentalism, as a fetishization of 'technique', is Clayton's Creedmoor rifle. The regulator's preferred method of killing is determined, in spite of the moral objections raised by Logan during their first meeting, by the simple fact that it 'accomplishes the task'. It doesn't matter that his prey, guilty of any crime warranting the death penalty or not, is given no opportunity to plead their case, make peace with God nor write a letter to their loved ones. Their executioner is unburdened with the need to look them in the eye – 'That, there; that makes all the difference', according to Logan. For Clayton, however, the thing that really makes all the difference is simply technique: 'the fact that it accomplishes the task'. All other considerations are disposable.

Throughout his tenure at Braxton's estate, Clayton makes numerous references to contracts, efficiency and vocational pride. His sense of self is not hampered by any anxiety over the division of labour. The mythic valuation of commitment evoked by his song to Little Todd – 'Life's Railway to Heaven' – mirrors that of the economic system which it is Clayton's job to defend. Like this hymn expressive of frontier spirit, Clayton never doubts his professional purpose nor his ability to carry it out. He runs on rails, unable to swerve from any appointed task, to which he devotes himself with an ironic and gleeful fanaticism. He is blind to the big picture – a fully autonomous agent who mistakes, with knowing relish, his own particular role in a larger economic system for the totality of

---

[10] Adorno and Horkheimer, *Dialectic of Enlightenment*, 155.
[11] See Ibid., 9. Instrumentalism might be compared to the 'subjective occasionalism' that Carl Schmitt used to characterize what I have, in turn, called Dark Romanticism; see Chapter 3.

that system and the value it possesses. Once his goal has been defined, every aspect of reality transforms into merely an adjunct to, or irrelevant frame for, its achievement; this includes those elements without which the goal would become meaningless. 'The real idol of late capitalism', wrote Ernest Mandel, 'is . . . the "specialist" who is blind to any overall context; the philosophical counterpart of such technological expertise is neo-positivism.'[12] Like this 'idol of late capitalism', Clayton is a specialist whose obsession with performance makes him wilfully blind to context, even to the extent of ignoring the intentions and wishes of his employer. Braxton gave Clayton his task, but now that the task exists, Braxton can go to hell. 'Always finish the work', Clayton aphorizes, 'and I don't give a damn whether or not I get paid.' For money cannot interest a man for whom the ideology of work is allowed to run to its illogical conclusion. Immediately before this statement, Clayton allegorized his task as the need to deal with a group of troublesome bats in a barn. The best way, Clayton says, is to trap all the bats inside the barn by waiting until sunrise. What exactly happens next is not related to Braxton, owner of the metaphorical barn, but at the end of the film, when Clayton attacks the gang's hideout, we will see him conclude his fable – by burning it down.

Clayton's 'bat hunt' functions as a metaphor for the unswerving devotion of the capitalist functionary whose blinkered devotion to efficient work entails a total disregard for anything beyond the confines of its self-contained and autonomous kingdom of means and ends. After dismissing Clayton for taking his job too seriously, Braxton immediately turns and berates his remaining employees for not working hard enough. The 'happy medium' that might be implied to exist somewhere between these two extreme degrees of commitment with which a worker can apply themselves to their job is invalidated by the near simultaneous presence of both, the ludicrousness of the contrast, and Braxton's assumed inability to see the continuum, which makes them merely variations of one and the same principle.

Law and disorder

On the surface, Clayton is a bricolage. His cultural hybridity is recognizable from the native American theme in his appearance, his somewhat unusual

---

[12] Mandel, *Late Capitalism*, 508.

Irish accent and his adoption of various costumes and disguises throughout the film. Like Odysseus, Clayton's method involves the transformative use of alien behaviours and outward appearances. He disguises himself as a preacher or an old maid in the same way that a hunter might break up their form with branches and leaves; yet, over the course of the film, the functional logic of such disguises conflicts with the absurdity and unconvincingness of their diegetic representation. When leading Little Todd's horse back to the gang's camp, Clayton wears a wide-brimmed farmer's hat. Later, Braxton finds him eating dinner dressed in white shirt, formal cap and braces, chewing a carrot. He plays typically Western instruments: the banjo and the harmonica. His very name – Robert E. Lee – is an appropriation.[13] All this material is adopted piecemeal, by a figure whose very existence seems to mock the idea of 'character' itself (and perhaps this brings us back to the reason why the film was not more of a critical and commercial success). This heterogeneity can be attributed, in part, to Brando's own performance choices: 'I don't understand who this character is', the actor admitted, 'I think he should be completely different every time we see him.'[14] There may be some connection here to the old Christian belief holding that the Devil, lacking the ability to 'create', as God creates, can only appropriate what already exists. The resulting ontology of evil is a perpetual presence in all things through ironic abstraction, like a mirror opposite of an omniscient deity.[15] In similar fashion, Clayton re-creates for himself, from bits and pieces, the exterior signs necessary to express a sense of identity.

Yet, this identity is also paradoxical, being both multiple and singular; Clayton is a chaotic melange of absorbed cultural elements, and, simultaneously, a single-minded embodiment of capitalist principles of action. Yes, Clayton is different every time we see him, but he is also always the same. Clayton's all-embracing absorption of difference marks the authoritarian pull of the unifying drive for totality – to bring the multiplicity of objective reality together under one name; as Adorno and Horkheimer note, even the idea of 'acceptance' can be articulated as an authoritarian impulse: 'the miracle of integration, the permeant act of grace by the authority who receives the defenceless person – once he has swallowed his

---

[13] From the infamous General in Chief of the Armies of the Confederate States, defender of the rights of slave owners.
[14] Cited in Wood, *Arthur Penn*, 234.
[15] Incidentally, one of the best places to observe this 're-creational' theological metaphysic at work is the music of Franz Liszt, particularly the final movements of the Piano Sonata in B minor (1854) and *Faust Symphony* (1857).

rebelliousness – signifies Fascism.'[16] Clayton's cultural appropriations give him a slippery identity as a Mephistophelian unifying force, one that his professional attitude directly allies with capitalism and its principles of rationality, as well as a broadly defined atmosphere of immorality and violence.

So, although Clayton functions as a generic representative of the law, he is also estranged – typically enough for Penn's films – from the classical paradigm of value ascription. Clayton's actions are seemingly at odds with ideas of justice, fairness, equality and dignity. Perhaps Robin Wood is wrong to suggest, therefore, that Brando's creation is the classical Western hero – defender of abstract justice – taken to its logical conclusion.[17] The murderous 'regulator' is closer to a metaphorical embodiment of the powers that defend capitalism by displaying no interest in 'the Law' at all.

From the outset, Clayton possesses an uncanny ability to discern the gang's true intentions. His professional intuition is unerringly accurate, as Logan and the film audience know all too well, and this undaunted certainty contributes to the film's ambiguous attitude concerning the value of instrumental thinking. No one ever accused the spirit of capitalism of being ineffectual. Logan's nemesis is, indeed, a force to be reckoned with.

Clayton's actions are often unpredictable. His behaviour follows hypothetical internal calculations, which are mismatched with the shocking representation of their results. We see Clayton do many bizarre things, yet each of them can be rationalized; indeed, he is sometimes at pains to explain them to other characters. His head grotesquely emerges from a horse's flank. Why? To prevent him being spotted whilst approaching the house. He is willing to burn down valuable property. Why? To kill some unwanted pests. He chases and impales a rabbit with a flying star, to practice its use as a weapon. He attacks the gang's hideout dressed as an old woman, to prevent his being spotted and recognized for the danger he presents. Although these interpretive hypotheses broadly make sense when encountered in their cinematic context, the actions themselves are, frankly, bizarre.

Clayton's final attack on the gang's cabin, for instance, seems somehow both archaic and modern. It is barbaric, yet deftly calculated. Faced with the prospect of assaulting an isolated cabin with an unknown number of criminal occupants, Clayton's strategy involves suspending a rope across the cabin, attaching to it a

---

[16] Adorno and Horkheimer, *Dialectic of Enlightenment*, 154.
[17] Wood, *Arthur Penn*, 173.

bottle of combustible fluid, running this bottle along the rope until it reaches the cabin and igniting it with a rifle. Clayton's attack is simultaneously ingenious, expertly determined, terrifyingly effective, and rather absurd. Like the scene of hanging, which begins the film, we are shown none of the diegetic preparations that proceed, explain and, in a sense, justify this act of violence. The violence that matters in a capitalist society is always already underway. By the time we realize what is happening, we have lost our chance to understand how it came about. The ultimate note of absurdity is struck by Clayton's unexplained appearance as an old woman. The costume choice is seemingly irrelevant, and simply renders the hunter's ancient technique of disguise the incomprehensible by-product of some arbitrary instrumentalism.

What is to be done, by an outsider such as Logan, when such madly efficient forces of darkness are set upon his tail?

Logan's condition

By the final act of *The Missouri Breaks*, Clayton has killed almost the entire gang. One was drowned in a river after being pulled off his horse, another was shot through the wall of a public outhouse, yet another whilst having sex and Calvin, startled from his bed by the cabin fire, was brutally impaled through the eye with a flying star. None of these victims were armed or posed any violent threat. The regulator's devastating arsenal found its targets at moments of profound human vulnerability: defecation, fornication and sleep. Only Logan is left alive, spared by Calvin's successfully convincing Clayton that the cabin fire claimed an extra victim. The cruelty and injustice of the represented killings, and the lack of 'fair play' involved in Clayton's calculating and sadistic actions, generate a distinct conventional narrative need for Logan to avenge his comrades with a heroic display of retribution. According to the norms of the Western genre, everything is building to a climactic stand-off between hero and villain. Such a resolution would unproblematically legitimize the values represented by Logan, and demonize those represented by Clayton. But this is not what happens.

Over the course of the film, Nicholson's protagonist has, in fact, not done very much. We first saw him driving stolen horses across the Montana countryside, and then robbing a train almost single-handed. He was an ideal embodiment of Western adventure and excitement. But ever since the gang purchased property on Braxton's estate and left him behind to tend the cabin, Logan has lain low. The hero of *The Missouri Breaks* has had an affair with the villain's daughter, spent a lot of time building a garden and failed to prevent or avenge the deaths of his comrades, and will continue to do so until almost the final scene. From a typical figure of generic action, Logan has, throughout the narrative, become less and less able to do things. Despite holding a gun several times, he never once shoots effectively.

Perhaps his character arc follows a crisis of utility, revolving around an (in) ability to transform objects into tools and ruptures into opportunities. In a quintessential Romantic narrative, Logan undergoes a profound alternation in his ability to act in the world. In opposition to Clayton's dynamic modernity – so extreme in its effect that it constantly relapses into its professed opposite: archaic myth – Logan finds himself reduced to a persistent inactivity that brings him into conflict with the narrative mode of the Western itself. Like private detective Harry Moseby (Gene Hackman) in *Night Moves* (1975), Logan is a protagonist who fails to live up to the expectations of their genre. As the film progresses, and the horrors perpetuated by Clayton begin to build to grotesque extremes, this inactivity will force Logan to find the means to fulfil his generic role, and counter violence with a violence of his own that is ultimately transformative. Where Clayton's professionalism takes purposeful activity to the point of absurdity, Logan's more 'human' attraction to sentiment prevents his unproblematic acceptance of the dynamic actions forced upon him by the film.

Towards the end of the narrative, Logan is on the run. With few remaining options, he barters away his last possessions for a little money and, unlikely enough, a clarinet. That the old trader whom he encounters has a clarinet to sell, and that Logan accepts it as compensation for his horses, are presented as mildly comical elements of generic excess contributing to that inconsistent 'reality effect' that emerges at times throughout the film. The clarinet is not an instrument typically associated with the Western genre, in the same way as Clayton's banjo or harmonica. Logan looks perplexed at his new and unwieldy possession, and rides off on his remaining horse, carrying the clarinet awkwardly in his hand.

When Logan is down on his luck and finds it necessary to make an honest trade to improve his lot, the idea of trade itself is rendered arbitrary, ludicrous and irrelevant to his real needs. Perhaps this moment in *The Missouri Breaks* offers a paradigm example of negative dialectics – stubbornly turning the category against itself so as to expose the false claim to universality by which

Figure 30 Logan (Jack Nicholson) playing a 'useless' clarinet whilst on the run. *The Missouri Breaks* (1976).

it functions: the idea of offering things for sale that no one wants to buy.[18] The clarinet is, in the context of the wider narrative at this point, a useless addition to Logan's possessions, and, as a stubbornly incongruous symbol of capitalism's irrationality, a correlate to Clayton's own madness. This incongruity is made comically apparent when Logan sits under a tree and attempts to play his new instrument. He succeeds in making only loud screeching sounds. For some reason, he finds the situation humorous and laughs aloud. But suddenly he turns his head, like an animal on the alert, listening, perhaps, to hear if he is alone. This image of a man sitting under a tree laughing whilst playing with a clarinet, momentarily on the alert for the sound of approaching danger – confused, traumatized, without purpose or goal, finding a false relaxation by exchanging hard-earned assets for a pointless luxurious possession – this image alone could function as an evocative critique of capitalism (Figure 30).

The 'wrong' behind it all – that economic ideology associated with the world of Clayton and Braxton – is more affectively evoked when Logan, passing through the scene of a former gangmate's assassination, discovers his friend's corpse in an open coffin propped against the side of a building. Logan's muted shock is accompanied by the pestering chatter of a salesman trying to encourage this potential customer to buy some clothes. The jocular sales pitch creates a distasteful contrast to this upsetting discovery, and Logan reacts violently, shaking the man away: 'I don't want the goddamn thing!' Here the cruel consequences of opposing the legitimate economic system are brought directly alongside the discourse and social relations, which form its everyday realization

---

[18] See Adorno, *Minima Moralia*, 68.

– the inappropriate meeting between a murdered and abused human body and the eternal proclamation to buy commodities creates a critical dialectic.

Homesickness

Let us go back a little and look at what brought our hero to this tortured condition between action and inaction, freedom and necessity, with a suggestive economic hue.

As Robin Wood noted, ever since *The Chase*, 'Penn has moved consistently outside established society to search for alternative (and always extremely vulnerable) groups embodying values of freedom, generosity, spontaneity and mutual human responsiveness: the Barrow gang of *Bonnie and Clyde*, the hippie community of *Alice's Restaurant* [1969], the rustlers of *The Missouri Breaks*.'[19] There are additional echoes of this theme in some of the films Wood does not mention, including the confused assemblage of paranoid runaways and trapped figures in *Mickey One,* and the titular group of *Four Friends* (1981), whose golden and optimistic school days are replaced by a fragmented and nostalgic disenchantment in the face of lost opportunities and disappointments. The gang's farmstead in *The Missouri Breaks*, situated on the edge of the wilderness, acts, as mentioned previously, as a frame or symbolic arena for the establishment and precarious development of alternative social arrangements and value systems – a space for what Morse Peckham called 'cultural transcendence'. As a Romantic subjectivity, Logan develops an experimental relationship with the idea of belonging.

Positioned between Braxton's estate, the wilderness and a utopian Garden of Eden, the sense of nostalgic comfort associated with the gang's cabin is fraught with tensions. When they construct their hideout, when Logan tends to the gardens and when he invites Jane to tea, there is a sense of both clinging on to something that is lost, and a feeling of something in the process of becoming. A Romantic 'homesickness' will force Logan to develop an ambiguous relationship with the space represented by the cabin. The only certainty of meaning the cabin possesses is one of ambivalence, created through a combination of factors that give it an ever-shifting essence as a diegetic construct: sanctuary, trap, business, home, prison, crucible of the future and temple of the past. The Romantic imperative for homesickness will only be validated, however, if the cabin refuses the normative hermeneutic imperative provided by each and every one of these

---

[19] Wood, *Arthur Penn*, 171.

types. Homesickness means never to return home, never to achieve certainty, but, rather, to keep unbounded the meaning and desire of every Romantic element at play in a representation.

The development of an alternative community creates a series of conflicts and problems, which result from its differentiation from the social totality. A process of change is shown to take place as the farmstead is emptied of the complex and problematic new system of alternative relations, and a confrontation is allowed to take place between one element of that adolescent system (Logan) and a promising new element (Jane). The couple begin a romantic relationship, which they keep secret from her father. This space for communication is set at a distance from consistency, calculation and economic considerations, and becomes a domain of human openness. Since the social totality represented by Braxton and Clayton has bastardized rationality into something alien, 'reason' becomes a dirty word in the new utopian space. Jane tells Logan that her mother 'ran off with the first unreasonable man she could find'. The concept of 'reason' must begin again. That is why the conversations between Jane and Logan often express a distinct sense of irrational distance between the two. Initially, they don't understand each other, yet they begin a relationship, meet, talk and make love. As is the case for so many Romantic heroes, the divine mystery of romantic attraction – 'love' – stands as a readily graspable metonym for this wider sense of mystery that now confronts Logan. His affair with Jane marks a dialogue with an Other, which, in its desirability and confounding inconsistency, offers a kind of 'truth' that Logan seems unwilling to reduce to a functionary of his own will. He finds Jane contradictory and perplexing. When she makes a move, he recoils. When he advances, she draws back. In one scene the couple ride on horseback face to face (Figure 31). When Jane asks if this might be described as 'lewd conduct?' Logan replies: 'I couldn't say for sure.' Jane's father, however, has a library of law books and knows absolutely what is right and wrong. In Logan and Jane's new world there is no order, only opportunity – an awkward constellation of things that are not set. This – in the most profound contrast to the kind of attitude towards the world and things represented by Clayton – is a dramatization of a subjective process of critical hermeneutics in the name of objective reason. It is a dance with an Other, with the potential to create something New through sheer uncertainty combined with a discipline of love.[20]

---

[20] The philosophy of Alain Badiou might be an interesting point of reference for such an interpretation, albeit one far too complex to address here, considering, as noted previously, its own complex relationships with both Romanticism and film.

Figure 31 Jane (Kathleen Lloyd) and Logan (Jack Nicholson) begin their uncertain relationship. *The Missouri Breaks* (1976).

However, as Carl Schmitt's critique of Romanticism made clear, remaining 'open' involves the prospect of remaining open to everything, including the idea of being 'closed'. Accordingly, despite playing with the condition of uncertainty, which allows the mute absence of cognition inherent in the Other to speak and reveal its truth-content, Logan is also negotiating elements of acquiescence and authoritarianism that counterpoint this development in problematic ways.

When the gang deliberate the course of action to be taken after Little Todd's death, Calvin's passionate suggestion that Braxton be killed in revenge is violently opposed by Logan. His authoritarian pronouncement is accompanied by his hammering a fist against the wall: 'We ain't gonna do it because I said we ain't gonna do it!' Even as a condition of his pacifism, Logan is shown here to be developing aspects of the authoritarian absolutism that has been more commonly associated with the film's antagonists. Their unwritten communal equality now under threat by Logan's outburst, another member of the gang says: 'Goddamn it, let's not start that stuff'. Calvin leaves the cabin without uttering another word of argument, perhaps because in response to such declamations – which justify their authority by appeal to a clenched fist – dialogue has no answer.

Calvin now seems to represent certain values that are at odds with Logan's ambiguous development. Calvin asks if Jane has a husband, and Logan says: 'She don't need one.' 'Boy, you're pretty far gone, ain't you?' Calvin replies, disapprovingly. 'That's the way it happens, ain't it, Cal?' 'I wouldn't know. Not since that dog put its tongue on the butter.' Logan's return to a domestic idyll is seen by Calvin to be a kind of slippage, and, in a sense, it is. Logan has partially and experimentally reverted from the more complete 'outsider' life of Calvin, and, with his garden and heterosexual relationship, has ventured some way towards the authorized ideal of familial and domestic existence implicit in the legitimate society represented by Braxton. The distance between Calvin and Logan at this point brings to the foreground the ultimately 'doomed' nature of Calvin's self-imposed exile, too. He forfeits legitimate society by abandoning reciprocal relationships with women, and, in the process, condemns his mission to a mythic sterility. Logan's own situation is neither one thing nor another; its liminality is made possible by the intervention of Jane, and may, perhaps, be a kind of Romantic upward spiral[21] – a 'rising above' the limitations of existence, yet tainted with the possibility that such a rising would lead to the ultimate corruption.

Failure to act, action as failure

The allocation of value to memory – the evocation of absent experiences from which we still have opportunities to learn – is an ambiguous element throughout *The Missouri Breaks*. In mythologizing tones, Braxton recounts the glories of the early West; Logan and the gang tell humorous stories of past sexual exploits and criminal endeavours; Jane gives testimony concerning the misplaced ideals and cruel injustices that are unrepresented by the dominant narratives of frontier mythology; Calvin cherishes an origin story of disillusionment and renunciation concerning the kind of life that is called normal. The only key character who does not remember – who does not value the past as a repository of truth – is Clayton. The regulator is obsessed with the present, and the present goal, always. The only time he refers to his past, whilst dressed as the preacher, it is revealed to be a lie concocted merely to draw his prey, Little Todd, into a false sense of security. Clayton bypasses the oppositional quality of myth – its difference from the immediately given – by becoming a physical embodiment of myth itself. The Other has been absorbed (evidenced through his symbolic bricolage of a persona), and so there is, as a result, no real Other from which to learn. The only quality of myth that remains in Clayton is the one which Roland Barthes identified: that which sees everything as 'natural' and therefore deems every act to be permissible.

---

[21] On the 'upward spiral' motif, see M. H. Abrams, *Natural Supernaturalism: Tradition and Revolution in Romantic Literature*, 1971 (New York: W. W. Norton and Co., 1973), 183–95.

In opposition to this demonic figure who doubts nothing, who is uncertain about nothing because they do not countenance an objective existence from which to learn, the film presents Logan as a spirit of resistance. Logan stands as a critical Romantic hero – a figure of uncertainty, who feels the primacy of the objective too keenly to act without hesitation, or to grasp reality as an instrument. If Clayton is the dynamic Dark half of Romanticism which turns subjectivity into absolute authority, Logan's inactivity is the ray of doubting, suffering, hope which refuses to do violence to the truth-content of the objective.

Yet, Logan does act. Eventually, he does take bloody vengeance upon Clayton and stands over the enfeebled Braxton, gun in hand and ready to kill. The stresses imposed upon the protagonist of *The Missouri Breaks* over the course of the narrative demand from him a retaliation of some kind; an equilibrium is required to satisfy the antagonisms and imbalances for which Clayton has been responsible. But how this narrative resolution is ultimately achieved creates serious consequences for the valuation of elements at play, and the metalinguistic 'goodness' of Logan as a hero. That twin threat of assimilation or destruction faced by many of Penn's protagonists, sometimes leaving them in ambiguous conditions between right and wrong, presence and absence – Bonnie and Clyde, Mickey, Sheriff Calder in *The Chase*, Danny in *Four Friends* – can be clearly discerned in *The Missouri Breaks*. Like so many Light Romantics, Logan is entangled in that aporetic doctrine of moral action that was once described so well by Georges Bataille:

> It is hard not to struggle in order to destroy an adversary. It is to offer oneself to death. To survive without betraying oneself requires a relentless, austere, agonising struggle: this is the only chance of maintaining that delirious purity which is never tied to logic and can never fit in to the mechanism of action – that purity which drags all its heroes into the mire of a growing guilt'.[22]

After he first learns of Little Todd's murder, Logan confronts Clayton at Braxton's home. He finds the regulator upstairs, lying in a bathtub overflowing with bubbles, and the pair engage in a rambling series of threats, taunts and evasions. The scene parodies the generic Western stand-off, since Logan's attempts to rouse Clayton to defend himself or plead for mercy are mockingly sidestepped by the nonchalant, slippery and, occasionally, bafflingly irrelevant responses of the disinterested and ironical regulator covered in scented foam. Clayton turns

---

[22] Georges Bataille, *Literature and Evil* (New York: Marion Boyars, 1985), 159.

away from Logan and leans over the side of the bath, perhaps challenging the 'hero' to literally shoot him in the back. Logan, however, is unwilling to take the bait. He contents himself by shooting through the side of the tub, causing water to pour onto the floor.

Logan's hesitation before pulling the trigger, and inability to take the 'necessary' action of avenging Little Todd, and securing, in the process, the lives of himself and his fellow gang members (from Clayton, at least), testifies to a constructed sense of 'goodness' in Logan as a character. His ability to act has, for whatever combination of practical considerations and moral principles, stalled at the moment when the immediate elimination of his enemy was possible. Perhaps Clayton's 'calculation' – turning his back on his would-be assassin – had the desired effect. Despite having his nemesis at his mercy, Logan ultimately could not bring himself to throw aside his scruples and kill a defenceless man.

Clayton's eventual death, therefore, presents a significant moral ambiguity. By showing himself now willing to kill without giving his victim a fair chance, Logan finally sinks to the level of his nemesis, and yet, he also complicates the action by investing it with elements of an opposed value system.

The long-awaited revenge is presented through a pair of isolated extreme close-ups of both characters' faces (Figure 32). Clayton wakes with a gasp, and Logan says: 'You know what woke you up? Lee, you just had your throat cut.' The regulator's own death is therefore the symbolic opposite of his eagle-eyed assassinations with a long-range rifle. Logan has killed a man whist being close enough to look him in the eyes. The 'humanity' of such an action is praiseworthy according to the moral values that Logan has already been shown to possess; the thing that makes 'all the difference', as he claimed earlier in the film, is

Figure 32 Logan (Jack Nicholson) murders Clayton in his sleep. *The Missouri Breaks* (1976).

reiterated through the successful action that concludes the narrative. In this sense, Logan's action is a victory. Yet, as Todd Berliner notes, murdering Clayton in his sleep, looking him in the eyes or not, is a surprisingly 'contemptible' action for the supposed hero of the film to perform.[23] By this fact, the very quality of dignity implied by looking someone in the eyes as they die becomes tainted. An unmistakable quality of scopophilic sadism creeps into the intensity of those almost point-of-view camera shots that portray the villain's final moments. We the audience, like Logan, are primed to relish the spectacle of Clayton finally receiving his just deserts.

Clayton's death presents the key moment for any interpretation that seeks to articulate Logan's story as an allegorical working-through of the relationship between reason, morality and action. Adorno and Horkheimer argued that one prototypical rationalist cultural trope is the Homeric gesture of self-sacrifice: Odysseus allowing himself to be tied to the ship's mast in order to safely pass the Sirens – privileged knowledge gained only at the cost of impotence. After being narratively 'impotent' throughout much of the film, Logan's murder of Clayton becomes, in a sense, his own self-sacrifice. Through this 'contemptible' action, he has lost a sure ideological foothold as the agency that resolves the narrative disequilibrium. At this climactic moment of *The Missouri Breaks*, the corrupted idea of myth itself has been sacrificed: Clayton, that fascinating embodiment of totalitarian absolutes, is no more. Yet, the price paid for this defeat is the very potential for our hero, Logan, to be considered a 'hero' at all.

The immorality saturating Logan's act of vengeance finds an evocative parallel in a pronouncement once made by Adorno: that honest acts of spontaneous injustice meting out a righteous revenge for acts of terror, evils though they may remain, are to be preferred to the dishonest 'purity' of an institutionalized mechanism of capital punishment. This is revealed (typically for Adorno) in memory of the Holocaust, and the idea of any possible restitution: 'If the men charged with torturing, along with their overseers and with the high and mighty protectors of the overseers, had been shot on the spot, this would have been more moral than putting a few on trial.'[24] The passionate violence of the avowedly irrational and unthinking act on the one hand, and the cold violence of the sanctioned mechanism that proclaims its rationality on the Other – one is honest in its injustice, the other is dishonest in its violent appropriation of the

---

[23] Todd Berliner, *Hollywood Incoherent: Narration in Seventies Cinema* (Austin: University of Texas Press, 2010), 40.
[24] Adorno, *Negative Dialectics*, 286.

spirit of justice itself. This logic is what perhaps makes Logan's abhorrent act preferable to the alternative. It is a lesser evil, for it is honest in its refusal to seem right and good.

Logan next confronts Braxton, determined to resolve the narrative tension concerning the landowner's responsibility for inviting the murderous regulator into the neighbourhood. He discovers that – simultaneously, it seems, with the removal of Brando's Mephistopheles – Faust himself has been reduced to a semi-comatose condition, in response to his daughter's determination to leave home. Braxton sits paralyzed in a chair, being fed soup by his loyal servant, Vern, the only one of his employees who is reported to have remained after their employer's sudden and crippling decline.

It is not any protest on the part of Jane that eventually causes Logan to change his mind and spare her father, but, rather, the pitiable conduct of Vern. Braxton's enfeebled employee displays a profound sense of loyalty to his master; he pitifully attempts to place himself between Braxton's limp figure and the Creedmoor rifle Logan holds before him as proof of the regulator's death. Vern declares that his master is all that he has left. The implication is that a lifetime of domestic servitude has rendered this worker, like Nelson the train guard, unable to face, or even to comprehend, the prospect of life outside the security of servitude. The system may be unequal and cruel, but, according to the positivistic truism alien to the Romantic critical imperative, 'it is what there is.' Alternatives can be frightening for people who are invested in keeping things the way they are, or for those who may be unable to imagine the possibility of change producing something better. Vern perhaps represents an entire social 'class'; he stands-in for all those who cannot afford the kind of cultural transcendence that is experienced by Logan. Does their 'love' of servitude stand in the way of the Romantic individual making genuine social change? Or do they, in this case, prevent the Romantic individual from becoming the very monster they wish to slay?

After a moment's pained hesitation, Logan throws the Creedmoor rifle through a nearby window, resolving, by this passionate outburst, not to take any murderous revenge upon Braxton. Logan's rejection of the rifle – the thing that serves to symbolize the potential for Logan to become like his erstwhile nemesis – is done seemingly on a fleeting whim. His openness to Vern's pitiable situation, or his openness to human Otherness and considerations that are alien to his immediate sense of self, has finally triumphed against his passionate determination to kill his enemy.

Perhaps these words written by Hölderlin can illuminate Logan's absorption and eventual rejection of these elements from Clayton: 'Since I am more liable to be destroyed than many other people I must try to extract some advantage from the things that have a destructive effect on me. I mustn't take them for what they are in themselves, but only insofar as they can be of use to my own truest life.'[25] This entails a tentative and experimental mode of life, or *Bildung* – remaining open and receptive to what is alien and unknown:

> Everything depends on the excellent not excluding the inferior, and the more beautiful not excluding the barbaric too much from amongst themselves, but not mixing too much either, but certainly and without passion recognising the distance between them and the others, and working and suffering out of this understanding. If they isolate themselves too much, they lose their effectivity, and they go under in their solitude. If they mix too much, no proper effectivity is possible either . . . they too servilely take up the alien, the more common into themselves, and are stifled by it.[26]

It is this openness that Carl Schmitt criticized as subjective occasionalism and saw to be Romanticism's problematic essence – rather than, in fact, the beginning of the end. Pick them up when they enable some necessary course of action; put them down before they corrupt irrevocably. Be open to what is different, not in order to absorb it into yourself, but, rather, to learn from it what you are not, or what you may lose by forgetting.

Narrative convention is satisfied, however, when Braxton wakes from his near lifeless condition and fires at Logan. This provides the necessary validation for the hero to then kill Braxton in self-defence. The logical justification for the semi-comatose villain's attack is not foregrounded, however, and the scene ends on an appropriately uneasy sense of closure.

The false ending

The Missouri Breaks presents the story of a gang of outsider entrepreneurs who take risks to succeed on the precarious outskirts of a competitive economic system, only to be destroyed by the ruthless, irrational and uncontrollable forces

---

[25] Hölderlin, Letters, No. 58, To Christian Ludwig Neuffer, 12 November 1798, 109.
[26] Friedrich Hölderlin, *Seven Maxims*, c.1799, in *Essays and Letters*, 240–3 (London: Penguin, 2009), 242.

unleashed by the system itself. In the process, the struggle between the film's hero and villain becomes a conflict between two philosophical perspectives, which, broadly speaking, represent the dynamic spirit of capitalism and a flattering spirit of self-negating Romanticism.

Economic rationality has no concept of an Other. It approaches every aspect of reality already knowing what it is, since it employs a quantitative paradigm of knowledge that allows it to measure everything and give no quarter to what is excluded. Its instrumental world view has no use for the Kantian 'thing-in-itself'. In Clayton, Enlightenment returns to the realm of myth, only now it is a version of myth that does not hold any objective mystery equally over all. What Horkheimer called the 'formalization' of reason – the transformation from objective to subjective reason – made this concept identical with an individual's capacity to adapt and survive in the immediate environment. This transformation robs reason of its capacity to question and hold to account the very social or ethical conditions of its environment and the principles according to which it operates:

> The individual, purified of all mythologies, including the mythology of objective reason, reacts automatically according to . . . economic and social forces (which) take on the character of blind natural powers that man, in order to preserve himself, must dominate by adjusting himself . . . . Pragmatic reason is not new. Yet, the philosophy behind it, the idea that reason, the highest faculty of man, is solely concerned with instruments, nay, is a mere instrument itself, is formulated more clearly and accepted more generally today than ever before. The principle of domination has become the idol to which everything is sacrificed.[27]

This false ideal of subjective reason can justify anything. It is as willing to serve the ends of totalitarianism and slavery as much as revolution and equality. Since pure veins of objective and subjective reason each contain the potential for totalitarianism, then 'the task of philosophy', Horkheimer argues:

> is not to stubbornly play the one against the other, but to foster a mutual critique . . . . Kant's maxim, 'The critical path alone is still open' . . . applies even more pertinently to the present situation. Since subjective reason is triumphing everywhere, with fatal results, the critique must necessarily be carried out with an emphasis on objective reason.[28]

---

[27] Horkheimer, *Eclipse of Reason*, 68–74.
[28] Ibid., 123.

This is precisely what films like *The Missouri Breaks* appear to offer. It is a Romantic drama of mutual critique, exposing the frailties and evils within Logan as well as Clayton, with a moral inclination towards the inactive Light Romanticism, which stems from objective reason.

With the rest of the gang dead, there is no suggestion that Logan will go back to his criminal activities. During his time with Jane, he has discovered an interest in ranching, and leaves the farm on a cart with a cow hitched up behind, presumably to begin again somewhere new. But is this a return to nature or a return to civilization? Do either of these have progressive potentials? Perhaps the ending of *The Missouri Breaks* is also a broadly conventional resolution, which upholds the dominant ideology by keeping the outsiders away from society, even though there is no consummation of the heterosexual couple. Similarly, there is no stable political content in the elements of love and forgiveness professed by the couples' parting words. Love and forgiveness, like Clayton's cultural assimilations, can just as easily facilitate the unifying pull of totality. The sense of hope lies, rather, in their extension of that sense of indeterminacy which has marked the negative elements of the film in opposition to subjective reason, and the economically determined need to succeed, account, explain and rationalize. After Logan kills her father, Jane says: 'I don't want to spend my life trying to get back at someone.' 'Why do you want to say that?' Logan asks. Her reply: 'No reason'.

The two faces of Romanticism, Light and Dark, are present here in the indeterminacy of *The Missouri Breaks*; in the irresolvable tensions between film as an aesthetic critique of capitalism and the film as an underperforming Hollywood commodity; in the film's violence as an attractive series of affects, and as an exposé of the violence inherent in the social totality; in the oppositional principles of reason that are embodied by its hero and villain; in the film's success as an entertaining genre movie and its failure as a bizarre and lopsided vehicle for Marlon Brando's reputedly 'bad' performance; and in its ideological function as a tool of distraction and recuperation for cinema-going workers, and its denunciation of the social system supporting a world that makes such escapism necessary.

When Robin Wood asked Arthur Penn about the common accusation that *Bonnie and Clyde* was a 'dangerous' film, because it supposedly encouraged revolt without any positive ideology or programme, Penn replied: 'I don't believe that there is revolt without a programme *which will emerge from it* . . . a revolt comes out (of) a social condition. I don't think it comes out of abstract goal definition, and an attempt to achieve these goals.'[29] True change cannot be predicted. In different ways, critical philosophy, from Novalis to Popper, Adorno, Rancière, Alain Badiou and beyond, has also shown us this. Change emerges from chance encounters, from suffering and striving, and is guided by a Romantic fidelity to an encounter with an objective truth that is allowed to communicate with us in a strange and indeterminate language.

---

[29] Wood, *Arthur Penn*, 149.

7

The tyranny of spectacle
Britannia Hospital (1982)

Lindsay Anderson's films owe a great deal to *Zéro de conduite* (1933). Blending satirical irony and surrealism, Jean Vigo's fantastic parable about a riotous student uprising has long been seen as a spiritual precursor to *If....* (1968).[1] Yet, despite the obvious narrative and aesthetic connections with Anderson's most celebrated film, the spirit of Vigo's work can be detected far beyond the grounds of the boarding school.[2] The poetic surrealism of *Zéro de conduite* may seem, in retrospect, like a manifesto for the entirety of Anderson and David Sherwin's 'Mick Travis trilogy'. The films often seem to function by creating precisely that intensification of the ordinary – a super-ordinariness that is simultaneously a crisis – described by Lukács.[3] We have already seen how the Brechtian *Verfremdungseffekt* strives for this kind of revelation: a new perspective on common things; an estrangement of the natural and reified; an incitement to independent thought. To a more radical degree than its predecessors, *Britannia Hospital* (1982) represents a complex and contested public world through a scandalous enhancement of the everyday. In doing so, it comes all the more directly into contact with the most significant paradoxes of Romantic aesthetics: the problem of artistic explanation set against aesthetic freedom, or that of the 'genius' in their relation to the social totality. Adorno once wrote: 'above all, one

---

[1] Hedling, *Lindsay Anderson*, 95–6.
[2] The casting of dwarf actor Marcus Powell as Sir Anthony in *Britannia Hospital*, an upper-class representative of the British Royal family, directly recalls the diminutive school master (Delphin) in Vigo's film. Both characters are pompous figures of social authority, crudely undermined by an absurd physical discontinuity between the representation of social and physical stature. The intertextual reference is indicative of Anderson's desire for the contextualization of the film and its satirical approach within the anti-establishment traditions of cinematic surrealism; see Hedling, *Lindsay Anderson*, 96, 181.
[3] 'On closer examination the structure of a crisis is seen to be no more than a heightening of the degree and intensity of the daily life of bourgeois society'; Lukács, *History and Class Consciousness*, 101.

should beware of seeking out the mighty, and 'expecting something' of them.'[4] Caught in a moment of superordinary crisis, the diegetic world seeks answers from 'the mighty', and by the final scene *Britannia Hospital* confronts, as forcibly as the other films considered in this book, the relationship between negation and freedom. It dramatizes the uncanny allure and ultimate horror of deifying categories of the certain, the strong and the affirmative – something reflected throughout the entirety of Romantic critical philosophy.

In *If. . . .*, *O Lucky Man!* (1973) and *Britannia Hospital*, Malcolm McDowell plays Mick Travis, an idealistic young man who, after rebelling against the oppressive ideologies of public school, fails to earn either fulfilment or fortune as a capitalist go-getter, humanitarian missionary or freelance journalist. The Mick Travis trilogy is ostensibly a tragic epic, straddling diverse genre categorizations and stylistic modes to detail the fall of 1960s political idealism, reflecting a sense of disillusionment over the rise of Right-wing economic ideology and the persistence of nationalist myth. In *Britannia Hospital*, the trilogy's 'hero' becomes a somewhat marginal figure; the narrative is, instead, dominated by a complex collective social crisis – a 'perfect storm' of political unrest – framed within a hospital setting allegorically representing human civilization in the modern Western world (Figure 33). Despite the characteristically 'British' themes, the critical rhetoric of *Britannia Hospital* targets something more expansive. The idea of nation functions as but one element of the concept of totality, in addition

Figure 33 Modern society on the verge of chaos in *Britannia Hospital* (1982).

[4] Adorno, *Minima Moralia*, 33.

to concepts such as positivism, subjective reason, the doctrine of action and hierarchical social organization. When seen as a thematic trilogy, the film returns to those grander themes of freedom, agency and identity mobilized in *If. . . .* and *O Lucky Man!*

'It's really hard to be anyone', Anderson explained in a contemporary interview; 'Either you go with the profit-making philosophy of Thatcher and Reagan, or you're left with a kind of anarchic despair – which is how you could characterize *Britannia Hospital*.'[5] Yet, it was on these very terms that critics thought the film 'embittered' and 'misanthropic', lacking subtlety and originality, and its satirical force blunted by 'an overriding pessimism'.[6] Commentators such as John Hill ultimately feel that the film's overall mood of 'populist' discontent aligns with the expression of various national anxieties 'to which Thatcherism had already started to offer its own solutions', and that the sneering tone validates the desire for strong leadership fulfilled in actuality by conservative figures such as Margaret Thatcher.[7] However, the film's political convictions are not quite so easy to pin down. Once again, the tension between the 'success' and 'failure' of the text illuminates interesting aspects of its Romantic form and content. Hill's reading seems to rest on the assumption that the film explains to audiences the question of power in ultimately unambiguous terms, without contradiction and interpretive inconsistency. As this chapter will attempt to demonstrate, however, the matter is considerably more complex.

Anderson's own belief that the Romantic idealism of his earlier films had ebbed away by the time of the later Mick Travis films points towards another element of their political ambiguity. Although critical consensus would have us see evidence of decline in Anderson's later work, we can attempt to explain it in a different way, one that does not defuse the critical potential of *Britannia Hospital*.[8] We can begin by marking perhaps the most significant evidence of Vigo's heritage in *If. . . .*: the latter's famous sequence in which Philips (Rupert Webster) intimately observes Wallace (Richard Warwick) perform gymnastics. It seems like a homage to a similar moment of slow motion in *Zéro de conduite*, when the rebelling schoolboys march through their wrecked dormitory carrying

---

[5] Cited in Stewart et al., 'An Interview with Lindsay Anderson', 5.
[6] Hedling, *Lindsay Anderson*, 183; Lenny Rubinstein cited in Rampell, et al., 'Revolution Is the Opium of the Intellectuals', 38. The film's negative reception has also been partly attributed to the initial timing of its release in 1982. A work so caustic about the British establishment was not fated to be well received during the height of the Falklands conflict, Pope John Paul II's historic visit to England and the FA Cup Final; see Hedling, *Lindsay Anderson*, 193.
[7] John Hill, *British Cinema in the 1980s: Issues and Themes* (Oxford: Clarendon Press, 1999), 141.
[8] See Hedling, *Lindsay Anderson*, 183; Rampell, et al., 'Revolution Is the Opium of the Intellectuals,' 38.

Figure 34 A moment of sublime freedom and spectacle in *Zéro de conduite* (1933).

Chinese lanterns in an atmosphere thick with feathers (Figure 34). These moments of transcendent spectacle become a fundamental object of *Britannia Hospital*'s own mode of filmic critique. As with the sales pitch in *O Lucky Man!*, when Blake's poetry was abused to garnish an ideology of profit, *If....*'s own cinematic Romanticism, inherited from Vigo, is betrayed by something darker. In the analysis of *Britannia Hospital* that follows, I will attempt to trace a certain movement of transcendental spectacle which began with *Zéro de conduite*'s playful moment of transcendental freedom, turned self-aware through *If....*'s youthful shattering of representative and sexual taboos, the tragic revelation of subjective aporia in *O Lucky Man!* and finally ending with a vision of political stupefaction in *Britannia Hospital*. What was once Vigo's innocent dream of cinematic purity has become, over the course of the trilogy, a problematic and ultimately self-alienating experience of power tied to a corrosive social totality. This narrative of loss, rather than evidencing a decline into political pessimism, as some critics have claimed, may allegorize the passing of pure Romantic idealism into a richer and more comprehensive experience of aesthetic critique.

Anderson's Brechtian approach was designed to induce audiences to 'think', or to stimulate them into perceiving anew the problematic world reflected in the films' allegorical mirrors.[9] Yet, this artistic desire is also burdened – as we have seen during discussion of that Romantic tension between freedom and

---

[9] Anderson, '*Britannia Hospital*', 157.

explanation – with an aura of authoritarianism, which needs to be negotiated. The topic comes full circle when we examine that element of transcendental spectacle which becomes so important to *Britannia Hospital*'s political content: the representation of diegetic acts of seeing, speaking and listening – involving the communication of knowledge, recognition of authority and the consolidation of values relating to individual freedom, community and even 'humanity' itself.

Satire and inequality

The film's method is to create a broad satirical portrait of society, egalitarian in the even-handedness of its mockery and the lack of privilege given to any diegetic point of view.[10] Yet, the work's own elevation above the ridiculed social melee accentuates the very quality of social distinction and illusion that it professes to denounce. Such works cannot escape their own ideological effects. The representation of a society, focusing only on its flaws and foibles, strives for a kind of critical distance regarding positivist association – a demythologizing of the current state of affairs and the institutions and practices that exonerate their failures. No perspective, even that of the work itself, is allowed to have an unproblematic authority over the represented elements; and, ideally, a kind of negative equality reigns over the diegetic world, recalling Karl Popper's democratic aphorism that we are all equal in our ignorance.[11] The ultimate message to emerge from such works is often a kind of humanistic pessimism, and the attempt to reflect the critique back honestly onto the process of artistic production results in the kind of ending we have already seen in O Lucky Man! In *Britannia Hospital*, however, the 'egalitarian' ambition of the satire causes new problems.

The initial question concerns the degree to which represented elements achieve the equality of critical representation desired by the form. The opening scenes establish an imbalance from the outset, and although previous commentators have noted that the film is particularly 'harsh' about trade unions, it is worth dwelling upon the complexities at play here, and how they serve to frame one of

---

[10] In its carnivalesque vividness, *Britannia Hospital* functions in a similar way to the Bruegel of *The Fight Between Carnival and Lent* (1559) or *The Netherlandish Proverbs* (1559).

[11] 'While differing widely in the various little bits we know, in our infinite ignorance we are all equal'; Popper, *Conjectures and Refutations*, 38.

the film's most important characters: Prof Millar (Graham Crowden), returning from *O Lucky Man!*[12]

An ambulance passes through a picket line outside the hospital, and although the strikers allow it to pass, they display little sympathy for the dying patient inside: 'He won't be playing (football) Saturday', jokes one. When the old man is wheeled into the intensive care unit, he is abandoned by the orderlies and medical staff, and melodramatically expires alone in a corridor to the ironical non-diegetic accompaniment of a muted 'Rule, Britannia!' The callousness that characterizes the strikers and workers in the opening scene creates an immediate impression that the film's target is class-based selfishness. This conjecture is soon counterbalanced by the conduct of Prof Millar, an upper-middle-class professional. He bursts through the picket line in a luxury car and sends a striker bouncing off his hood. Rolling down his window, Millar contemptuously calls the strikers 'Insects!' and drives away. As he parks outside a modern and imposing building next to the hospital, we see his own name prominently displayed on its façade.

This opening sequence apparently strives to create a kind of satirical equality between negatively valued represented elements. Both the neglectful workers and the reckless Prof Millar are shown to make up 'equal' parts of what is wrong with the fictional world. However, this equality is potentially discounted by the narrative succession of emotively weighted events. The audience, having witnessed the uncaring treatment of a weak and dying old man, are primed to assign a greater sense of positive value to Millar, who bursts so violently and humorously into the film and contemptuously assaults the callous strikers. Although, logically, Millar knows nothing about the mistreatment of the old man, and the cinematic assignment of responsibility to the hospital workers, nor, we assume, as the film progresses and we find out more about his character, would he care even if he did. Yet, in the succession of diegetic events created by scene structuring, it is almost as if Millar is 'taking revenge', from a metalinguistic perspective, for the injustice of the previous scene. If these interpretive possibilities take hold, then the film encourages audiences to side with Millar from his first appearance: cavaliering into the hospital grounds and displaying a 'just' contempt for the strikers. These valuations are complicated as the narrative progresses, but *Britannia Hospital* never shakes off this inherent ambiguity surrounding the values it ascribes to the elements from which the satire is constructed. Something is wrong with the social totality, no doubt; but not all are equal in their objectionableness.

---

[12] Hedling, *Lindsay Anderson*, 180.

The contrast between these two points is illustrative:

1) Throughout the film, Millar's experiments are represented through a comical use of sublime inflation. The mysterious research project named 'Genesis' is veiled behind generic science fiction and horror clichés, giving it and its creator a sense of grandiose significance turned ludicrous. Millar openly compares himself to 'God' on many occasions, as befits the 'mad scientist' cultural type. Yet, the cinematic representation of his work creates a sense of disproportion that complicates the humorous effect. Genesis is shrouded in a representational absence evocative of the sublime awe associated with *2001: A Space Odyssey* (1968), and its very mystery becomes a marker not only of its 'seriousness', but also of its creator's genuine value as a 'genius' – a unique and superior individual.
2) The introduction of Genesis is followed by a scene in the ICU that is completely different in its rhetorical method and ideological effect. Following a terrorist bombing, a large number of injured people arrive at the hospital, and a group of orderlies refuse to clear the corridor of obstacles due to insufficient overtime conditions. The humour of the scene derives, in part, from a disproportion between the human concerns that are at stake in the diegesis (the medical treatment of hundreds of injured people) and the central problem which needs to be resolved (the presence of 'sausages' in the worker's complimentary breakfast being negotiated as compensation for overtime). When the sausage issue is resolved, the injured people can be treated.

What is important to recognize about these two points is the difference in rhetorical method the film employs to achieve its satirical effect, and the resultant degree to which audiences are primed to value the object of critique. Whereas the ICU staff are rendered 'bad' due to their represented willingness to sacrifice the physical well-being of others on account of a hot breakfast, Millar is 'bad' to a potentially lesser degree due to the abstraction of the (supposedly) negative element – one whose negativity is far more liable to a positive moral interpretation. His 'absurdity' is given no cognitively graspable diegetic object (such as the injured people) against which to measure and define itself. Genesis is a genuinely sublime absence, which does not humorously invalidate the ironic Godlike awe of Millar as a character. Consequently, audiences are potentially not so able to identify his pretensions with any contemptible human fault befitting the satirical agenda, as is the case with the ICU orderlies, but are, rather, closer to categorizing Millar as a 'superior' being, as he does himself.

This ambiguity will surface repeatedly as the film progresses, ultimately leading to the final scene – the public unveiling of Genesis – which mobilizes many Romantic tropes concerning genius, spectacle, political agency and (in) activity.

Sublimity and science

Throughout the Mick Travis trilogy, it is possible to detect a continuity in the enigmatic role allocated to scientific themes. This development contributes to the cinematic representation of diegetic acts of sensory and cognitive experience that bear upon the idea of Romantic inaction.

The first notable event in the trilogy occurs towards the finale of *If. . . .* as the rebellious schoolboys are clearing out the cellar. They discover a wooden cabinet filled with bottles and jars containing dissected animals, organs and a human foetus, the last of which Travis examines closely. The scene is given a mysterious quality by the questioning musical tones on the soundtrack, absence of dialogue and the selection of this moment as one of *If. . . .*'s ethereal black and white sequences. The strange girl (Christine Noonan) suddenly appears inexplicably, takes the jar from Travis' hands and places it back in the cabinet. The narrative advances without further reference to the discovery, and the rebels soon discover the stockpile of weapons, which ultimately provides them with the means to symbolically disassociate themselves from official society at the film's denouement. The scene functions as a mysterious interlude. Like the previous monochrome sequence in the gymnasium, its narrative extraneousness creates a sense of profound yet indeterminate meaning. Some interpretations have suggested that the foetus symbolizes the dead and sterile ideology of the official society, either that, or the promise of a new beginning, mirroring the ending of *2001: A Space Odyssey*.[13]

Reading retrospectively, the sublime awe that characterizes this moment becomes particularly significant to the political interpretation of *Britannia Hospital*, during which the 'sublime science' theme returns in stronger, more troubling force in reference to political agency. *Britannia Hospital* is explicitly

---

[13] Hedling, *Lindsay Anderson*, 93; Izod, et al., *Lindsay Anderson*, 131.

Figure 35 The mysteries of science and humanity. Travis (Malcolm McDowell) encounters an intertextual reference in *Britannia Hospital* (1982).

linked to this thematic heritage by the telling moment when Travis encounters another foetus in a jar whilst exploring Millar's lab (Figure 35). Considering the peculiar aura that accompanies these scenes, it seems likely that there is something more going on here than the use of embalmed foetuses as symbolism for the moribund nature of British establishment, the ambiguous possibility of a new beginning, the simple equation of scientism with immorality or the appropriation of resources from the science fiction or horror genres. The question of scientific morality is presented here as a fragment of that broader exploration of individual agency that underlies the trilogy.

By the time of *O Lucky Man!*, science is already playing a much larger role; but now the mysterious quality that surrounded the cabinet has been augmented by a decided feeling of helplessness and horror. The scene at Prof Millar's clinic, during which Travis discovers the terrible fate of his fellow volunteer – horrific, unexpected and comic – plainly evokes the genre tropes, which return in *Britannia Hospital*. Like other products of institutional authority, science is given a negative treatment throughout *O Lucky Man!* In other sequences, Travis witnesses a nuclear explosion and the devastating effects of chemical weapons – all of which are, as we have seen, presented as results of the corrupt and unstable social totality that forms the object of the film's critical address. As in *If....*, science remains something politically unspeakable, and plays a significant role in the moral darkness and pessimism that permeates the represented world. A complete dissociation is created between the grandiloquent and positivistic discourse surrounding science, and what is shown to be its cruelly inhuman realization. The kind of science represented in *O Lucky Man!* reduces the human body to its most vulnerable, invaded and damaged conditions, and relates that experience to a harmful social totality associated, primarily, with affirmative and pro-capitalist ideologies. *Britannia Hospital* promotes these corporeal motifs and turns them into a central theme. The narrative is filled with bodies that are damaged and dying, bloated and shrunken, incised and dissected, either marching to and fro or hobbled and comatose. The film gives all these conditions a different meaning and presents through them a dynamic and living world, filled with variety and opinion, yet one suffering from all manner of social ills allegorized in bodily form.

There is a quality of paralysis and anxiety that science brings to these films, and it is surely explicable in many ways. Yet, it seems to invite one particular interpretation which corresponds to the overarching method of political critique. There is a reason why science, in these films, almost exclusively equates to medical science, with its connotations of bodily examination, judgement and treatment. It is more than just a science of the body, but, rather, of the 'the body politic' – the free individual as multiplicity, or multiplicity as individual; objectified, divided, fragmented and injured; judged and segmented, grouped and partitioned, ordered into positions, defended against infections; its individual parts arranged into permutations judged necessary and appropriate by competing political interests who hold an intuitive and unspoken ideal of a 'true' and organic whole.

The final scene of *Britannia Hospital* returns the Mick Travis trilogy to that moment of sublime awe that the presence of science and deathly stillness first created in *If . . . .* when the Crusaders found the cabinet in the basement. Millar's great experiment, Genesis, is observed by ranks of silent humans – violently political subjects fallen into mute order and passivity in the presence of a dynamic and charismatic genius – stunned into an awesome silence by the presence of 'man remade'. A super-subject without a body, Genesis is divorced from the allegorized materialistic and economic concerns that have plagued the narrative, and so can function as an image of their problematic transcendence. The uniform stillness that reigns over the final few minutes of the film – which is all the more shocking for the complex and intense dynamism apparent throughout the rest of the narrative – becomes both the satire's greatest triumph, as well as its profoundest moment of ideological negation.

Before analysing these pivotal scenes, we must look very carefully at all that has gone into them.

The one who speaks

In both *O Lucky Man!* and *Britannia Hospital*, Prof Millar's charismatic persona, wide-eyed stare and seemingly illimitable idealistic candour about the furtherment of humanity recalls the 'mad scientist' cultural type made popular by countless science fiction stories. The idea that science is an ambivalent and potentially destructive force has a long cultural history. From the oft-retold stories of Faust and Frankenstein through to the infamous army medical experiments and nuclear research of the 1940s, the scientist is burdened with the potential to evoke a malleable and persistent series of ambiguous connotations. Some stereotypical tropes of the scientist figure include a lack of empathy, unconcern for traditional conceptions of morality, and a monomaniacal devotion to their work, all of which are employed in the characterization of Millar. His sharp suits and well-groomed appearance, unassailable confidence, compelling social abilities and statuesque figure seem to turn him into something relating to capitalist business iconography – a exemplar of the contemporary Thatcherite ideology of competition (Figure 36). At times, he seems like an amalgam of two characters from *Metropolis* (1927): Rotwang (Rudolf Klein-Rogge), the prototypical cinematic mad scientist, fired by passionate visions and egocentric desires, and Joh Fredersen (Alfred Abel), the ruthless and robotic businessman, willing to sacrifice human lives for a standard of personal power and glory objectified by an awe-inspiring social system. Integrating both cultural types – the mad scientist and the amoral businessman – Graham Crowden's character

Figure 36 The business-like 'mad scientist' Prof Millar (Graham Crowden) in *Britannia Hospital* (1982).

comes to embody the principle that ends justify means, and that the glory of dynamic human progress and 'the greater good' outweighs individual freedom.

Millar is certainly the film's villain. He is not only a monomaniacal and narcissistic advocate of eugenics, but also a murderer and a cannibal. In one scene, he liquidizes a human brain and eats, with sinister relish, a chunk of flesh plucked from his dissection knife. He justifies the most 'monstrous' ethical actions by citing his own duty as a prophet of scientific progress. His voluminous declamations seek to depoliticize themselves by a claim to represent, as he puts it, the 'pure, benevolent spirit of science'. Millar's power to mesmerize his public mythologizes his right to speak on behalf of the future. This claim to be operating from a higher ethical perspective, distinct from that of the material condition of society itself, in order to selflessly ensure the general betterment of the species – this claim is evocative of the problematic figure of the Romantic genius. It is a trope that finds potent realization and diverse political association in the works of Schiller, Nietzsche, Wagner and Hitler, respectively.[14]

Yet, at the same time, Millar is a formidable figure of personal value. A white male professional, tall and charismatic, confident and assured, a master of language, with his name in the title of an independent scientific institution, and being, now, in *Britannia Hospital*, at a very particular age – towards the 'wiser' end of middle-aged, not yet afflicted with any apparent physical or mental impairments as the specific result of his maturity – Millar is a conglomeration of culturally generated signifiers of authority and significance. The ambiguity that ultimately surrounds Millar is hardly unique to cinematic depictions of villainy, yet it comes to play a particularly important role in defining the film's own metalinguistic attitude. Although Millar is explained to be a ludicrous and dangerously insane character, his status as a genuinely talented and unique individual is buttressed by the extraordinary things that he is shown to achieve within the films' diegetic reality. In Millar's own words – uttered with a combination of hubristic pride and Romantic poeticism – his work consists of nothing less than 'Man remade'. His experiments, although only varyingly qualified successes, are shown to make powerful impressions on witnesses. His achievements elicit an awed appreciation, framed as quietist passivity, in the face of something genuinely affecting, and they do not proceed from categorically 'false' scientific attributes. Yes, his 'human experiment' goes on a rampage and must be put down; and yes, Genesis comes to resemble a broken record; but

---

[14] See Kitchen, *Romanticism and Film*, 33.

Millar does, indeed, bring these remarkable things into creation. As he says himself: 'My transplants *work*', no matter what else they may do. His powers are shown to be as 'real', if not as absolute, as those of God.

Not only this, but Millar's authority as a political element is shown to be primarily dependent on the explanatory power of audiovisual representation – the performance of verbal or non-verbal communication as the spectacle of 'truth' (not unlike 'the Word from the Lord' evoked by *Mickey One* [1965]). Over the course of the film, Millar is shown to pontificate for the benefit of a television crew who are making some kind of documentary profile. Led by Peter (Peter Mancini), the recording crew hang on Millar's every word, evidently considering his quasi-scientific rambling to be 'televisual gold', and Crowden's performance invests Millar with a compelling charisma. He is explicitly shown to be not only a skilled scientist, but also a professional 'professor' – an expert and magnetic imparter of verbal explanation.

Millar's function in *Britannia Hospital* can be illuminated by considering Jacques Rancière's interpretation of the term 'auctor', or 'the one who speaks'. From a linguistic root shared with 'author' and associated with the idea of an educator, explicator or salesman, an auctor is not first and foremost an intellectual, but a 'guarantor', 'a *master* of words'.[15] An auctor works with rhetoric in a form that occludes the violence of explanation itself; by building connections, divisions and identities, they seek 'to unite people by apprehending meaning; to pacify by virtue of a strength that precedes the exercise of power'.[16] As Rancière puts it: 'The auctor is a specialist in messages, one who is able to discern meaning in the noise of the world';[17] in other words, they derive their being from the pragmatic construction of a fictive coherence and certainty from the ultimately irreducible multiplicity of objective reality. Possessing a capital of knowledge hewn from a deformed objective reality, therefore, Millar is a 'professor' who overrules the conjectural nature of the verb 'profess' – sign of the invitation to dialogue inherent to higher education. He is an auctor, or the result of a subjective judgement that those to whom he pontificates are unable to understand things for themselves.[18] This judgement establishes, as a fundamental root of inequality, the hierarchical relationship between those who speak and those who listen. The violence of explanation takes the form of the old tyrannical relationship between

---

[15] Rancière, *On the Shores of Politics*, 10.
[16] Ibid.
[17] Ibid., 9.
[18] See Rancière, *The Ignorant Schoolmaster*, 6; see also Kitchen, *Romanticism and Film*, 10.

teacher and student critiqued in Rancière's pedagogical theory, one based upon an inherent social distinction between intellects of different quantitative content, rather than the formal quality of intelligence itself.[19] Its ultimate effect is one of social distinction: the implicit valuation of action and certainty against passivity and negation, and the resultant separation of those individuals who are judged to fall either side of the line. The one who speaks ('declaims' – to offer speech, without invitation to dialogue) must be certain of what is said, and can therefore be connected, like Clayton in *The Missouri Breaks* (1976), with the Dark Romantic schema outlined in Part One.

For *Britannia Hospital*, the inevitable by-product of this process is the mythologization of the individual voice – the one who is certain enough to speak – and, moreover, its false transformation into 'the voice of humanity'. The film's ending and its metanarrational content is predicated on Millar's rhetoric achieving this political effect. Building throughout the film, we see Millar consistently operate according to an implicit process of violence in language by articulating a false equivalency between his personal significance and that of the human race as a whole. When a staff member says: 'A big day for you, Professor!' Millar's corrective reply equates his individual will with that of the world spirit: 'A big day for mankind!'

Millar's power comes as no surprise, for all things that are of significance in the world of *Britannia Hospital* are guaranteed by the authority of spectacle. Throughout the narrative we are shown that a Royal visit to the hospital requires the addition of banners, flags, costumes, carpets, music and all manner of multimedia hoopla. The social totality represented by the hospital officials and Royal guests is shown to be obsessed with ritual display – protocol and decorum – not only because it mythologizes the established order, but also because it equates spectacle, or affirmative expression, with value itself. As a result of its ambiguous relationship with the idea of production, the activity of 'putting on a show' to mark a special occasion recalls the archaic powers accredited to magic. Just as some things contribute to the performance of myth by being put on display, so too must their causes and costs – the materiality of labour behind such spectacle – remain hidden. It is telling that the hospital officials are just as eager to orchestrate what the Royal visitors *do not* see as what they do. Because of this willingness to police the sensorial fabric (as Rancière might say) of an objective material reality, all such phantasmagorical spectacle contains

---

[19] Rancière, *The Ignorant Schoolmaster*, 4–8.

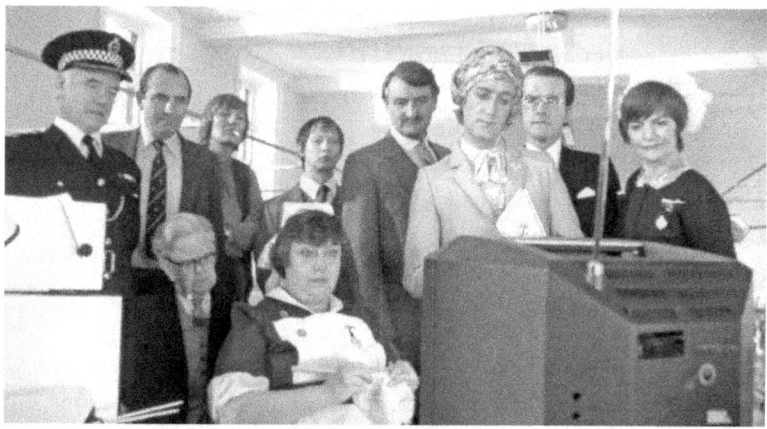

Figure 37 A moment of distraction – the hospital inspection party stops to observe the televised rocket launch. *Britannia Hospital* (1982).

the nascent spirit of irrationality.[20] It is for this reason that diegetic experiences of seeing, speaking and listening, as sites for the performance of social power, have such an important role in the political interpretation of films, and moments of audiovisual display combined with diegetic spectatorship have a special significance in *Britannia Hospital*.

In one telling scene, the group of official visitors, inspecting the hospital in advance of the Royal visit, silently watch the launch of a rocket on a portable television (Figure 37). This event has no obvious narrative significance, and the characters soon continue their tour. But the story stops for this brief moment during which individuals are curiously enraptured by the spectacle of human progress – a progress made possible by science, and carrying a weight of associated values regarding activity, practical achievement and the idea of 'progress' itself. This atypical moment of static diegetic spectatorship functions a prelude to the film's dark finale.

Tellingly, this scene is shortly followed by one in which the same tour group visit Sir Hubert (Arthur Lowe), a terminally ill politician who expires whilst delivering the famous 'this sceptred isle' speech from Shakespeare's *Richard II* (1595). The original runs thus:

> This royal throne of kings, this sceptred isle,
> This earth of majesty, this seat of Mars,

[20] See Rancière, *The Politics of Aesthetics*, 7.

> This other Eden, demi-paradise,
> This fortress built by Nature for her self
> Against infection and the hand of war,
> This happy breed of men, this little world,
> This precious stone set in a silver sea
> Which serves it in the office of a wall
> Or as a moat defensive to a house,
> Against the envy of less happier lands,
> This blessed plot, this earth, this realm, this England . . .²¹

With the visitors crowded at the foot of his deathbed, Sir Hubert removes his oxygen mask to deliver these last words. In cultural representations, John of Gaunt's speech can often function as a patriotic hymn aggrandizing the English nation. In this abridged context, such sentiments might be symbolic of the moribund condition of the 'better' aspects of traditional cultural heritage. If so, the dying politician becomes – according to the logic of the satire – another ludicrous figure preaching a national ideology out of touch with reality. But the expurgated lines, known to audiences more familiar with Shakespeare, include the following:

> This land of such dear souls, this dear, dear land,
> Dear for her reputation through the world,
> Is now leased out – I die pronouncing it –
> Like to a tenement or pelting farm.
> England, bound in with the triumphant sea,
> Whose rocky shore beats back the envious siege
> Of wat'ry Neptune, is now bound in with shame,
> With inky blots and rotten parchment bonds.
> That England that was wont to conquer others
> Hath made a shameful conquest of itself.²²

This poignant rebuke might be directed at the society depicted in *Britannia Hospital*. This is the only scene in which the inspection party wear protective face masks, and it is almost as if they do not want to become infected with the unwelcome 'truth' imparted by this tragic John of Gaunt. Whether his poetic disillusionment is meant to be mocked or sincerely mourned is open to interpretation, of course; it is impossible to decisively allocate its critical force

---

[21] William Shakespeare, *King Richard the Second*, 1595, in *The Complete Works of William Shakespeare* (London and Glasgow: Collins, 1954), Act 2, scene 1, 454.
[22] Ibid.

to either the object or the metalanguage, specifically. But such acts of speaking and listening play vital and conflicted roles throughout the film, constructing a complex network of political associations and possibilities. Shakespeare (that most iconic and richly evocative of explicators) returns in the final scene with Millar and Genesis, and any positive value ascribed to the Bard's words will also render the conclusion of the film all the more ambiguous.

Intensifying the ordinary

Most characters in *Britannia Hospital* remain oblivious of the extraordinary experience awaiting them at the end of the film. For the other hospital staff, Prof Millar's 'demonstration' is but one event in a crowded programme marking the visit of 'HRH' – Her Royal Highness (Gladys Crosbie). Spectacle and deception become the general rule, as the staff, led by the busy chief administrator Mr Potter (Leonard Rossiter), oversee the Royal preparations whilst dealing with all manner of problems: strikers, hundreds of casualties from a nearby terrorist attack and a growing crowd of protestors outside the front gates, irate at the presence of a pampered private patient, the reviled African dictator, President Ngami (Val Pringle). Also supervising the events of the day are representatives of the Palace Sir Anthony (Marcus Powell) and Lady Felicity (John Bett), police Chief Superintendent Johns (Fulton Mackay), the senior hospital executive Mr Figg (John Moffatt) and head of the medical staff Sir Geoffrey (Peter Jeffrey). This group makes up a kind of 'ruling class' – a microcosm of the social elite, including the aristocrats and professionals who materially and symbolically benefit from social cohesion. Their struggle to keep the Royal visit on track becomes synonymous with the need to maintain the stability of hierarchical society itself.

Mr Figg explains that this special day requires a 'plan of campaign' realized with 'clockwork precision', mixing technological and military metaphors which evoke ideas of calculated organization and its violent enforcement. This defensive imperative is reinforced by the elites' often being directly contrasted with the massed forces seeking to challenge its authority (the protestors and strikers calling for 'equality'). The hospital disc jockey (Bernard Griffiths) perhaps unintentionally misrepresents the sound of chanting protestors outside the hospital grounds as a patriotic display of enthusiasm for the Royal visitors, and, indeed, throughout the film the two developments become increasingly linked as a species of provocation and reprisal. The absurd practices of official society elicit a kind of unplanned popular retribution. Matters are slowly 'coming to a head' as a result of that intensification of the ordinary occasioned by ritual exposure of the 'heart' of society itself – HRH – and what that exposure spontaneously brings forth. This 'perfect storm' of political activity, constructed by the film as part of its critical method, equates the represented events as the coming-to-fruition of tensions and flaws inherent to this fictionalized exaggeration of modern society in the developed world.

More specifically, *Britannia Hospital* places emphasis on the misuse of representative responsibility, and further suggests that the structural organization of society perpetuates such misuse. For example, Phyllis (Joan Plowright) is one of several mid-level hospital officials who abuse their position by surreptitiously blackmailing Mr Potter to secure an invitation to the Royal lunch. But this is not something attributable to the will of individual characters who might be abusing their positions; the selfishness of the upper-lower-class managers is enmeshed within a general organization which permits tribalism and corruption. Anyone given social responsibility, the message seems to be, is placed in a position where corruption is not only possible but also conveniently advocated by the mythology of the social system as a whole – the Royal lunch becomes, in its very potency as a locus of social value, the grand justification of every petty connivance characters enact on its behalf. The liberal sentiment that 'Britannia belongs to the People now', as Phyllis claims, supposedly on behalf of her workers, rings hollow in the face of the elitist values to which this 'emancipation' is uncritically attuned.

No positive alternative is allowed. No perspective is free from the corruption that marks the whole. Ben Keating (Robin Askwith), the leader of the strike, is also shown to be hypocritical and self-serving, despite his professed belief in egalitarianism. 'It's the same for everyone, or nothing at all', he declares before his supporters, whilst readily agreeing to a labour settlement that only partially meets their demands because it is offered with underhand personal advantages. Potter's seductive talk of MBEs, OBEs and a personal invitation to the Royal lunch is enough to displace Keating's socialist ideals. The mythic nature of the objects that Potter rhetorically dangles before the union rep is underlined by the anti-realism of the following scene. Keating stands before his co-workers and affirms the false victory they have won over Potter. The hospital administrator delivers a meliorating official statement dense with ideological mystifications that serve the dominant economic and social structure (made of individual valuations, which are, incidentally, diametrically opposed to Light Romanticism): 'the British working man . . . and woman will always put unity before anarchy,

Figure 38 Mr Potter (Leonard Rossiter) placates the strikers in *Britannia Hospital* (1982).

loyalty before self, common sense before disruptive strike. God bless you all!' (Figure 38) This glowing display of affirmation convinces most of the workers, who do not see it, as the audience are primed to, as a hollow performance of self-serving officialdom. As if to radicalize the mythic nature of Potter's sentiments, a representative of Fortnum & Mason (Valentine Dyall) steps forward and begins singing 'Auld Lang Syne' – a traditional hymn of British cultural togetherness. In one of the film's more anti-realist moments of comedy, the management and strikers join hands and sing. Following token acts of dissent, we see bribery and betrayal forgotten in the peal of the old unity.

Mr Potter is the lynchpin of official hospital organization. More so than many other characters, Potter is shown to be good at his job: capable, knowledgeable, inventive, calm under pressure and devoted to his institution. When public disturbance is on the verge of rendering the Royal visit untenable, Potter refuses to bend, unlike his dependent superior Mr Figg. Due to his iconic role in *The Fall and Rise of Reginald Perrin* (1976–9), however, Leonard Rossiter's cultural image evokes the existential disillusionment of the middle-class professional. In one scene, he delivers a remarkable and stirring speech on vocational commitment, which mixes pathos and bathos, sincerity and comic overinflation:

> I love this hospital! Its my whole life. Its been wife, mother, child to me. I've given it everything. And nothing is going to wreck it. Nothing!

Potter's love for the social totality represented by the hospital marks his own state of dependency, becoming an object of both humour and pity. Recalling

Nelson the train guard from *The Missouri Breaks*, and Adorno and Horkheimer's comment about people who are 'bound up with the system' – who accept the capitalist *weltanschauung*, play by its rules and enjoy its comforting rewards – Potter's passionate outburst reads as a symptom of this displaced value, in the form of a risible and yet poignant neurosis.[23] Unusually, when Brechtian distancing slips from the film's aesthetic approach, its critical force appears to gain a momentarily heightened profundity. As a result of his loyalty, Potter becomes a tragi-comic figure; a troubling point of identification for anyone who, like many a potential viewer, may have given everything to their profession and yet feel, deep down below their salary and social status, when they find themselves comparing their vocation to a spouse, parent, or child, that they have also been robbed of something.

Like a father, Potter has a thorough knowledge of his loved one from top to bottom. When he and assistant Biles (Brian Pettifer, returning once again from *If. . . .* and *O Lucky Man!*) go into the maintenance area to restore the hospital's power, the chief administrator is shown to know even how to work the boilers. Also like a father, he thinks nothing of defending his loved one with violence. A disgruntled worker suddenly appears and attempts to stop Biles from restoring power; determined that nothing should harm his beloved hospital, Potter picks up a shovel and strikes the worker. As electricity is restored and Potter returns upstairs, Biles and the audience discover that the campaigning manager has committed manslaughter. A deep wound on the worker's head, a growing pool of blood on the floor, unblinking eyes and an ominous musical cue on the non-diegetic soundtrack, all suggest that the man is dead. Potter was the proactive organizer, intent on protecting the interests of his treasured institution. We and Biles are left to question whether he knows he has killed someone, or if he would really care if he did know. Perhaps his manager's brain, operating at a time of crisis, would unthinkingly consider the death of an uncooperative worker to be merely another problem 'solved'. As that diabolic spirit of capitalism from *The Missouri Breaks* might say: 'It accomplished the task.'

Potter is not alone in his institutionalization. The secretary, Ms Tinker (Barbara Hicks), affectionately moulds her actions to facilitate Potter's pragmatic dynamism. She anticipates his arrival in the office, receives his coat, hands him documents and imparts verbal information, all of which the preoccupied executive meets without ceremony. Rushing to his meeting with

---

[23] Adorno and Horkheimer, *Dialectic of Enlightenment*, 150.

the 'important people', Potter omits to close the office door, and Ms Tinker shuts it with a smiling air of spousal affection. Despite Potter's more 'obvious' value to hospital operations, therefore, he is shown to be equally dependent upon the unacknowledged contribution of others in the system. Whilst the official delegation agitatedly discuss their options after the hospital is blockaded by the makings of a popular riot, a missile is thrown through Potter's office window, injuring Phyllis. In the confusion, the group tend to the wounded delegate, scramble to the phones and shutter the windows, leaving the office in gloom. Through the bustle, the office scene showcases a hierarchy of dependency. Ms Tinker notices that everyone is standing in the dark, and casually switches on the light. No one notices the change. The phones are also not in working order today, and Sir Anthony is accidentally connected to Battersea Dog's Home and a minicab company. A third time, Supt Johns humbly dials on the peer's behalf, and the call is finally put through. Tending to Phyllis' injury, Sir Jeffrey asks for tweezers, procured from the pocket of another secretary. Subordinates accomplish basic actions that are, for various reasons, beyond the ability of their superiors. The more illustrious the individual, it seems, the greater their degree of unrecognized dependence upon people below them in the social structure. But, again, the film refuses to privilege these subordinates with any greater value as a result of their quiet consistency. Ms Tinker's thoughtfulness is humorously contrasted with the more 'serious' actions of the others. The chaotic scene in Potter's office is perhaps when the film's satirical social matrix is at its keenest – Ms Tinker's housekeeping becomes just as absurd a gesture as the fact that the agitated elites were sitting in the gloom in the first place.

The clamouring protestors outside suddenly present the Royal delegation with a serious problem. It has become impossible to ignore the alarming size and volatility of the riotous crowd beyond the hospital gates. Popular discontent has been fermenting in the world beyond and seems now to have mutated into mass insurrection. The strikers join forces with a political march protesting the presence of the African dictator in the private wing, and the mob is now held back by the police. Eventually, a figure emerges to galvanize the crowd's resentment. Elijah Odingu (Rufus Collins) directs the protestors' rage not only against the reviled Ngami, but also against his 'capitalist' protectors (Figure 39).

For all his questionable actions, Mr Potter is shown to be instrumental in maintaining the official arrangements. By going out to bargain with Odingu, he shows genuine ingenuity and courage, successfully managing to negotiate safe passage for ambulances containing, unbeknownst to the resentful crowd, the

Figure 39 Elijia Odingu (Rufus Collins) galvanises the protestors in *Britannia Hospital* (1982).

Royal entourage in disguise. In return for this concession on behalf of what are initially believed to be civilians injured in terrorist attacks, Potter betrays the non-essential privileged dependents, including Ngami, and sends them out to meet the wrath of the mob. Odingu has won his battle against privilege and inequality; yet Potter's ingenuity has allowed the ultimate mythic embodiment of social distinction itself to slip in under the wire. The Royal family then parade about as a tactless reminder of the ultimate unchangeability of the system. The effect is to make a mockery of the people's victory. It contrasts Odingu's championing of equality and humane feeling with the triumph of a contemptuous lie. The protestors display an understandable indignation when faced with a deceptive, hypocritical and absurd vision of the social elite, and, when the bandages and blankets are removed from the fake patients, to reveal uniformed representatives and HRH herself, the patriotic non-diegetic music makes what is being revealed seem like a sham itself: the pomp, ceremony and grandeur of social distinction as a concept. The trick that got them through the protestors mirrors the trick that characterizes the real thing.

Yet, *Britannia Hospital* still presents a broadly negative view of popular revolutionary praxis. As we have seen, critical philosophy refuses to advocate such activity for reasons that illuminate aspects of a Light Romanticism. The refusal to participate in affirmative action avoids perpetuating the wrong inherent in praxis itself, yet this refusal is burdened with a guilt reflected in the poetics of modern art. The idea of revolutionary praxis contains the spirit of the totality it wishes to overthrow. Indeed, by the final scene, *Britannia Hospital* shows us a vision of a society which, after having undergone a radical experience of political upheaval, appears to be on the verge of congealing again in the form of an awesome and monolithic tyranny. The dissenting public are shown to be broadly selfish, vindictive and easily manipulated; in Anderson's own terms, they simply follow 'the person who shouts loudest', like the crowd in Shakespeare's *Julius Caesar* (1599).[24] However, a sincere desire for justice, equality and rational discussion is occasionally apparent through their churning passions, and, as events progress, the belligerence of the protestors becomes validated by the hypocrisies, absurdities and criminal activities perpetrated by society's guardians.

Yet, when the rebels eventually overwhelm the police and force their way into the heart of elite society, they are easily quelled by Millar's numbing charisma. Even though their riotous actions have brought matters to a head, by the final scene, the prospect of political change will be swamped by a sublime experience of mute spectatorship. The protestors' efforts to bring about social equality become flattened, along with the similarly futile actions of their official antagonists. They are equated in insignificance, but only under the shadow of Miller's spectacle of tyranny.

The man without qualities

What, then, of Mick Travis – the 'hero' of Anderson's trilogy? Although he is the leading figure within a clearly defined and sympathetic group in *If....*, and this centrality becomes even more pronounced in *O Lucky Man!*, Travis' function in

Figure 40 Travis (Malcolm McDowell) investigates Prof Millar's sinister experiments in *Britannia Hospital* (1982).

---

[24] Rampell, et al., 'Revolution Is the Opium of the Intellectuals', 36.

Britannia Hospital is very different. Compared to the battle between the elites and the protestors, his story is largely a narrative sideshow (Figure 40).

There is no doubt about the new dominant figure in the narrative. The magnetic Millar is concerned with the destiny of the human race. Millar speaks for everyone, and, in so doing, creates himself – the Dark Romantic auctor – an ego that creates the illusion in others of having transcended the self by speaking on behalf of something larger, such as a nation, a race or an ideal. Travis, on the other hand, does the exact opposite. In *Britannia Hospital*, as in *O Lucky Man!*, he is concerned largely with himself; individual freedom, health, safety, monetary remuneration and professional satisfaction – these are his primary concerns. Yet, by so declaring, he paradoxically speaks for humanity at large. His role as an allegorical Everyman necessitates that he become a figure that transcends the subjective almost 'accidentally'. In *If....* he was largely undifferentiated from the group of innocent Crusaders, who stood for a Romantic ideal of freedom, albeit one that was problematically naïve. Travis breaks from this idea of the communal subject at the start of *O Lucky Man!* when he attempts to outshine his co-workers at the coffee factory, and spends much of his time after being released from prison attempting to regain that lost paradise. His efforts, whether to convince the drunken homeless of the Brotherhood of Man or, now, to work with an incompetent team of investigative journalists to bring the villainous Millar to justice, are doomed to failure. The fate that awaits this figure of modern subjectivity – vessel of humanity's illusions and anxieties in the modern developed world, suffering in the shadow of a forgotten ideal – brings him to a very curious condition. Yet, his efforts to play a role in the diegetic world of *Britannia Hospital* hinge, like so much else, upon the ambiguous powers of spectacle: that which is seen, recognized and valued.

Although Travis now heads a team of investigative journalists, the capitalist ideology that guided him in *O Lucky Man!* seems firmly in place once more. 'Gotta find something to sell. Something the people want to buy', he says, monetizing his desire to expose the unethical experiments of Prof Millar. His fellow journalists, Sammy (Frank Grimes) and Red (Mark Hamill), are youthful and cocksure; ensconced in a van down the street, they get high on drugs and become ineffectual backup.

Aided by Nurse Amanda Persil (Marsha Hunt), Travis manages to gain entry to Millar's private labs. He is there to 'get the dirt' on Millar – to inveigle his camera into the villain's secrets; yet the documentary crew, tripping around on Millar's heels, secure copious footage of the very kind of ethically dubious medical procedures that Travis seeks to capture. He hides in a cupboard and pokes his high-tech wireless camera through a crack in order to film: merely the TV crew, already documenting Millar's every move. They have just recorded him liquidizing and devouring a human brain. In this context, Travis' efforts to 'get a scoop' seem rather toothless. The value of the exposé is deflated by being merely a guerrilla attempt to record what the permitted crew are already documenting. He and Amanda are going to great lengths to smuggle an 'unruly' camera into a secret operating theatre; the documentary team, however, already have front row seats. Travis' probing camera – which assumes all the fearsome power of the gun it cosmetically resembles – actually lacks any such power (at this point in the film).

When Travis encounters that second foetus in a jar whilst exploring Millar's labs, it may, indeed, function as a simple intertextual reference to *If. . . .* or underscore Millar's ethically questionable methods. But if the muted strings on the musical soundtrack have an air of disappointment about them, then the scene might provoke a feeling of metanarrational regret. As an elegiac summation of Travis' character development, we may feel the gulf between the ideal of Romantic alterity that he once represented, to the sorry state of clueless complacency which has, on the whole, characterized his fictional being ever since. Travis looks up from his discovery, attracted by the sound of a whistle. Opening a conveniently placed hatch, he observes several dozen doctors and nurses rehearsing a complex medical procedure in an ominous operating theatre. This is the room in which Travis will meet his end – dissected and reconstructed as a monstrous hybrid of the human hopes and passions he has embodied across three films.

From a shot of Mr Figg reverently kissing the hand of HRH, the film cuts back to this theatre, and Millar finally sealing Travis' fate as the fulfilment of this, his first, 'human', experiment. For the Professor's jigsaw-like construction of body parts into a racially diverse whole seems like nothing less than an attempt to fashion a perfect human, freed from the flaws that have shown to pervade the world of *Britannia Hospital*. If the Travis of *O Lucky Man!* was too isolated, over-individualistic and lacking the sense of social cohesion necessary for a perfect society, then Millar's construction of a new subject from bits and pieces, appropriated from all forms of humanity, seems like a nightmarish realization of its opposite. The individual has been absorbed into the totality. The hybridized and violent result of Millar's 'humane solution' is not so far removed from Marlon Brando's devilish embodiment of the capitalist spirit. Heralded by a great 'genius' who proclaims to reveal the ultimate calculated transcendence of humanity's divided nature, the destruction of Travis' individualism might even be interpreted as a grotesque allegory of Marxist socialism. If we fancifully chose to interpret the failure of Millar's 'humane solution' as an allegory of Marxist praxis – its scientific pretensions in Marx and Engels, its utopian promise in the charisma of Lenin and its disastrous realization in state communism – then the film itself does not give us many points to contradict such a reading. Millar (Marx), the visionary ideologue, sees his history-making creation wreak havoc indiscriminately, and the utopian dream brought to ruin.

As in *O Lucky Man!*, a moment of stillness and pain bears the burden of a tragic revelation. Playing Frankenstein, Millar wakes his monstrous creation on the operating table and says: 'Welcome to the world!' The New Man gradually gains consciousness, and Malcolm McDowell's piercing eyes look up into space and slowly reveal pained emotions, as if once again on the verge of tears (Figure 41). Given the immediate context of Millar's welcoming words, the New Man's internal suffering is suggested to be the result of perceiving abstractly the present state of human civilization represented by *Britannia Hospital*.

The momentary gaze becomes a sign of metanarrational disappointment, reproach and also of truth – a sign of the objective 'wrong', responsibility of no single subjectivity, which characterizes the allegorical diegesis. The supreme generic moment of subjective power – when Frankenstein would traditionally proclaim triumphantly his usurpation of Godlike creativity ('It's alive!') – becomes something else. Filmic stillness is again utilized as a vessel for an enigmatic truth that refuses to be unproblematically integrated into the

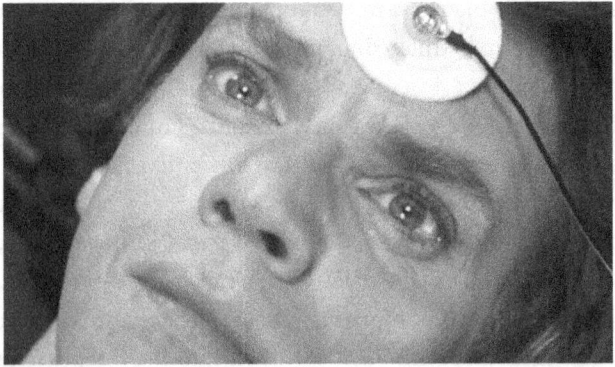

Figure 41 Millar's 'New Man' (Malcolm McDowell) contemplates the world into which he has been born. *Britannia Hospital* (1982).

cinematic story – the pull of narrative action. It momentarily offers something halfway between story and excess. Travis' face, which has lost its identity *as* Travis' face, is a non-event that demands a new name. Perhaps reflected in those shining eyes are all the dreams of *If . . . .*'s Crusaders, all the pain and betrayal of *O Lucky Man!* and the realization that Travis, the hero of Sherwin and Anderson's epic *Bildungsroman*, has failed to 'do his duty', or even to know what it might have been.

At this moment, I believe we find the perfect illustration of the transition between Light and Dark Romanticism discussed in Part One of this book. To move from thought to praxis is to embrace failure and betray the 'empty infinity' of freedom as pure negation. Morse Peckham believed that the Romantic experience found fulfilment in the realization – later described so well by Adorno – that all expression of being is violence. Morality then, as we have seen, is recast as an intolerable passivity. If all action is violence, then Millar's New Man epitomizes the pure aggression that marks the disastrous transition from thought to act – from Light to Dark. When faced with a society so evidently wracked with terrible things, it is more than a tragic fulfilment of generic convention when the New Man's poignant moment of revelation is lost in bloodshed. A flash of indeterminate truth revealed in filmic stillness is lost in the riptide of cinematic spectacle. Thought is lost in the violent and numbing act.

The New Man bites Millar's hand, and, in the desperate struggle to separate the two, the head tears away from the body. As a symbol of the new modern subject-as-bricolage, the creature loses the seat of individuality, and the power of an implicitly collective and unthinking rage takes over. Divided between the head and the body, the New Man becomes, like Hamlet, a symbol of the hopelessness of present conditions: freedom's dependency upon historical institutions and reified categories as well as the essential violence that underlies them. The doomed existence of the New Man is only a result of Millar's narcissism, just as *Britannia Hospital* as an artwork is only the result of the filmmakers' expression.

But something new and uncertain yet remains. It is only after Travis has lost all control, lying unconscious and defeated in Millar's operating room, that an unexpected ray of hope appears; something which recalls, even in Travis' apocalyptic failure, the disruptive potential of the Romantic Crusader he left behind on the school rooftop. The camera that the investigative reporter impotently wielded like a gun does contain a vestige of power. Travis' work, distorted by the ideology of capitalism in his talk of supply and demand, is, after all illusions are smothered, nothing less than the Romantic striving to place an unauthorized camera – to enact something like a redistribution of the sensible fabric of political and aesthetic reality.

The opportunity appears as a gap in Millar's orchestrated world of appearances. Before the Professor begins experimenting on the captured Travis, he turns to the director of the documentary crew and says: 'Not this one, Peter'. In this moment we see that the investigative journalist's efforts to intervene in the sensorial fabric – where perceptual experience equates to politics – were not totally without potential. Despite the documentary crew's privileged insight into Millar's grandest projects, there are still some things that the great man will not have them see;, some things which it is within his power to withhold from perception. The power of the gaze functions as Millar's combined ability to hold the eye of the camera and his authority to send it away. In the words 'Not this one, Peter', the value of Travis' unruly camera is reaffirmed, even after the destruction of its controlling hand. This is why there is so much potential in the moment when Amanda, Travis' collaborator, picks up the camera, kisses it, and says 'Darling, your work will go on', however clichéd and unconvincing the line may seem. The riotous climax will be precipitated when she broadcasts images of HRH to the reporter's van, which is now occupied by protestors roused to storm the gates of the hospital after seeing this proof of Potter's betrayal.

To recall Rancière's discussion of Schelling, perhaps this is a moment when film imagines its potential to achieve the Absolute, through exploring and renegotiating the divide between the objective eye of the camera and the subjective eye of the filmmaker. The unauthorized, uncontrolled and largely unplanned image is still shown to have the power to subvert the distribution of the sensible. Travis' work – for all its misguided selfishness and disappointment – has a potential value that is in sympathy with the interpretable metalanguage of the film itself. Travis' unruly camera has the right 'spirit': a Romantic spirit. Shaped like a weapon, its disregard for boundaries and *doxa*, its incessant desire to criticize, to find things to attack, to see under the surface: it shares all this with *Britannia Hospital* itself. Yet, it also shares the film's failure. The author who wields this supposedly objective eye of truth inevitably fails by transforming its objectivity into something else – a meaningful expression – a fiction which, as Travis himself is at pains to explain, is contextualized, marketed and understood as a product: 'Something people want to buy'. Travis cannot succeed and expose Millar any more than *Britannia Hospital* as a satire can overthrow the dominant social system and its pervasive myths and hypocrisies. Travis' failure as a free individual, as well as *Britannia Hospital*'s failure as a film – these things reflect the aporetic condition of modern art itself.

The moment of crisis

So much for Travis the hero. His alienated suffering has been eclipsed by that of humanity as a whole, squabbling in Potter's office and pressing against the hospital gates. In its desire to transcend a self-interested individualism, perhaps *Britannia Hospital* is 'post-Romantic', as Anderson affirmed. But the film's Romanticism persists in refusing to acknowledge any productive alternative to the truth-content experienced by the suffering and immobile subject. Alternative images of 'truth' do emerge – like Adorno's fireworks and *Mickey One*'s broken nose – but their validity remains transient, un-programmatic and flawed.

There is one such shot that endows the unruly public beyond the railings with a sense of poetic validation. In a sudden change of register, the tone of irony accompanying the sterile pomp and ceremony of the Royal entourage makes way for another image of pregnant stillness. As the social elite troop across the hospital grounds to Millar's lab, patriotic music blurs the diegetic boundaries and swells to accompany the angry crowd observing this proof of their betrayal. The camera tracks horizontally across the figures pressed against the railings; their faces crane forward as their hands hold the bars, accentuating their exclusion from the privileged world flaunted before them (Figure 42). The film turns the resources of class distinction into the means of disclosing a

Figure 42 The protestors are given a poignant moment of filmic validation. *Britannia Hospital* (1982).

certain unexpected value; the mythic music and the iron bars – the 'tools' used to ensure the separation of the people – become symbols of their freedom through negation: signs of what they are denied. Their grievances are given a nobility which is all the more potent because of the way the momentary sincerity of the representation contrasts with the film's otherwise ironic tone.

The crowd resume their shouting, breach the gates and engage ranks of police officers wearing riot gear. Outside the labs, the Royal party stand to attention as the inauguration ceremony begins. A band plays the British national anthem, and as the riot continues to this anempathetic accompaniment it is almost as if the filmic rhetoric compensates for the absence of the infamous and officially omitted middle verse:

> O Lord our God arise,
> Scatter her enemies,
> And make them fall:
> Confound their politics,
> Frustrate their knavish tricks,
> On Thee our hopes we fix:
> God save us all.

The mythic idealism crystallized in the patriotic music is recontextualized as a hypocritical and violent realization of social power. 'Scatter her enemies' becomes the spectacle of an SPG officer punching a harmless woman; 'Confound their politics' becomes Lady Felicity cursing the working classes with crude profanity that clashes comically with her social status; 'Frustrate their knavish tricks' becomes Potter betraying the private patients and protestors for a 'greater good'; and 'God save us all' becomes the subsequent desperate scramble of the Royal delegation to find shelter from the mob in Millar's lab.

Throughout the film, various factions have been vying for significance. The narrative has been densely packed with union action, terrorist attacks, technological glitches, personal jealousies, monstrous experiments, class tensions, besieging rioters and a nightmare of logistical rigmarole. The success of the Royal visit has become a metaphor for proper functioning of the power structures synonymous with modern civilization itself. The filmic allegory positions the popular uprising as a challenge to the hegemony of the dominant political and cultural arrangement of human affairs. As a 'state of the nation' satire, *Britannia Hospital* radicalizes its final scenes by subsuming all the narrative's class struggles, prejudices and individual desires within an epic allegorical framework. This sense of building to a grand and apocalyptic summary perspective means that the climactic monologue is able to address the entirety of the social fabric woven by the film and perform something like a metanarrational judgement.

With the police overwhelmed by the onslaught of popular resentment, spilling, finally, through the establishment's last redoubt, Millar emerges above the melee and shouts down the crowd. Speaking on his usual grand scale, the Professor quells the angry mob of 'Little men' and invites them to follow him. Odingu leads the public throng into a lecture theatre to witness Millar's revelation – to see and hear 'what the Future means'. Indeed, the film's tone has now raised the pitch of events to a level that matches Millar's previously absurd grandiloquence. *Britannia Hospital*, like Millar himself, has all the whilst been talking about the condition of humanity in general; it is therefore not a surprise to end the film on his terms, and to finally equate his previously disproportionate rhetoric with that of the satire itself. Millar must fulfil his destiny as a fictional character. He becomes a perfect embodiment of Dark Romanticism, offering a moment of cultural transcendence that is nothing less than pure totality: explanation as authoritarian apocalypse.

A shameful conquest

Millar's motionless audience are told that humanity is living on the verge of 'a new era'. 'I am going to show you the face of that new era!', he proclaims, standing

Figure 43 Millar (Graham Crowden) prepares to reveal his sublime creation, Genesis. *Britannia Hospital* (1982).

in the middle of an austere stage – an expanse of black decorated with white and chrome shapes, evoking not only *2001: A Space Odyssey*, but also fascist propaganda. An aesthetic of bold, clinical and linear structures evokes ideas of the superhuman, the posthuman or the inhuman (Figure 43).

Millar delivers a potent monologue on the self-destructive tendencies of the human race. He speaks from a stage that has become, as Walter Benjamin described on behalf of Brechtian epic theatre, 'a public platform'[25] – a space for direct critical address. He professes faith in the power of the human brain to overcome racial and class differences, and to set aside conflict in the name of a transcendental evolution to post-humanity. The Professor finally reveals Genesis, his second attempt (after the failure with Travis) to produce 'Man remade'. Revealed from under a pyramidal case, Millar's great answer to humankind's perpetual strife is an abnormal and pulsating disembodied brain, looking somewhat like an atomic bomb cloud. Over an awed silence from the spellbound crowd, the new being's faltering first words bring the film to a close: the 'What piece of work is a man' speech from *Hamlet* (c.1601). As if it were a broken record, Genesis repeats the line 'How like a God . . ', which becomes both an affirmation and a question.

This final sequence is unlike the rest of the film. The mode of metanarrational address has changed, and the film's matrix of politicized belligerents – its central diegetic and narrative content – has transformed into a passive array of spectators. The potentially chilling effect of this transformation is partly a result of their similarity, now, to a cinema audience.[26] Millar becomes the sole active figure in the diegesis. When he first invited the discontented public to join his demonstration, the protestors took their seats next to the officials and dignitaries; although neither party seemed enthusiastic about their new neighbours, Millar became the cause of a temporary and uneasy kind of equality. When Odingu sat next to Phyllis, Keating next to Lady Felicity and everyone gave each other an uncertain look, society became flattened – defined by a simpler distinction, between Millar on one hand and humanity on the other. Millar's speech pacifies all the other diegetic elements, including satirical class tensions, power struggles, selfish plots and criminal activities. The world around him is stunned into an uncertain silence.

Part of the ambiguity surrounding Graham Crowden's character results from the interesting possibility that a great deal of what he says in this climactic speech might be considered 'true' by many potential film viewers. Millar discourses

---

[25] Benjamin, 'What is Epic Theatre?' (second version), 22.
[26] See Hedling, *Lindsay Anderson*, 180.

charismatically about the devastating effects of climate change, prejudice, war and social distinction. He seems to have all the facts at his fingertips: 'two-thirds' of all plant species, 55 per cent of the animal kingdom' and 70 per cent of our mineral resources' will be extinguished by the end of the century. Indeed, Miller expresses political opinions that align with the most radical members of the audience; his passionate accusation that 'a tiny minority indulge themselves in absurd and extravagant luxury' might have been spoken by Odingu. Although these moral accusations chime with contemporary standards of humanitarian ethics, they contain a hidden violence, and eventually Millar's speech begins to demonstrate more clearly its underlying hostility to principles of freedom.

His subject is the self-mastery of the human race; our ability to achieve things on compounding standards of possibility, transcending the condition of our ancestors, and our potential to change the future in ways that are currently unimaginable. This theme is communicated alongside a sublime awe for the human brain and its capacity to comprehend and create. Millar bamboozles his audience by employing the vanity of positivism, evoking a profoundly affective experience of universal narcissism where the 'glory' of human achievement has the effect of a drug. Yet, this progressive idealism – a positivity which finds its determining value in the rational and historical improvement of the human condition – is brought into an irresolvable political tension with the method of its filmic presentation: the duality of passive and active; those who speak and those who listen; the subject of knowledge and those who are its object. If the audience members represent a self-consciously dynamic humanity (which Hegel might have understood by using the term 'Spirit'), then they are objectified by Millar's explanatory authority. Spirit is transformed into social capital.

Ultimately, Millar claims that the real enemy to human destiny is freedom – freedom in the form of choice. Man chooses, Millar says accusatorily, to 'annihilate itself'. If humans wage war and destroy the world around them through the exercise of free will, then the rational thing is to remove that freedom. The Professor's argument provides the framework for a 'rationalistic' form of social planning and eugenics, inviting the destruction of freedom and its abstract embodiment in the autonomous individual. That destruction is precisely what Genesis represents, not only as a diegetic element but also as a filmic experience.

Putting aside their differences, forgetting their grievances and claiming a vestige of equality that promises to answer all their questions, the social world of *Britannia Hospital* achieves a kind of problematic cultural transcendence.

Figure 44 Humanity, metonymically represented by Mr Potter (Leonard Rossiter), contemplates a politically ambiguous infinite. *Britannia Hospital* (1982).

Sitting passive before a metaphysical crisis occasioned by the narrative, the faces of Potter, Odingu and the rest, shown in close-up, become signs of a profound Light Romantic inaction (Figure 44). Even at their moment of most transcendent value – as the words 'How like an angel ... how like a God', spoken by Genesis, sound against their individual faces – they become the image of a social totality so 'perfect' it is ready to be contained in 'a matchbox', as Millar had threatened. It is almost as if we have been privileged to walk behind a painting by C. D. Friedrich and see those transfixed observers from the front. In these images, the 'empty infinities' of negative freedom encounter the spectre of political quietism: thralldom to the tyrany of spectacle. Their similarity to a cinema audience is not accidental. The film's method of 'aesthetic education' demands that we recognize those faces as our own. Like the artwork itself, this moment of cultural transcendence has been orchestrated by one who does not doubt, nor one who doubts their right to speak for others. As 'the one who speaks', an artist knows that a conscious violence is the only honest way to speak at all.

The false ending

In an article about *Britannia Hospital*, Lindsay Anderson differentiates between the 'intellect' and 'intelligence'.[27] Although he does not explain this difference in any great detail, it is possible to follow his lead and interpret the end of the Mick

---

[27] Anderson, '*Britannia Hospital*', 157.

Travis trilogy in reference to this distinction. We might think of the intellect as the unequal, historically determined and accumulated distribution of knowledge and skills possessed by any particular individual, whilst intelligence might be understood as the formal, equal and innate capacity of any human being to think rationally. According to this distinction, intelligence becomes the prerequisite for intellect. A similar formulation has been used by Jacques Rancière in his discussion of the concrete social realization of political reason itself in the act of speaking and listening.[28] In the presence of an auctor who speaks in the name of humanity at large, the social capacity for reason – embodied by the idea of the 'human', which Millar puts on trial at the end of *Britannia Hospital* – is presented with a complete imbalance of the distinction between intellect and intelligence. This imbalance has rendered the majority mute and in bondage to the sublime performance of political power. Through a reduction of the capacity for reason to the mute act of listening, humanity forfeits, to the rule of a tyrant, the necessary other half of that relation. This is an experience of social power articulated as the presentation of a distinction between active and inactive, speaking and silent, but one that yet contains the radical potential to redistribute the meanings of such terms.

By listening to Millar, the audience – a collection of figures we know to be dynamic, angry at a society which is not perfect, yet full of a diverse and colourful life – become things; silent, receptive and still. Yet, this does not make them as objectified and politically quietist as the presentation of events makes them appear at first. Like Travis at the end of *O Lucky Man!*, Millar's audience are allowed an indeterminate moment of stillness conjured by raw explanatory violence. But even as this moment is experienced as the effect of naked force (Anderson's slap with the script is replaced here by the violence of Millar's rhetoric), there remains the possibility for something genuinely New to occur.

Millar's message, in twisted form, becomes the message of the film itself: 'an appeal to the intelligence', just as Anderson claimed:

> The challenge at the end is a question, not an answer ... the film does say, I hope, that we must mistrust institutions, power, the instincts for power within us, and in that way I think *Britannia Hospital* is an anarchist film. It puts the responsibility squarely on the individual to develop first the intelligence and the moral awareness by which alone Man can control his destiny.[29]

---

[28] Rancière, *On the Shores of Politics*, 81–2.
[29] Cited in Rampell, et al., 'Revolution Is the Opium of the Intellectuals', 36.

Don't go to authority figures and expect something of them, as Adorno warned. You've got to think for yourselves, even if you have to be told to do it. Like the figure of the filmmaker behind the camera, Millar performs the paradox of aesthetic education: the act of unfreedom, which is necessary to make freedom sensible as a possibility. Anderson's films seem to dramatize, philosophically, the explanatory violence that is also the seed of emancipation.

By falling into a condition of uncertain thought, the humanity of *Britannia Hospital* has become 'open'. But to what? Emerging from this space of freedom is simply that greatest of betrayals: a 'new' voice speaking 'old' words – a voice, in fact, deprived of all vestige of humanity save an ironic validation of the power which gives it life. Like Arthur Lowe's dying politician, Genesis recites broken passages of Shakespeare, falling back on a trustworthy political myth because it suffers from a related trauma. These bodies take on the burden of the body politic, which, divided, alienated, pulled in different directions and beaten, displays a terrifying willingness to abandon its own vitality through participation in a group experience of sublimity. All this is engineered by a man of boundless activity whose political presence is erased by his own speech. Millar's actions as a Romantic genius create a space for something different, but fill it with something deathly, inhuman and spouting the same old recycled myths. Despite this, the audience's lack of reaction to Millar's new humanity contains, in its passive negation of determinate action or expression, the possibility of freedom, a freedom that would, as always, only be the freedom not to affirm.

Britannia Hospital ends, not with a vision of apocalyptic violence, nor with our heroes going back to work, the director stepping onto the screen like God or an uneasy ride into the sunset, but with a similar moment of sublime diegetic excess in which action collapses into a reflective stillness. Horkheimer put it bluntly: 'All hope lies in thought'[30] – intolerable reflection rather than productive and successful activity. Critical philosophy, like Anderson and Millar, places faith in human intelligence to reason 'aesthetically', with genuine and indeterminate freedom. *Britannia Hospital* creates a powerful moment for such thought. It creates an empty infinity dominated by a charismatic individual in whose presence we can only sit passive, immobile, disembodied, and yet, through the techniques of Romantic critique, catch ourselves in the act of falling silent.

---

[30] Adorno and Horkheimer, *Towards a New Manifesto*, 27; see also Adorno, 'Resignation', 293.

Appendix

Comparison of terms

The table below indicates rough distinctions between two broadly defined poles of Romanticism, as they are discussed in this book. These entirely rhetorical quasi-structuralist relationships may be helpful in guiding the reader through the philosophical analysis presented in the early chapters. 'Capitalism' belongs in the Dark column, although it is difficult to assign a satisfying corresponding term. Like Romanticism, 'Art' contains features relating to both sides, as the opening chapters make clear. Art is Light in terms of aesthetic indeterminacy, for example, and Dark in terms of meaningful expression.

Light Romanticism	Dark Romanticism
Negation	Affirmation
Freedom	Explanation
Quality	Quantity
Inaction	Action
Film	Cinema
Infinity	Totality
Loss	Profit
Dionysus	Apollo
Objective	Subjective
Uncertainty	Certainty
Incoherence	Coherence
Open	Closed
Pain	Pleasure
Meaningless	Meaningful
Failure	Success
Disagreement	Agreement
Punctum	Stadium
Unproductive	Productive
Useless	Useful

Bibliography

Abrams, M. H. *Natural Supernaturalism: Tradition and Revolution in Romantic Literature*. 1971. New York: W. W. Norton and Co., 1973.

Adorno, Theodor W. *Aesthetic Theory*. 1970. London and New York: Bloomsbury, 2017.

Adorno, Theodor W. 'Education after Auschwitz'. 1967. In *Critical Models: Interventions and Catchwords*, 191–204. New York: Columbia University Press, 2005.

Adorno, Theodor W. *History and Freedom: Lectures, 1964–1965*. Cambridge: Polity Press, 2006.

Adorno, Theodor W. *In Search of Wagner*. 1952. London and New York: Verso, 1991.

Adorno, Theodor W. *Lectures on Negative Dialectics*. 1965–6. Cambridge: Polity Press, 2008.

Adorno, Theodor W. 'Marginalia to Theory and Praxis'. 1969. In *Critical Models: Interventions and Catchwords*, 259–78. New York: Columbia University Press, 2005.

Adorno, Theodor W. *Minima Moralia: Reflections from a Damaged Life*. 1951. London and New York: Verso, 1987.

Adorno, Theodor W. *Negative Dialectics*. 1966. New York: The Continuum International Publishing Group, 2007.

Adorno, Theodor W. 'Notes on Kafka'. 1953. In *Can One Live After Auschwitz? A Philosophical Reader*, ed. Rolf Tidemann, 211–39. Stanford: Stanford University Press, 2003.

Adorno, Theodor W. 'Opinion Delusion Society'. 1963. In *Critical Models: Interventions and Catchwords*, 105–22. New York: Columbia University Press, 2005.

Adorno, Theodor W. 'Parataxis: On Hölderlin's Late Poetry'. 1963. In *Notes to Literature, Volume Two*, ed. Rolf Tidemann, 109–49. New York: Columbia University Press, 1992.

Adorno, Theodor W. 'Resignation'. 1969. In *Critical Models: Interventions and Catchwords*, 289–93. New York: Columbia University Press, 2005.

Adorno, Theodor W. 'The Stars Down to Earth'. 1974. In *The Stars Down to Earth and Other Essays on the Irrational in Culture*, ed. Stephen Crook, 46–171. London and New York: Routledge, 1994.

Adorno, Theodor W. and Max Horkheimer. *Dialectic of Enlightenment*. 1947. London and New York: Verso, 1997.

Adorno, Theodor W. and Max Horkheimer. *Towards a New Manifesto*. 1989. London and New York: Verso, 2019.

Albert, Hans. *Treatise on Critical Reason*. 1968. Princeton: Princeton University Press, 1985.

Anderson, Lindsay. 'Britannia Hospital'. 1994. In *Never Apologize: The Collected Writings*, ed. Paul Ryan, 148–59. London: Plexus, 2004.
Anderson, Lindsay. 'British Cinema: The Historical Imperative'. 1984. In *Never Apologize: The Collected Writings*, ed. Paul Ryan, 390–7. London: Plexus, 2004.
Anderson, Lindsay. *The Diaries*, ed. Paul Sutton. London: Methuen, 2004.
Anderson, Lindsay. 'The Film Artist – Freedom and Responsibility!'. In *Never Apologize: The Collected Writings*, ed. Paul Ryan, 210–14. London: Plexus, 2004.
Anderson, Lindsay. 'Get Out and Push!'. 1957. In *Never Apologize: The Collected Writings*, ed. Paul Ryan, 233–51. London: Plexus, 2004.
Anderson, Lindsay. 'How *If*.... Came About'. In *Never Apologize: The Collected Writings*, ed. Paul Ryan, 108–11. London: Plexus, 2004.
Anderson, Lindsay. 'Notes for a Preface'. In *Never Apologize: The Collected Writings*, ed. Paul Ryan, 120–3. London: Plexus, 2004.
Anderson, Lindsay. 'O Lucky Man!'. 1994. In *Never Apologize: The Collected Writings*, ed. Paul Ryan, 126–8. London: Plexus, 2004.
Anderson, Lindsay. 'School to Screen'. In *Never Apologize: The Collected Writings*, ed. Paul Ryan, 112–15. London: Plexus, 2004.
Anderson, Lindsay. 'Stand Up! Stand Up!'. 1956. In *Never Apologize: The Collected Writings*, ed. Paul Ryan, 218–32. London: Plexus, 2004.
Anderson, Lindsay. 'Stripping the Veils Away'. 1973. In *Never Apologize: The Collected Writings*, ed. Paul Ryan, 129–36. London: Plexus, 2004.
Bakhtin, M. M. *The Dialogic Imagination: Four Essays*. 1975. Austin: University of Texas Press, 1996.
Barthes, Roland. *Camera Lucida*. 1980. London: Vintage Books, 2000.
Barthes, Roland. *Criticism and Truth*. 1966. London and New York: Continuum, 2007.
Barthes, Roland. *Mythologies*. 1957. London: Vintage Books, 2009.
Bartley III, W. W. 'Alienation Alienated: The Economics of Knowledge *Versus* the Psychology and Sociology of Knowledge'. In *Evolutionary Epistemology, Theory of Rationality, and the Sociology of Knowledge*, ed. Gerard Radnitzky and W. W. Bartley III, 423–51. La Salle: Open Court, 1987.
Bataille, Georges. *Literature and Evil*. New York: Marion Boyars, 1985.
Benjamin, Walter. *The Origin of German Tragic Drama*. 1963. London and New York: Verso, 2009.
Benjamin, Walter. 'What is Epic Theatre?' (first version). 1966. In *Understanding Brecht*, 1–13. London: NLB, 1973.
Benjamin, Walter. 'What is Epic Theatre?' (second version). 1939. In *Understanding Brecht*, 15–22. London: NLB, 1973.
Berlin, Isiah. *The Roots of Romanticism*. 1965, ed. Henry Hardy. London: Pimlico, 2000.
Berliner, Todd. *Hollywood Incoherent: Narration in Seventies Cinema*. Austin: University of Texas Press, 2010.

Bernstein, Richard J. *The New Constellation: The Ethical-Political Horizons of Modernity/Postmodernity*. Cambridge: Polity Press, 1991.

Blake, William. 'The Marriage of Heaven and Hell'. c.1790–93. In *Complete Writings*, ed. Geoffrey Keynes, 148–60. London: Oxford University Press, 1966.

Bourdieu, Pierre. *Language and Symbolic Power*. 1991. Cambridge: Polity Press, 2018.

Braudel, Fernand. *Civilisation and Capitalism: 15th–18th Century, Vol. 2, The Wheels of Commerce*. 1979. London: William Collins Sons and Co., 1983.

Bronk, Richard. *The Romantic Economist: Imagination in Economics*. Cambridge: Cambridge University Press, 2009.

Browning, Robert. 'Epilogue'. 1889. In *Robert Browning's Poetry*, ed. James F. Loucks and Andrew M. Stauffer, 485. New York: W. W. Norton and Co., 1979.

Buck-Morss, Susan. *The Origin of Negative Dialectics: Theodor W. Adorno, Walter Benjamin, and the Frankfurt Institute*. New York: The Free Press, 1977.

Callinicos, Alex. *Against Postmodernism: A Marxist Critique*. Cambridge: Polity Press, 1989.

Canby, Vincent. '"The Missouri Breaks", Offbeat Western'. In *The New York Times*, 20 May 1976. https://www.nytimes.com/1976/05/20/archives/missouri-breaks-offbeat-western.html; accessed 1 March 2021.

Carlyle, Thomas. *The Works of Thomas Carlyle, Vol 10 – Past and Present*. 1843. Cambridge: Cambridge University Press, 2010.

Chaikin, Michael and Cronin, Paul. 'A Summing Up'. 2007. In *Arthur Penn: Interviews*, ed. Michael Chaiken and Paul Cronin, 200–13. Jackson: University Press of Mississippi, 2008.

Coleridge, Samuel Taylor. 'Kubla Kahn'. 1816. In *Poems*, ed. J. B. Beer, 167–8. London: J. M. Dent and Sons Ltd., 1963.

Colletti, Lucio. *From Rousseau to Lenin*. 1969. London: NLB, 1972.

Combs, Richard. 'Arthur Penn'. 1981. In *Arthur Penn: Interviews*, ed. Michael Chaiken and Paul Cronin, 133–45. Jackson: University Press of Mississippi, 2008.

Conrad, Joseph. *Heart of Darkness*. 1902. London and New York: Alfred A. Knopf – Everyman's Library, 1993.

Crowdus, Gary and Richard Porton. 'The Importance of a Singular Guiding Vision: An Interview with Arthur Penn'. In *Cinéaste*, Vol. 20/2 (1993): 4–16.

Cunningham, Frank R. 'Lindsay Anderson's *O Lucky Man*! and the Romantic Tradition'. In *Literature/Film Quarterly*, Vol. 2/3 (1974): 256–61.

Deleuze, Gilles. *Cinema 2: The Time-Image*. 1985. London and New York: Continuum, 2005.

Dostoevsky, Fyodor. *Notes from Underground*. 1864. London and New York: Alfred A. Knopf – Everyman's Library, 2004.

Dostoevsky, Fyodor. *Winter Notes on Summer Impressions*. 1863. Richmond: Oneworld Classics Ltd., 2008.

Fichte, Johann Gottlieb. *The Vocation of Man*. 1799. In *The Popular Works of Johann Gottlieb Fichte, Vol. 1*, 321–478. Bristol: Thoemmes Press, 1999.

Fichte, Johann Gottlieb. *The Vocation of the Scholar*. 1794. In *The Popular Works of Johann Gottlieb Fichte, Vol. 1*, 149–205. Bristol: Thoemmes Press, 1999.

Frank, Manfred. *The Philosophical Foundations of Early German Romanticism*. Albany: State University of New York Press, 2004.

Fuller, Steve. 'Karl Popper and the Reconstitution of the Rationalist Left'. In *Karl Popper: A Centenary Assessment, Volume III – Science*, 2006, ed. Ian Jarvie, Karl Milford and David Miller, 181–96. Milton Keynes: College Publications, 2015.

Gallagher, Catherine. 'The Romantics and the Political Economists'. In *The Cambridge History of English Romantic Literature*, ed. James Chandler, 71–100. Cambridge: Cambridge University Press, 2009.

Goethe, Johann Wolfgang von. *Wilhelm Meister's Apprenticeship*. 1796. London: J. M. Dent and Sons, 1944.

Gogol, Nikolai. *Dead Souls*. 1842–52. New York: Alfred A. Knopf – Everyman's Library, 2004.

Goldmann, Lucien. *Immanuel Kant*. 1967. London: Verso, 2011.

Gorz, André. *Critique of Economic Reason*. 1988. New York and London: Verso, 1989.

Griffin, Dustin. *Satire: A Critical Reintroduction*. Lexington: University Press of Kentucky, 1994.

Habermas, Jürgen. *The Philosophical Discourse of Modernity*. 1985. Cambridge: Polity Press, 1998.

Hedling, Erik. *Lindsay Anderson: Maverick Film-Maker*. London and Washington: Cassell, 1998.

Hegel, Georg Wilhelm Friedrich. *Introductory Lectures on Aesthetics*. 1820–29. London: Penguin Books, 2004.

Hegel, Georg Wilhelm Friedrich. *The Phenomenology of Spirit*. 1807. Oxford: Oxford University Press, 1976.

Highet, Gibert. *The Anatomy of Satire*. Princeton: Princeton University Press, 1962.

Hill, John. *British Cinema in the 1980s: Issues and Themes*. Oxford: Clarendon Press, 1999.

Hölderlin, Friedrich. Letter 58. To Christian Ludwig Neuffer. 1798. In *Essays and Letters*, 108–10. London: Penguin, 2009.

Hölderlin, Friedrich, (et al.). 'The Oldest Program for a System of German Idealism'. c.1795. In *Essays and Letters*, 341–2. London: Penguin, 2009.

Hölderlin, Friedrich. *Seven Maxims*. c.1799. In *Essays and Letters*, 240–3. London: Penguin, 2009.

Hölderlin, Friedrich. 'There is a Natural State . . .'. c.1794. In *Essays and Letters*, 227–8. London: Penguin, 2009.

Horkheimer, Max. *Eclipse of Reason*. 1947. London and New York: Bloomsbury, 2013.

Horkheimer, Max. 'Traditional and Critical Theory'. In *Critical Theory: Selected Essays*. 1968, 188–243. Lexington, NY: The Continuum Publishing Company, 2002.

Izod, John, et al. *Lindsay Anderson: Cinema Authorship*. Manchester: Manchester University Press, 2012.

James, Henry. *The Wings of the Dove*. 1902. London and New York: Alfred A. Knopf – Everyman's Library, 1997.

Jameson, Fredric. *The Political Unconscious*. 1981. London and New York: Routledge, 2002.

Jameson, Fredric. *Signatures of the Visible*. 1992. London and New York: Routledge, 2007.

Kant, Immanuel. *Critique of Judgement*. 1790. Indianapolis and Cambridge: Hackett Publishing Company, 1987.

Kant, Immanuel. *Critique of Pure Reason*. 1781. Indianapolis and Cambridge: Hackett Publishing Company, 1996.

Kant, Immanuel. 'What is Enlightenment?'. 1784. In *Political Writings*, 54–60. Cambridge: Cambridge University Press, 2000.

Kellner, Douglas. 'Brecht's Marxist Aesthetic: The Korsch Connection'. In *Bertolt Brecht: Political Theory and Literary Practice*, ed. Betty Nance Weber and Hubert Heinen, 29–42. Manchester: Manchester University Press, 1980.

Kitchen, Will. *Romanticism and Film: Franz Liszt and Audio-Visual Explanation*. London and New York: Bloomsbury Academic, 2020.

Kleist, Heinrich von. Letter to Ulrike von Kleist, Berlin, 5 February 1801 (extracts). In *Selected Writings*, ed. David Constantine, 420–1. Indianapolis and Cambridge: Hackett Publishing Company, 1997.

Kleist, Heinrich von. 'Reflection: A Paradox'. 1810. In *Selected Writings*, ed. David Constantine, 410. Indianapolis and Cambridge: Hackett Publishing Company, 1997.

Kolker, Robert. *A Cinema of Loneliness*, 4th edition. Oxford: Oxford University Press, 2011.

Kompridis, Nikolas. *Critique and Disclosure: Critical Theory between Past and Future*. Cambridge and London: The MIT Press, 2011.

Lawrence, Joseph P. 'Translator's Introduction: The Ecstasy of Freedom'. 2019. In *The Ages of the World*. 1811, ed. Friedrich Wilhelm Joseph Schelling, 1–52. Albany: State University of New York Press, 2019.

Löey, Michael. *Georg Lukács – From Romanticism to Bolshevism*. 1976. London: NLB, 1979.

Löey, Michael and Robert Sayre. *Romanticism Against the Tide of Modernity*. Durham and London: Duke University Press, 2001.

Lukács, Georg. *The Destruction of Reason*. 1954. Delhi: Aakar Books, 2017.

Lukács, Georg. *History and Class Consciousness: Studies in Marxist Dialectics*. 1923. Cambridge, MA: The MIT Press, 1988.

Lyotard, Jean-François. *Acinemas: Lyotard's Philosophy of Film*, ed. Graham Jones and Ashley Woodward. Edinburgh: Edinburgh University Press, 2017.

MacCabe, Colin. 'Realism and the Cinema: Notes on some Brechtian Theses'. 1974. In *Tracking the Signifier – Theoretical Essays: Film Linguistics, Literature*, 33–57. Minneapolis: University of Minnesota Press, 1985.

Mandel, Ernest. *Late Capitalism*. 1972. London: NLB, 1975.
Mann, Thomas. 'Mario and the Magician'. In *Collected Stories*, 603–50. London: Everyman's Library, 2001.
Marcuse, Herbert. 'A Note on Dialectic'. 1960. In *The Essential Frankfurt School Reader*, ed. Andrew Arato and Eike Gebhardt, 444–51. New York: Continuum, 2002.
Marcuse, Herbert. *One-Dimensional Man: Studies in the Ideology of Advanced Industrial Society*. 1964. London and New York: Routledge, 2010.
McVeagh, John. *Tradefull Merchants: The Portrayal of the Capitalist in Literature*. London: Routledge and Kegan Paul, Ltd., 1981.
Mereghetti, Paolo. 'America Has Changed'. 1990. In *Arthur Penn: Interviews*, ed. Michael Chaiken and Paul Cronin, 172–5. Jackson: University Press of Mississippi, 2008.
Moretti, Franco. 'The Spell of Indecision'. In *Marxism and the Interpretation of Culture*, ed. Cary Nelson and Lawrence Grossberg, 339–44. MacMillan Education Ltd., 1988.
Moretti, Franco. *The Way of the World: The Bildungsroman in European Culture*. London and New York: Verso, 1987.
Mourenza, Daniel. *Walter Benjamin and the Aesthetics of Film*. Amsterdam: Amsterdam University Press, 2020.
Novalis (Friedrich von Hardenberg). *Fichte Studies*. 1795–96. Cambridge: Cambridge University Press, 2003.
Novalis (Friedrich von Hardenberg). *General Draft*. c.1799. In *Philosophical Writings*, ed. Margaret Mahony Stoljar, 121–36. Albany: State University of New York, 1997.
Novalis (Friedrich von Hardenberg). *Last Fragments*. c.1799–1800. In *Philosophical Writings*, ed. Margaret Mahony Stoljar, 153–65. Albany: State University of New York, 1997.
Novalis (Friedrich von Hardenberg). *Logological Fragments I*. c.1798. In *Philosophical Writings*, ed. Margaret Mahony Stoljar, 47–66. Albany: State University of New York, 1997.
Novalis (Friedrich von Hardenberg). *Logological Fragments II*. c.1798. In *Philosophical Writings*, ed. Margaret Mahony Stoljar, 67–84. Albany: State University of New York, 1997.
Novalis (Friedrich von Hardenberg). *Miscellaneous Observations*. c.1798. In *Philosophical Writings*, ed. Margaret Mahony Stoljar, 23–46. Albany: State University of New York, 1997.
Peckham, Morse. *Explanation and Power: The Control of Human Behavior*. New York: The Seabury Press, 1979.
Peckham, Morse. 'The Problem of the Nineteenth Century'. 1955. In *The Triumph of Romanticism*, 87–104. Columbia: University of South Carolina Press, 1970.
Peckham, Morse. *Romanticism and Ideology*. Hanover and London: Wesleyan University Press, 1995.
Peckham, Morse. 'Toward a Theory of Romanticism'. 1950. In *The Triumph of Romanticism*, 3–26. Columbia: University of South Carolina Press, 1970.

Peckham, Morse. 'Toward a Theory of Romanticism: II. Reconsiderations'. 1960. In *The Triumph of Romanticism*, 27–35. Columbia: University of South Carolina Press, 1970.

Peckham, Morse. *Victorian Revolutionaries: Speculations on Some Heroes of a Culture Crisis*. 1970. Piscataway: Transaction Publishers, 2010.

Pevear, Richard. 'Introduction'. In *Dead Souls*. 1842–52, Nikolai Gogol, ix–xxii. New York: Alfred A. Knopf – Everyman's Library, 2004.

Popper, Karl. *Conjectures and Refutations: The Growth of Scientific Knowledge*. 1963. London and New York: Routledge, 2002.

Popper, Karl. *The Logic of Scientific Discovery*. 1935. London and New York: Routledge, 2002.

Popper, Karl. *Objective Knowledge: An Evolutionary Approach*. Oxford: The Clarendon Press, 1979.

Rampell, E. and Lenny Rubenstein. 'Revolution Is the Opium of the Intellectuals: An Interview with Lindsay Anderson'. *Cinéaste*, Vol. 12/4 (1983): 36–8.

Rancière, Jacques. *Film Fables*. 2001. London and New York: Bloomsbury, 2016.

Rancière, Jacques. *The Ignorant Schoolmaster: Five Lessons in Intellectual Emancipation*. 1987. Stanford: Stanford University Press, 1991.

Rancière, Jacques. *The Intervals of Cinema*. London and New York: Verso, 2014.

Rancière, Jacques. *The Lost Thread: The Democracy of Modern Fiction*. 2014. London and New York: Bloomsbury, 2017.

Rancière, Jacques. *On the Shores of Politics*. 1992. London and New York: Verso, 2007.

Rancière, Jacques. *The Politics of Aesthetics*. 2000, ed. Gabriel Rockhill. London: Bloomsbury, 2017.

Ray, Robert B. *A Certain Tendency of the Hollywood Cinema, 1930–1980*. Princeton: Princeton University Press, 1985.

Ricœur, Paul. 'The Model of the Text: Meaningful Action Considered as a Text'. 1971. In *Hermeneutics and the Human Sciences*, ed. John B. Thompson, 159–83. 1981. Cambridge: Cambridge University Press, 2016.

Ryan, Michael and Douglas Kellner. *Camera Politica: The Politics and Ideology of Contemporary Hollywood Film*. Bloomington and Indianapolis: Indiana University Press, 1988.

Schelling, Friedrich Wilhelm Joseph. *The Philosophy of Art*. 1802–03. Minneapolis: University of Minnesota Press, 1989.

Schelling, Friedrich Wilhelm Joseph. *System of Transcendental Idealism*. 1800. Charlottesville: University Press of Virginia, 2001.

Schiller, Friedrich. *On the Aesthetic Education of Man*. 1795. London: Penguin Books, 2016.

Schlegel, Friedrich. '*Athenäum* Fragments'. 1798. In *Theory as Practice: A Critical Anthology of Early German Romantic Writings*, ed. Jochen Schulte-Sasse et al., 319–26. Minneapolis: University of Minnesota Press, 1997.

Schlegel, Friedrich. 'Fragments on Literature and Poesy'. 1797. In *Theory as Practice: A Critical Anthology of Early German Romantic Writings*, ed. Jochen Schulte-Sasse et al., 329–35. Minneapolis: University of Minnesota Press, 1997.

Schlegel, Friedrich. 'Ideas'. 1800. In *Theory as Practice: A Critical Anthology of Early German Romantic Writings*, ed. Jochen Schulte-Sasse et al., 326–8. Minneapolis: University of Minnesota Press, 1997.

Schlegel, Friedrich. 'On Incomprehensibility'. 1800. In *Theory as Practice: A Critical Anthology of Early German Romantic Writings*, ed. Jochen Schulte-Sasse et al., 118–28. Minneapolis: University of Minnesota Press, 1997.

Schmitt, Carl. *Political Romanticism*. 1919. Brunswick and London: Transaction Publishers, 2011.

Schumpeter, Joseph A. *Capitalism, Socialism and Democracy*. 1943. London and New York: Routledge, 2010.

Segaloff, Nat. *Arthur Penn: American Director*. 2011. 2nd edition. Sarasota: Bear Manor Media, 2020.

Shakespeare, William. *The Complete Works of William Shakespeare*. London and Glasgow: Collins, 1954.

Sinnerbrink, Robert. *New Philosophies of Film: Thinking Images*. London and New York: Continuum International Publishing Group, 2011.

Stewart, Scott and Lester Friedman. 'An Interview with Lindsay Anderson'. In *Film Criticism*, Vol. 16/1–2 (1991–92): 4–17.

Sussex, Elizabeth. *Lindsay Anderson*. London: Movie Magazine Ltd., 1969.

Thompson, E. P. *The Romantics: Wordsworth, Coleridge, Thelwall*. Woodbridge: The Merlin Press, 1997.

Thompson, E. P. *William Morris: Romantic to Revolutionary*. 1955. New York: Pantheon Books, 1976.

Walker, Alan. *Franz Liszt: The Virtuoso Years, 1811–1847*. London: Faber and Faber, 1983.

Weber, Max. *The Protestant Ethic and the Spirit of Capitalism*. 1904–05. Minola: Dover Publications Inc., 2003.

Wollen, Peter. 'The Last New Wave: Modernism in the British Films of the Thatcher Era'. In *Fires Were Started: British Cinema and Thatcherism*. ed. Lester D. Friedman, 30–44. London: Wallflower Press, 1993.

Wood, Robin. *Arthur Penn*. New edition. Detroit: Wayne State University Press, 2014.

Wright, Will. *Sixguns and Society: A Structural Study of the Western*. Berkeley: University of California Press, 1975.

Yeats, William Butler. 'The Second Coming'. 1919. In *Poems*. London: Faber and Faber Ltd., 2000.

Index

2001: A Space Odyssey (1968)
    213–14, 238

Abrams, Meyer Howard   49 n.5
Adorno, Theodor   14, 22, 28, 33–4, 39,
    49–52, 79–83, 93–7, 103, 110 n.5,
    139, 145–6, 153, 164, 168, 174, 176,
    182–5, 187, 190, 201, 206–8, 226,
    233, 242
  and aesthetics   7–10, 40–5, 67–72, 74,
    87, 99, 130, 235
  Aesthetic Theory (1970)   7–8, 40,
    67, 71
  Dialectic of Enlightenment
    (1947)   145, 147
  Negative Dialectics (1966)   34, 60,
    70–1, 80, 93
  and Romanticism   57–61, 63–5, 73–4,
    78, 87, 96
Aesthetic education (Schiller)   12, 16,
    35–9, 53, 56, 242
Albert, Hans   47, 52, 56–7
Alice in Wonderland (1865)   144
Alice's Restaurant (1969)   23, 31, 33,
    195
allegory   34–40, 110, 143
Althusser, Louis   14
Anderson, Lindsay   4, 12, 15–16,
    19–46, 73–4, 102, 117, 141–3,
    163, 170–6, 207, 209–10, 229, 233,
    235, 240–2
Apollo and Dionysus   11, 67
Aristotle   101
Auschwitz   40, 56, 59, 73, 79, 99

Badiou, Alain   75 n.109, 196 n.20,
    206
Bakhtin, Mikhail   35
Balzac, Honoré de   100, 145
  Comédie humaine (1829–48)
    145
Barthes, Roland   9, 11, 35, 42, 76, 198

Bartley III, William Warren   102
Bataille, Georges   199
Bazin, André   4, 6, 100
Beatty, Warren   42
Beethoven, Ludwig van   7–8, 88
Benjamin, Walter   35, 38, 238
Berlin, Isiah   1, 49
Bernstein, Richard J.   4, 48
Bicycle Thieves (1948)   20
Bildungsroman   97, 143, 145, 161, 171,
    175, 176, 233
Blake, William   23, 26, 61, 174, 210
Bonnie and Clyde (1967)   15, 21, 23, 27,
    32, 39, 177, 180, 195, 205
Bordwell, David   16
Bourdieu, Pierre   182
Bowie, Andrew   47
Brando, Marlon   177, 182, 186, 190–1,
    202, 205, 231
Braudel, Fernand   92 n.64
Brecht, Bertolt   28, 30, 33, 35–8, 142,
    171, 173–4, 176, 180, 226, 238
  'alienation' (*Verfremdungseffekt*)   26,
    143, 207
Britannia Hospital (1982)   27, 31, 40, 45,
    102, 158 n.21, 207–42
Browning, Robert   73, 166–7
  Asolando (1889)   166–7
Bruegel the Elder, Pieter   211 n.10
Bulloch, Jeremy   171
Bunyan, John   36

Callinicos, Alex   6, 61
Carlyle, Thomas   55 n.24, 61, 73
Cavell, Stanley   16
The Chase (1966)   23
Chinatown (1974)   177
Citizen Kane (1941)   121
Coleridge, Samuel Taylor   29, 61, 169
    n.30, 174
Colletti, Lucio   59 n.34
communism   59

Conrad, Joseph   100, 109, 140, 163, 173
  Heart of Darkness (1899)   109, 139, 163
critical rationalism   14, 16, 48–9, 56–60, 64, 82, 93
critical theory   14–16, 47, 49, 56, 59–67, 82, 102, 171
Crowden, Graham   163 n.25, 173, 217, 219, 238
cultural transcendence (Peckham)   5, 14, 58, 61, 66, 72, 74, 78–9, 82, 86–8, 90, 102, 132, 195, 237, 239
Cunningham, Frank   29, 143, 174
Currie, Greg   16

Darwin, Charles   56
Defoe, Daniel   144
  Colonel Jack (1722)   144
Deleuze, Gilles   4, 6, 16, 19, 100
Der letzte mann (1924)   174
Derrida, Jacques   4
De Sica, Vittorio   4, 19
Dionysus. *See* Apollo and Dionysus
La dolce vita (1961)   112
Dostoevsky, Fyodor   75, 97, 100
  Notes from Underground (1864)   34, 89–92
Dr Strangelove (1964)   121

economic rationality   4, 51, 55–6, 61, 95, 150, 154, 163, 165, 170, 181, 185, 187–8, 204
Eisenstein, Sergei   6, 41
Elgar, Edward   175
  The Dream of Gerontius (1901)   175
Engels, Friedrich   55, 232

The Fall and Rise of Reginald Perrin (1976–9)   225
Fichte, Johann Gottlieb   3, 51–2, 91–3, 148, 170
  The Vocation of Man (1799)   3, 91, 170
  The Vocation of the Scholar (1794)   91
Flaubert, Gustave   8, 88, 100
Ford, John   23
Foucault, Michel   4, 14

Four Friends (1981)   23, 40, 97–8, 195, 199
Frank, Manfred   52, 84, 93
Frankin, Benjamin   209
Free Cinema   27
French Revolution, the   7, 88, 170
Freud, Sigmund   56
Friedrich, Caspar David   3, 7, 240
Frye, Northrop   49 n.5

Gainsborough Pictures   26
German Idealism   21, 54, 78
The Godfather (1972)   177
Goethe, Johann Wolfgang von   145, 173, 176
  Wilhelm Meister's Apprenticeship (1796)   145, 155
Gogol, Nikolai   100, 144, 175
  Dead Souls (1842)   144, 146, 162
Goldberg, Rube   129
Gordon, Adam Lindsay   168
Gorz, André   187
Greenaway, Peter   26

Habermas, Jürgen   4, 48, 59 n.34, 67
Hamlet (c1601)   79–81, 83, 87, 91, 102, 238
Hammer Film Productions   26
Hayek, Friedrich August von   51, 56, 57, 59, 102
Hedling, Erik   26, 28, 30, 142 n.3
Hegel, Georg Wilhelm Friedrich   51, 54, 58–60, 70, 99, 239
Heidegger, Martin   50 n.9
Hellman, Lillian   136 n.19
Hepburn, Audrey   112
Highet, Gilbert   34 n.53
Hill, John   209
Hitler, Adolf   78
Hölderlin, Friedrich   40, 43, 47, 52–3, 57, 64, 203
Hollywood   3–4, 23–4, 132, 137, 178, 205
Horkheimer, Max   51, 59–61, 65, 82, 145, 170–2, 182–90, 201, 204, 226, 242
  Dialectic of Enlightenment (1947)   145, 147
House Un-American Activities Committee   108, 136

If.... (1968)   21, 27, 31, 37, 39, 141, 146, 149, 171, 176, 207–10, 214–16, 226, 229–31, 233
Instrumentalism   188
Is That All There Is? (1992)   28, 44, 60, 65

James, Henry   100, 110, 126
  The Wings of the Dove (1902)   125–6
Jameson, Fredric   14, 83 n.27, 177 n.1
Jarman, Derek   26
Jaws (1975)   177
Julius Caesar (1599)   229

Kafka, Franz   36, 109, 111
  The Castle (1926)   111
Kant, Immanuel   7–8, 33, 49–55, 66–70, 72–3, 78, 81–2, 95, 99, 109, 204
  Critique of Judgement (1790)   52
  Critique of Pure Reason (1781)   49
  'What is Enlightenment?' (1784)   54, 66
Keats, John   23, 61, 100
Kellner, Douglas   13, 15–16
Kermode, Frank   49 n.5
Kierkegaard, Søren Aabye   50 n.9
Kleist, Heinrich von   95, 109, 173
Kolker, Robert Phillip   15, 31, 33, 46
Kompridis, Nikolas   6, 47–8, 59
Korsch, Karl   36, 38
Kracauer, Siegfried   100

Lancaster, Burt   24
Last Tango in Paris (1972)   177
Lawrence, David Herbert   23
Lenin, Vladimir Ilyich Ulyanov   232
Liszt, Franz   6, 54, 103, 128 n.16, 190 n.15
  Faust Symphony (1957)   190 n.15
  Piano Sonata in B Minor (154)   128 n.16, 190 n.15
Löey, Michael   62
Loren, Sophia   112
Lowe, Arthur   163 n.25, 173, 242
Lukács, Georg   50 n.9, 62, 73, 81, 95, 208
Lyotard, Jean-François   10 n.22

MacCabe, Colin   30, 33, 36
McCarthyism   108, 111, 132
McDowell, Malcolm   22, 27, 141–2, 148, 152, 157, 172–3, 208, 215, 229, 232
Malebranche, Nicolas   84
Mandel, Ernest   189
Mann, Thomas   97
Marcuse, Hebert   59, 65–7
Marx, Karl   14, 15, 40, 47, 50, 55, 56, 59, 61, 62, 66, 78, 147, 171, 232
Marxism   14, 15, 30, 34, 36, 47, 50, 54, 55, 59, 66, 74, 83, 111, 130, 232
Mary Poppins (1964)   127
Mastroianni, Marcello   112
Méliès, Georges   8
Metropolis (1927)   114, 217
Metz, Christian   6
Mickey One (1965)   23–4, 32, 40–2, 45, 48, 65, 101–2, 107–40, 143, 162, 173, 178, 187, 195, 219, 235
Midnight Cowboy (1969)   16
Millán-Zaibert, Elizabeth   47
The Miracle Worker (1962)   23
The Missouri Breaks (1976)   23, 40, 45, 102, 177–206, 220, 226
Moretti, Franco   54, 83, 88–9, 145
Morris, William   61
Müller, Adam   1, 83
Murnau, Friedrich Wilhelm   174

Nietzsche, Friedrich   50 n.9, 62 n.45, 73 n.106, 79, 148, 164, 218
Night Moves (1975)   22 n.4, 23, 193
Novalis (Friedrich von Hardenberg)   6, 9, 11, 37, 47–8, 52–3, 57, 62, 64, 66, 67, 71–2, 85, 88 n.48, 94, 96, 101, 206

O Dreamland (1953)   117–18
Olivier, Laurence   26
O Lucky Man! (1973)   12, 13, 27, 29–31, 32 n.45, 33, 35, 38, 40, 45, 102 n.94, 134, 141–76, 178, 186, 208–12, 215, 217, 226, 229–33, 241
One Flew Over the Cuckoo's Nest (1975)   177
Ozu, Yasujirō   4, 19, 38

Paganini, Niccolò 7
Pasolini, Pier Paolo 41
Peckham, Morse 5–6, 14, 24, 29, 32 n.45, 45, 47–8, 56, 58, 66, 72–3, 77–8, 93 n.65, 102, 195, 233
Penn, Arthur 4, 15, 16, 19–46, 73–4, 77–8, 97, 102, 108, 111, 132, 136, 177, 180, 191, 195, 199, 205
Popper, Karl 1, 20, 33, 47–8, 51–2, 56–60, 63–4, 73, 93 n.68, 102, 157, 206, 211
positivism 2, 7, 43, 48, 50–1, 54–6, 59, 63–4, 91, 100, 132, 152, 157, 165, 186–7, 189, 202, 209, 215, 239
Powell, Marcus 207 n.2
Powell, Michael 26
pragmatism 51–2, 56, 58, 67–9, 73, 162, 173, 204, 219
Pressburger, Emeric 26
Price, Alan 102 n.94, 147–9, 160–1, 166, 174

Rancière, Jacques 2–16, 19, 22, 28, 37–8, 40, 43, 45, 47, 67–8, 72, 74–7, 82, 100–3, 139, 174, 206, 219–21, 234, 241
  'regimes of art' 3, 5–13, 19, 22, 37, 42–3, 45, 56, 65, 67–9, 71, 76–7, 99–102, 127–8, 140, 149
Ravel, Maurice 127
Ray, Robert B. 15, 23
Reagan, Ronald 209
Reed, Carol 26
Richard II (1595) 221
Richardson, Ralph 163 n.25, 173
Ricœur, Paul 20
Roberts, Rachel 173
Robinson, William Heath 129
Romanticism (Light and Dark) 2–3, 5, 8, 11–12, 49–50, 62, 72, 77–80, 82–3, 85–93, 97–8, 102, 139, 143, 167, 173, 178, 188, 199, 205, 220, 224, 228, 230, 233, 237, 240, 243
Rorty, Richard 4
Rossiter, Leonard 225
Rousseau, Jean-Jacques 100

Ruskin, John 61
Russell, Ken 26
Ryan, Michael 13, 15–16

Saltus, Edgar 73 n.106
Satire 30, 32, 34–40, 46, 128–9, 143, 173, 211–14, 234, 236–7
Sayre, Robert 47, 62
Schelling, Friedrich Wilhelm Joseph 6, 8, 9, 34, 50 n.9, 58 n.32, 88 n.48, 99, 234
  System of Transcendental Idealism (1800) 8, 40, 53, 72
Schiller, Friedrich 35, 40, 48, 54–5, 59, 66, 92–5, 173, 218
  Letters on the Aesthetic Education of Man (1795) 8, 47, 54, 66, 92–3, 147
Schlegel, Friedrich 47, 52, 57, 63–4, 66–7, 87, 88 n.48, 96, 128
Schmitt, Carl 1–2, 21, 78, 82–8, 90, 95, 97, 188 n.11, 197, 203
Schopenhauer, Arthur 50 n.9, 73 n.106
Schumpeter, Joseph 61 n.41, 185
Segaloff, Nat 24
Senacour, Étienne Pivert de 100
Shakespeare, William 79–80, 221–3, 229, 242
Sherwin, David 207
Simmel, Georg 5 n.9
Sinnerbrink, Robert 16
Sismondi, Jean Charles Léonard de 61
Smith, Murray 16
Star Wars (1977) 13
Sullivan's Travels (1941) 143 n.5
Swift, Jonathan 36

Thatcher, Margaret 209
Thelwall, John 169–70 n.30
They Shoot Horses, Don't They? (1969) 16
Thompson, Edward Palmer 169–70
Tinguely, Jean 129
The Train (1965) 24
Turgenev, Ivan 100

Vigo, Jean 207, 209–10
Visconti, Luchino 19, 38

Voltaire   36
   Candide (1759)   143 n.4

Wagner, Richard   6, 8, 40, 54, 78, 100, 218
Weber, Max   92, 109, 125, 134, 147, 162
Wood, Robin   15, 22–3, 40, 110, 115, 180, 191, 195, 205

Wordsworth, William   61, 169 n.30
Wright, Will   182 n.4

Xenophanes   57

Yeats, William Butler   23, 103

Zéro de conduite (1933)   207–10

www.ingramcontent.com/pod-product-compliance
Lightning Source LLC
Chambersburg PA
CBHW070027010526
44117CB00011B/1739